ALSO BY WILLIAM BRYANT LOGAN

Oak: The Frame of Civilization

Dirt: The Ecstatic Skin of the Earth

Air

The Restless Shaper of the World

WILLIAM BRYANT LOGAN

W. W. NORTON & COMPANY

New York • London

For information about permission to reproduce selections from this book,
write to Permissions, W. W. Norton & Company, Inc.,
500 Fifth Avenue, New York, NY 10110

For information about special discounts for bulk purchases, please contact
W. W. Norton Special Sales at specialsales@wwnorton.com or 800-233-4830

Manufacturing by Courier Westford
Book design by Chris Welch
Production manager: Louise Mattarelliano

Library of Congress Cataloging-in-Publication Data

Logan, William Bryant.
Air : the restless shaper of the world / William Bryant Logan. — 1st ed.
p. cm.
Includes bibliographical references and index.
ISBN 978-0-393-06798-9 (hardcover)
1. Air. 2. Air—Social aspects. 3. Atmosphere. I. Title.
QC866.L64 2012
551.5—dc23
2012013823

W. W. Norton & Company, Inc.
500 Fifth Avenue, New York, N.Y. 10110
www.wwnorton.com

W. W. Norton & Company Ltd.
Castle House, 75/76 Wells Street, London W1T 3QT

1 2 3 4 5 6 7 8 9 0

For Sam, Jacob, Eliza, and their grandmother Jean

Contents

Floating

Contents

Spinning

Flying

Telling

Calling

Breathing

Contents

Shining

Acknowledgments

So many people gave me their generous help in the research and preparation of this book. I am deeply grateful to them all.

Special thanks are owed to John Haines and Joe Witte. The former, who is the retired New York State Mycologist and appears twice in *Air*, was wonderfully generous with his time and his knowledge. The spore sucker was his invention. It was delightful to work with him in what Mary Banning would have called "the debatable world of the fleshy fungi." Meteorologist Joe Witte both inspired me with his knowledge and his images and resources, and helped me to find numerous people in the world of weather forecasting who were crucial to the book.

Among the National Weather Service forecasters who were tremendously helpful were Brandon Smith of the Upton, New York, station and Steve DeRienzo, Kimberly McMahon, and science officer Warren Snyder, of the Albany, New York station. They helped me not only on the specific sections in which they are mentioned but also offered many useful comments about the predictability of the weather in general.

Atmospheric scientist Kerry Emanuel helped me a great deal,

both in the understanding of general weather phenomena and in the realm of weather forecasting. He also provided memories and comments regarding the work of Edward Lorenz. Howard Bluestein, of the University of Oklahoma, patiently explained to me his work on tornado genesis and also helped to elucidate the character of Edward Lorenz.

The climate scientists Gavin Schmidt and Kostas Trisgaridis of the Goddard Institute for Space Studies were both amazingly forthcoming in helping me to understand the roles of aerosols in a changing climate and the way in which climate models are generated and used.

A special word of thanks is due my sister-in-law Maud Humphrey, late administrator of the Art Department at the University of Kansas, who put me in touch with Professor Sally Cornelison. The professor found a reference that helped me solve questions about Bellini's iconography.

Dr. Jesse Roman and Dr. Robert Powell, both prominent pulmonologists in Louisville, Kentucky, helped me to understand respiratory disease as it relates to both indoor and outdoor air pollution. I met both men at the wonderful Sacred Air Festival, organized as the latest in their annual Festivals of Faiths, by Christy and Owsley Brown.

University of Washington astronomer Donald Brownlee—an important contributor to my favorite book, *Global Biogeochemical Systems*—helped me understand the different atmospheres on Earth, Venus, and Mars.

Kari Castle and Wayne and Paula Sanger made me understand their passion for hang gliding. It was a pleasure to listen to them and to watch the Sangers and their South African friend Adrian fly.

David Oguss and Captain Richard Siano—both pilots of deep experience and humanity—train working pilots using simulators and classroom training. Oguss put me through the paces of a flight simulator for a private jet, and both men talked with me at length about their experiences as teachers and pilots.

I also owe thanks not only for the expertise but also for the patience of my flying instructor, Brian Monga, of Air Fleet Training. He was always cheerful and helpful.

Chad Jemison and everyone at the Edmund Niles Huyck Preserve in upstate New York were so helpful in providing me access to all the information they had about creatures living on the preserve.

As always, the New York Public Library was an invaluable resource for my research. I am grateful for my space in the Wertheim Study, and in particular to librarian Jay Barksdale.

It was a very great pleasure to work with my editor, Alane Salierno Mason, whose sensitive, intelligent editing and questions have become an important part of my writing process. Her assistant, Denise Scarfi, patiently fielded endless questions about illustrations, forms, and deadlines with grace and good humor, despite my tardiness and occasional hysteria.

So many friends have helped me with their reflections both directly and indirectly on the subject matter of this book. I want to thank especially Steven O'Connor, whose thoughts always inspire and challenge me, and David Sassoon, whose conversation and climate blog are very important to me. I also want to thank three priests whom I have been lucky enough to know. The Very Reverend James Parks Morton has been a source of inspiration to me for more than two decades. The Reverend Ray Donohue delights me with his broad knowledge, his concise and illuminating sermons, and his deep humanity. Father Mark Lane is warm and generous, and his intelligence always hits the nail on the head.

Finally, I owe a great debt to my wife, Nora H. Logan, for her fine illustrations. It is lovely to see her enlivening work with pen and ink. In addition, she was a constant source of controversy and inspiration as I tried to talk with her about what I was writing. And many thanks to my daughter, Eliza Logan, who on short notice managed to track down and get permission for all the photographs in *Air*.

I have certainly neglected to mention at least a few people, and I will be kicking myself about it. I ask them to forgive my addled pate.

For the use I have made of what others were generous enough to tell me, I alone am responsible.

And in this bright confusion we are bound
Like anything to everything around.

—Edwin Denby

Introduction

At 3:30 p.m. on September 16, 2010, Brandon Smith left home, bound for his shift at the Upton office of the National Weather Service. At about 4:00 p.m., Aline and Billy Levakis climbed into their Lexus and left their home, going to visit relatives. At 4:30 p.m., I was working at my desk in downtown Brooklyn and getting ready to walk the dog. I was right in the middle of something difficult, so I put off the walk until later.

Smith arrived at the station, an unprepossessing beige cookie-cutter building on the sprawling, pine-barren grounds of Brookhaven National Laboratory on Long Island. The building is wedged into a cut-out space in a pine forest, but it would fit as well into a mall. It has few windows, and these are high above the heads of those working inside. The old joke about weather forecasters not looking out the window, then, is at least half true. You can look out the window all right, but all you can see are pine branches or sky. Still, the weather forecasters do not want for data.

Forecasters at Upton sit in front of a three-headed workstation. Three large flat-panel monitors face them, at center and to the left and right. Each of these screens can be divided into four segments. With a few keystrokes, the forecasters can call up any of dozens of models that predict what the weather might be. They can also call up any and all data from weather satellites, not to mention Upton's own radar or the radar from Newark, LaGuardia, or Kennedy airport. Since the airport radars refresh every minute, while the in-house radar updates information only every seven minutes, they get not only different pictures of the air but also fresher ones. They can also call up any other data, including the results of weather balloon launches anywhere in the world, and the reports from aircraft and ships at sea.

On September 16, Smith was to go on duty at 4:00 p.m. It was a humid day in early autumn, with the temperature in the high 70s. He knew there might be afternoon thunderstorms, but nothing big was on the horizon. The off-going shift of forecasters briefed the incoming shift on what they had been seeing. Out west in Pennsylvania they saw what might be the beginning of big thunderstorms. One forecaster said that he had detected possible rotation in one of them.

If warm air rises quickly and spins at the same time, a vortex may develop, and if the spin persists and propagates, both low and aloft, you may get a tornado. A tornado in New York? Not likely, but not impossible either.

Smith sat down at his workstation and started querying the weather models, complex computer simulations of the atmosphere. Were the conditions right for the thunderstorms to become severe? Was rotation possible? Most global models work on too broad a grid to detect small-scale things like thunderstorms, but by looking at the finer grids of the North American Mesoscale (NAM) model, he might get an idea of the potential for enough upwelling warm air to form a major squall line.

He had not been sitting more than a few minutes when he abandoned the models. The squall line—or as acronym-loving weatherpeople call it, a QLCS or Quasi-Linear Convective System—was emphatically holding together. As it crossed northern New Jersey, the radar showed increasingly frequent lighting strikes, represented as white streaks on the screen. From one or two scattered across the screen, the streaks had multiplied, like the arrival of a flock of starlings, until they were practically obscuring the colored images of the moving clouds.

He called up the SkewT diagram with the latest data gathered from planes taking off and landing at Newark airport. A SkewT chart shows how temperature and wind vary as the aircraft ascends or descends through the atmosphere. This report had been taken at about 3:40 p.m. Not absolutely fresh data, but a real picture of what had been happening in the air.

Smith noticed two things. First, the temperature line showed a steady and rather steep decline from the surface of the earth well aloft into the upper air. A parcel of warm air will keep rising until it cools to the temperature of the air it meets aloft. There, it will condense, and rain might fall. If the air aloft is much colder than the surface air, the warm moist ball of surface air can rise fast and far, carrying its load of wetness with it. Second, the spread between temperature and dew point indicated a lot of water in the air, better than an inch and a half of possible rain. Big thunderstorms were likely.

Smith was getting ready to issue a severe thunderstorm warning when he noticed something else. The winds at the surface were from the southeast at about ten knots. The winds just a couple hundred feet aloft were twenty knots from the south, and just a little above that they were screaming from the southwest at fifty knots. If that wasn't enough to put a spin on a rising column of air, nothing was. He was getting rotation, from the surface up, perhaps enough to join the high spin of the thunderstorm to the surface of the earth.

The wind from the southeast is coming right off the ocean, he thought, so it is bringing in even more moisture. The rain out there is falling hard and fast, with large raindrops. If he were a forecaster in Oklahoma or Kansas—where the surrounding air is dry—he could get a good overall radar image of the storms. When a sickle-shaped form appears on the edge of convective clouds, the plains forecaster predicts a tornado and issues a warning. In coastal New York, heavy wet rainfall in warm humid air obscures any such tornado signature.

How was Smith to tell, then?

And how to tell in time?

He switched over to the Newark Doppler radar in New Jersey. The Doppler radar not only refreshes every minute but also tells him whether the wind is coming toward the radar or away from it. It assigns a color and color intensity for winds coming from different directions. He would be able to determine velocity to help gauge the severity of the storms, and also whether there were winds blowing in contrary directions.

This is what he saw: A thick swath of bright-green air was blowing hard toward the radar. Right beside it, bright-red air was rushing away from the radar. The line between them was sharp, and there was the suggestion of a spinning hook. Such fast, contrary winds could hardly not produce rotation. Smith issued a tornado warning.

At about the same time, I went to check the weather report on my computer. It had begun to rain, and I wondered if we were about to get a thunderstorm. I thought I would walk the dog if we weren't going to get soaked. Otherwise, I would wait. The top of the screen at the Weather Underground website for Brooklyn read "Tornado Warning." I thought I had called up Brooklyn, Oklahoma, by mistake. I looked out the window. The rain was falling hard. A gust rattled the window pane. Not walking the dog just yet, I thought.

The first twister made a waterspout off the south tip of Staten Island, turned out to sea, and fell apart. A second, stronger one started up at the north tip of the island, caromed off an industrial neighborhood in Bayonne, New Jersey, and jumped across the water to Brooklyn.

Five minutes had passed. I went to the window to see if we could go out yet. The air had turned the yellow green of rotting lettuce. The rain was not falling anymore. It was blowing sideways down the street as though it were in an awful hurry to get to Queens.

The Levakises' Lexis turned left on the on-ramp and drove onto the Grand Central Parkway.

At Upton, Smith was scrolling fast through the radar screens: Upton, LaGuardia, JFK.

The tornado pushed on into southern Queens. The rain slacked on State Street. I went out with Orion and turned left to follow our usual route. "Oh shit," I breathed. Between 3rd Avenue and Nevins, the whole of State Street was littered with tree parts: London plane, Norway maple, linden, honey locust. A big old black locust had failed from the base out of a small front garden, crushing two cars and two other trees.

In southern Queens the tornado lifted. The air was still spinning aloft but no longer at ground level. Fierce updrafts were sucking the warm wet air high into the atmosphere, where way aloft it became cold heavy air. But for a few minutes this heavy and increasing pool of cold air was held in place by the updrafts. In essence, it was like a water balloon that you fill and fill and fill, wondering if and when it will burst.

Then the updrafts stopped. The balloon burst. The cold air fell like lead from the sky, and when it hit the ground, it spread out in an arc like a billowing skirt. The storm had already been moving at forty miles per hour north into Queens, and the burst of falling air hit the ground at eighty miles per hour. So the winds out ahead of the advancing squalls were suddenly traveling in a broad arc at 120 miles per hour.

Smith was at the radar. He saw a broad red bow form out ahead of the storm. It was at least two and a half miles wide: a macroburst.

At the Queens Museum of Art, two mature linden trees were

ripped straight out of the ground, roots and all, with a five-foot-deep mass of soil. The tops of trees broke from their trunks. In Forest Hills, whole rows of eighty-foot-tall trees were toppled. They were spread over the ground in the shape of the macroburst arc.

But Smith was staring at the Doppler radar coming out of Kennedy airport. Again, he had the green stream and the red stream running into one another, only this time the red turned yellow and then orange. Color indicates wind speed. The orange represented winds at eighty to one hundred knots. Another tornado, and a stronger one.

The straight-line winds of the macroburst had run into the almost still air north of them, jarring the whole air mass into a second round of spinning. This is not an uncommon phenomenon with tornadoes. Weatherpeople call it a bookend vortex.

This tornado spun up on the edge of the Grand Central Parkway. Looking at it afterward in the field, Smith and his colleague could see exactly where the tornado had begun again, because the trees were splintered and their branches tossed in all directions.

As the storm hit, Aline Levakis was driving. The couple had just passed Jewel Avenue. The sky was green, the rain driving, and the air full of leaves, twigs, and debris. She had to pull over. At that moment, a large branch tore loose from an overhanging tree. It landed on the car, crushing the driver's side of the passenger compartment. Billy Levakis, only slightly wounded, held his wife's hand as she died. They had changed seats only ten minutes before.

For Brandon Smith, the weather was a problem that he had solved admirably. Unfortunately, he could not solve it until a few minutes before it occurred. For me, the weather was first an annoyance and then a matter of wonder. It occurred to me only later that if by chance I had not checked the forecast and had instead taken the dog for a walk, Orion and I might have ended up under that locust tree. For the Levakises, the weather changed irrevocably the course and ends of their lives.

~⁀

The air cannot be owned. It cannot be controlled. It cannot be contained. It has no borders or boundaries. It is hot or cold, thick or thin, heavy or light, wet or dry as it pleases. It appears and disappears at will. It spins, rises, falls, swirls, spurts, mounts up, swoops down, expands, contracts, tumbles, jets, sprays, mixes, flows, sinks, stays, or rests. It is as quick to change as dirt is slow. It penetrates the soil; it mixes in the sea. It can stand human plans on their heads or sweep them out the door like dried leaves. It changes the world. It changes the fate of creatures and the destiny of peoples.

The air is a single, moving fluid that stretches from the heavens to the earth. The higher you go in the air, the less there is of it, but it never actually ends. About halfway from the earth to the moon—say, a hundred thousand miles aloft—one molecule of the air may meet another only every week or so, and the solar wind is as likely to send that molecule into interplanetary space as back down toward the earth. Still, there is just a touch of the air even way up there.

Almost all the moving fluid of the air, however, is found within sixty miles of the earth's surface. If you had the right car and a road that went straight up, no traffic and no stoplights, you could drive there in under an hour. At the surface of the earth, that thin, all-encompassing sphere of air weighs about five hundred trillion tons, enough to drive it deep into soils and diffuse it into the water. (Nothing breathes water. Fish and all the flora of the ocean extract their air *from* the water.) Right at the surface of the earth is a microscopically thin layer of air that the force of friction keeps almost completely still. Nowhere else is the air ever still.

The air is the theater of the world, only it is the strangest of theaters. It creates and is created by its actors, and is itself both stage and actor. The air is the great protagonist. All flesh is made from the carbon dioxide in the air. All creatures breathe it to sustain their lives. It makes, delivers, and drops the rain and snow that vivify all life on earth. It carries spores to new homes; pollen to waiting anthers; and insects, bats, and birds to one another. Bacteria live and reproduce in it. It is neither mystical nor poetical to assert, as does the *I-Ching*, "The clouds pass, and the rain does its work, and all individual beings flow into their forms."

The air is the great antagonist. It brings the pathogens and decomposers that decay the dead or destroy the living. It carries the pests that devour a crop of corn or kill thirty billion trees. It makes the storms that drown the main street of Schoharie, New York, in twelve feet of water; erode thousands of tons of topsoil; topple buildings; and drive a wheat stalk through a telephone pole in Tell, Texas.

The air stirs the pot. It changes its course over the face of the earth, and where once rain fell dependably at a certain season, it suddenly does not fall at all. The Mayan civilization collapses. The T'ang Dynasty in China falls. The Old Kingdom of Egypt is destroyed. Where once southerly winds brought warm air, now northerlies bring arctic air: the Viking colonists of Greenland arrive in 956 but before 1500 they have either died or moved away.

The air thickens the plot. Twice, the Mongols fail to invade Japan, their fleets mauled by typhoons. (The Japanese dubbed the storms *kamikaze*, "Divine Winds.") In 1588, the Spanish Armada is destroyed when a powerful Atlantic storm piles up more than half the fleet on the rocky beaches of Ireland. Never again are the Spanish a threat to invade England.

The air is the great stage. Odors rise, waft, and diffuse through it. Chemical signals so transmitted are the most widespread form of communication on the earth. Sound is propagated through the air, making it the medium of every call, all language, each incantation or song. And every object that has a color or that shines—from the ever-changing sky itself, to the blue field of forget-me-nots, to the black and yellow back of a garden spider, the candy-apple red of a dragonfly, that blue-spotted eft hiding beneath the pallid lips of a hen-of-the-woods mushroom—does so in the ambit of the air.

Living beings make and sustain the theater of the air. Using the water vapor from the air and soil, carbon dioxide from the atmosphere, and energy from the sun, plants make both the structural components of their cells and the food to feed them. One step in the process releases oxygen into the air. Most of this oxygen is inhaled by animals and taken in by plant cells, both of which give off carbon dioxide.

Photosynthesis and respiration would balance one another were it not for death. Much of a dead being is dissolved into the air again, but some is not. Some cellular carbon is buried in the soil, or sinks through the water to the bottom of the sea. There, it is more effectively entombed than in any grave. The release of oxygen in photosynthesis thus exceeds the release of carbon by respiration. The atmosphere is about 20 percent oxygen because of the dead.

The theater of the air covers the whole world. It has no walls, but it does have a roof, and this roof is made of oxygen. Before there was oxygen free in the air, no life could live on the land or exposed in the open air. Ultraviolet radiation blasts cells apart. When the usual double-oxygen molecule—O_2—rises to the top of air, however, it absorbs this radiation, and the molecule is blasted apart. It may recombine shortly after into another dioxygen, or it may instead make trioxygen, O_3, better known as ozone.

This drama high in the air creates the roof of the world. Not only does the oxygen shield living beings from ultraviolet rays, it also caps the restless motion of the air. It is a rule of life that a warmer fluid rises through a colder one, but not vice versa. When the warm is on top of the cold, it makes a lid in the air.

When oxygen absorbs radiation, making ozone in the upper air, the temperature rises. Just beneath that point, the temperature has reached a nadir. From an average 57 degrees Fahrenheit (14 degrees

Celsius) at the earth's surface it has sunk to –71 degrees (–22 degrees Celsius). But from the bottom to the top of the ozone-making stratosphere, the temperature rises to +28 degrees (–2 degrees Celsius).

Weather cannot push through the warm worldwide inversion. The fast-rising columns of air in the strongest summer thunderstorm cells punch up into this layer, but they cannot continue to rise through it. The warmer air of the stratosphere stops them. Instead, the cloud tops bob up and down there, like corks on the ocean waves. The anvil-shaped top of the biggest thunderheads—the flattened crest of clouds that looks like the wave of Elvis Presley's curls—marks the place where the rising air hits the stratospheric roof.

All the action happens below. Oxygen is a major player. So are water vapor and carbon dioxide, though they account for only a tiny fraction of the volume of the air. More than 78 percent of the gas in the air is nitrogen. Like oxygen, it usually occurs as a double molecule, dinitrogen, N_2. Unlike oxygen, it forms a strong bond with itself and remains uninterested in other combinations.

Yet without nitrogen, the living have no proteins, and without proteins no enzymes, no behavior, no reproduction, no skins. A few organisms—whose ancestors lived before oxygen was free in the atmosphere—are able to take nitrogen from air. From these come ultimately the organic world of nitrogen. Again and again, the materials are recycled from one creature to another and back into the air again. But without this first fixation, there is no life.

Likewise, if there were no death and no decomposers, the nitrogen would build up in the dirt, deserting the air. Insects' strong exoskeletons are made of nitrogen-containing chitin. If this material alone were not decayed and decomposed by fungi, bacteria, and the sun, the atmosphere would have been bare of nitrogen within forty million years of the insects' arrival.

Beneath this roof live all the earth's actors, and the air is freest of them all. As both stage and actor, it is the archetype of freedom.

From one point of view, we know very well what the air will do. It will get warmer in one season, cooler in another. Rain or snow or hail will sometimes fall. Fog might form, or a deck of gray stratus, or heaps of cumulus, or towering nimbus clouds, issuing lightning, thunder, and tornadoes, or the long trailing wisps of cirrus clouds, like an old woman's hair. The wind might rise or fall. It will likely be more westerly than not if we live north of the equator, though it can be northerly, southerly, and even easterly. It might whisper or roar, rise or fall, spin or run straight and true. We know that all of these things will happen.

But we do not know in advance when the events will occur, where they will occur, how much or how little weather they will bring, or what the results will be. Just so, we know that a person is born, lives a life of a certain average span, and faces the same need to eat, to sleep, to love and be loved, to age and die. But just what will become of any individual mewling, puking infant is beyond the skill of anyone to predict. It is a matter of fate, which is to say, of freedom.

The air is set in motion when the sun strikes the sphere of the earth. Near the equator it strikes more directly, near the poles more obliquely. Therefore, the former is heated more than the latter. Air that is hotter rises, and as it does, it flows north toward the cooler regions. As the warm air heads north, it cools. The rising air near the equator lowers the pressure beneath it at the planet's surface. The colder air from the poles is denser and so under greater pressure. The cold dense air flows south along the surface, warming as it goes.

Warm air heads north aloft and cools. Cool air heads south beneath and warms. This is the fundamental movement of the dance, but because the planet spins as this exchange occurs, the air is deflected west or east, according to where it is on the face of the globe. What began with this simple impulse soon ramifies into an unpredictable, ever-shifting pattern of moving air, some wetter and some drier, some hotter and some cooler, some in streamlines, some in gyres, some in eddies that span a thousand miles.

Introduction

Anyone who has ever looked at a weather map can visualize the patterns in an instant. In the northern temperate zone, a general flow from west to east is interrupted by waves that rise or fall through the latitudes, by rising and falling zones of pressure, and by the sweeps of fronts marked warm or cold and colored red or blue on the maps. The patterns are easily recognizable, but it is very likely that the same exact pattern has not repeated even once in the history of the world.

In 1947 Dave Fultz at the University of Chicago demonstrated this freedom of the air in a most unexpected way. He used an old dishpan. He set it on a turntable so he could vary the speed at which he turned it. He set up a system to heat it in the middle and cool it at the edges. He filled the dishpan with water, invented a dye to trace the way the fluid moved, and started fiddling with the knobs. He rotated it faster and slower; he heated the water more or less at the center; he cooled the water more or less at the edge. He kept careful track of what he saw. Granted, Fultz used water, not air, and his pan was more like a shallow cylinder than a globe, but one could guess that the water would behave something like the air in the atmosphere, responding to the heating and the turning.

Fiddling around and keeping track, Fultz found what he saw in his dishpan fascinating. A slow rate of rotation with moderate heating in the center caused the water to have a steady, unvarying, streamlined, round-the-world flow. With a faster rotation but a high contrast in temperature between the center and the edges, he instead got the fluid to flow in regular, unvarying waves. When he changed the heating and cooling, he sometimes created a vacillating pattern. In other words, the regular pattern of waves would appear for a time, then disappear, then appear again. And with certain combinations of moderate heating and cooling with moderate speed of rotation, he found the flow of the fluid to be completely unpredictable. There would be large waves and smaller waves, but they would appear and disappear

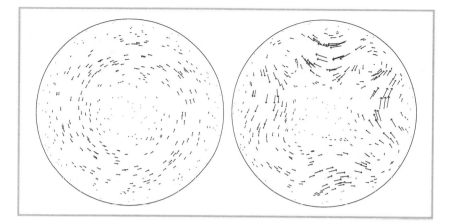

Two of the four regimes in the dishpan experiment. At left, the regime of pure streamlines. At right, a regularly varying pattern. (Courtesy of the American Meteorological Society)

with no predictable pattern at all. This last regime bore an uncanny resemblance to weather maps.

When the dishpan propagated regular and unvarying waves, the only unknown was how big they would be. Once started, they would continue ad infinitum. When the pattern vacillated between making waves of one sort and then waves of another sort, one did not know ahead of time either the size of the wave sets or the period in which they would arrive. Once they had recurred two or three times, however, one could write it all down in equations and be sure that so long as the heating and the rotation did not vary, the pattern would continue indefinitely.

The regime that looked like our weather maps was a different story. The same things were obviously happening over and over, but they were not happening at the same place, or at measurable time intervals, and the waves were bigger and smaller, eddying and swirling, without any single pattern. There was rhythm, there was order, but it could not be abstracted from the actual events.

It is astonishing to think that our planet might have been arranged

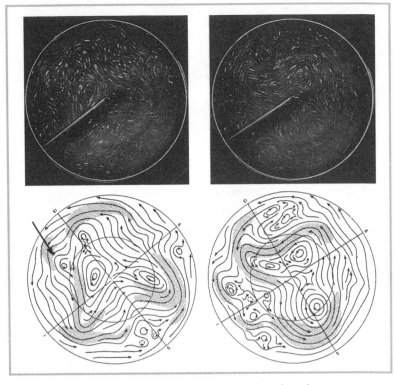

Two states of the dishpan in successive rotations, when the movement is unpredictable. (Courtesy of the American Meteorological Society)

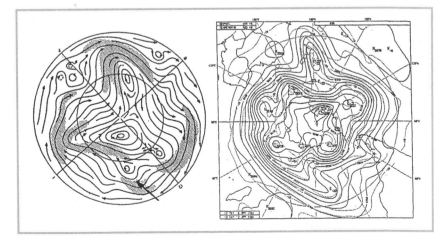

The fourth regime bears an uncanny resemblance to weather maps. At left, the dishpan. At right, a 500 MB weather map. (Courtesy of the American Meteorological Society)

so that its air would flow in any of the other three regimes. But it was not. The air of the earth is free.

～

Only subjects exist, with the accidents which inhere in them, the action which emanates from them, and the relations which they bear to one another.

—*Jacques Maritain*

One hot August day in New York, many years ago, I got off a subway car in upper Manhattan. The air-conditioning was broken. I was sweating, almost stifled, very cranky. As the door opened, it revealed an advertising poster for a movie called Zardoz. (I never saw the film.) The tag line atop the poster read, "I have seen the future. And it doesn't work."

At the time I was wiping my brow and gasping for breath.

"Precisely!" I thought.

I had just finished translating a poem by Federico García Lorca entitled "La Aurora," or "The Dawn." The poet had written it during his trip to New York in 1929, at the beginning of the Great Depression. In it, García Lorca had written, "We're bound for the jungle of numbers and laws / The artless games, the fruitless sweats." Stumbling out of the airless train toward a meeting with an exercise bicycle, I felt strongly that I was experiencing both.

But there was something else written on that *Zardoz* poster, though not by its makers. Someone had scribbled in thick black magic marker, "The theories of Creation and Evolution are BOTH right, White Man!"

That sentence gave me hope, and I have never been able to get it out of my mind. Evolution shows beautifully the music of variation and combination among all living beings, but it is weak and wooden when it comes to motive. Creation, on the other hand, is all about the motive, but it insists on a simple and unchanging story line that excludes most of what we delightedly observe. Where would we be if *both* were true? We would be living in the world of the begotten, of what is born, alive, and bound to die. We would be in the place that the French philosopher Jacques Maritain called "the world of nature and adventure." There is a supple and irreducible order to nature— like the similar but never identical patterns in the air—but it works itself out as a story of adventure whose end is not known and whose purpose is only surmised as we reach the end of each chapter. In such a world, wonder—not certainty—is the great joy.

One afternoon on another hot August day, twenty-five years later, I got tangled in dragonflies. I was walking up an aisle of lawn cut among islands of staghorn sumac, red-hipped rugosa roses, brambles, and goldenrod. The principal aisle led down to a broader lawn and in it an ancient apple tree, the last of a former orchard. Beyond that lay a house. Side aisles branched off along the main aisle at odd angles, each leading off into the same landscape of scrub islets.

I had to carry my trash and bottles through this labyrinth to the road. I had just passed the apple tree and was laboring uphill into the maze when I felt a small concussion near my right ear, like a tiny gust or perhaps the wake of a toy boat. I walked a few more steps, put my burdens down, and felt around my ear. No damage.

Then I saw what had done it. A blue dragonfly about three inches long with two black rings on his abdomen was making straight for me down the middle of the main aisle. Half an inch before my face, he pulled up, zigged in a jagged step forty-five degrees right, then zagged back, passing within an inch of my occipital lobe, stirring the hair on the back of my head. I turned to see him jerk stepwise in rising and diving feints around the bole of the apple tree and head back toward me, only this time he seemed to have four or five companions diving out of side aisles toward him, under him, over him. I kept turning and now I could see that there were more of them. Every side aisle disgorged them in threes and fives. All told, there must have been three dozen at the least.

All were flying swift, indescribable patterns. The red sumac flowers at eight to twelve feet up appeared to be one terminus; the yellow goldenrod flowers at about three feet high another. The apple tree marked one boundary; the edge where the lawn gave way to woods another. They went no higher than the highest sumac staghorns, above which a bird might have snagged them. They brushed the grass at the bottom.

Sometimes they seemed to be chasing one another. Often, they seemed to be chasing the air itself. They did not fly in elegant arabesques so much as in twisting angles. They turned as swiftly and as steeply as you can flex a finger or a wrist. One moment, they were going in one direction, the next they had pivoted anywhere from 90 to 180 degrees, as though they had come to a turn in some invisible tunnel in the air. (Indeed, it is possible that they were flying the microclimate of air currents among those islands.) One touched a sumac flower and pivoted. Another lit briefly on a goldenrod. Occasionally, each would stop dead in the air, hovering, as if to reconnoiter, then dash off again. Once or twice, a flying dragonfly actually backed up and side-stepped, before zipping off again.

When I stopped among the dragonflies, they did not change the game. Nor did they make me an enemy target. Instead, they incorporated me into the course. I had twenty or thirty more near misses, some passing so close I could hear the sizzling whirr of wings, but I was soon entirely unconcerned that one would hit me. I realized that the air did not lead into me, but around me, and they were paying attention to the air. It was like watching blue fireworks in broad daylight. I tried to puzzle out a pattern, but there was none that I could grasp.

If I had lain down and kept very still on the grass, perhaps I would have seen that they were chasing tiny bugs. And with the technology now available I could certainly have filmed and mapped their flight. I could have learned how matchless as fliers are the dragonflies. They can move one of their wings to stall position while beating another so fast it produces tremendous lift. The result is a 360-degree turn in less than one-thirtieth of a second. I could have seen how they use their large heavy heads like plumb bobs, to help them tell up from down and maintain orientation in their zigzag flight. I could have studied how their amazing multiple eyes with almost 360 degrees of view can fix a target and converge unerringly on it at what to an insect is blinding speed.

Learning these things increases my wonder at the dragonfly, but the deepest wonder is that we coincide in that place and that time, each taking our place in the air. There is a supple way that the world is ordained to work and change, but how it will actually change is unpredictable. It depends on chance meeting. It depends on adventure, a word that in its Latin derivation means "to come to, or to reach."

Did the world change because I ran into dragonflies on an August afternoon? Yes, it did. Some dragonflies may have lived longer or shorter, on its account. (I notice several flying gulls taking an interest in the game, perhaps with a meal of dragonfly in mind.) Or mated or not mated. Or maybe the twist of their wings moved the air in such a way that three thousand miles away and two weeks into the future, a typhoon got under way.

There is no way to know how large an effect may branch from the littlest cause.

The world is open; the stage and its actors are free.

~

If the world is made of nature and adventure, then it is a story. There is action and response. There are happenings that change the world forever for each and for all. For one, it may be a tornado that kills his wife, for another a thunderstorm that drives him into a doorway where he meets his future bride. The accepted adult response to such a world is to protect against it. So much of our response to adventure is to control and eliminate it, because it brings danger and uncertainty. The child's response is rather to accept and indeed embrace it. How wonderful that I should be buried in dragonflies! How amazing to be suddenly soaked to the skin!

To an alert child, the air and sky are actors. It is the purpose of this book to bring the air alive for the rest of us. We know so little about the air. It so constantly bathes us that we think of it only when it does something unpleasant: oh, the air is so polluted! Or when the weather is bad: it's raining cats and dogs! Or when it becomes a danger: global warming is killing the planet! Or when it brings us something really special: I have never seen such a sunset!

But the air in every moment is a special gift. There is no other planet within twenty parsecs that has the like of it, and perhaps there is no other place anywhere at all that has such air. The air is the archetype of restless immanence. It is full of invisible movements and invisible contents. Through what it does and what it brings, it makes and unmakes the world it envelops. There is no actor more powerful on this earth, yet for the most part we studiedly ignore it.

Our success as a species has filled the air with the leavings of our lives, changing its behavior in ways that are dangerous to us and to many other species. It is an irony of the postwar period that we regarded pollution as our chief "problem" in the air. Indeed it was— and still is—a serious threat, and it has had consequences other than increasing the frequency of respiratory diseases. It was, for example, a primary cause of the deadly drought in the Sahel of Africa. Still, unbeknownst to us, the pollution was damping the greenhouse warming caused by our pumping more and more carbon into the air. Global temperatures actually declined slightly from 1945 until the 1970s.

When we started to reduce pollution, we unmasked the more serious problem of climate change. We seem to be between a rock and a hard place: more pollution, less warming, or less pollution, more warming. It is like one of those long balloons. When you squeeze one end, the other expands.

In a civilization based on exchange and consumption, rather than on work and contemplation, everything is reduced to a problem to be solved. Preferably, the solution should involve the making and sale of products and services. Yet every solution creates another problem, because in truth, both the air and the rest of us are not problems to be solved but mysteries in which we live. Mysteries, as the French existentialist Gabriel Marcel knew, are not matters that are beyond us. They are matters that envelop us.

The air is the archetype of such a mystery. In this book, I propose that we get to know it not only as a problem, but also as a wonder. We will discover the air by means of what happens in it and through it.

The air is never empty, although mostly it seems to be. Floating invisible through it are gases, dust, fungi and bacteria, pollen, and liquid and solid particles called aerosols. Unseen though they may be, each plays its part in the concert of the world. Some decay the dead, some make rain fall and bring increase, some promote health or seed disease.

The air is spinning. All the phenomena of weather and climate come from the restless motions of the air, the gyres, and all their permutations that bring rain, snow, fog, hail, sleet, black ice, tornadoes, hurricanes, the layers and the heaps of the clouds, the rising smoke of the chimneys. We can't control the weather, but nevertheless the weather changes as we change the contents of the air.

The air is the medium of flight. It is a remarkable thing that solid objects leave the ground, but they do. Leaves, bits of bark, candy wrappers, airplanes, birds, insects or bats, all are translated through the air through the law of wings.

All creatures tell each other stories and call to one another through the medium of the air. Sometimes the telling is by chemical signals, by odors, scents, perfumes, stenches. Sometimes, the calling is by means of waves that travel through it—compressing and expanding the front of the air—to make the range of sounds, their harmonies and discords.

All that is alive exchanges gases with the air by means of the phenomenon of breath, and whatever we breathe out is breathed in by some other living thing. The energy to live is derived from these exchanges in the air.

Finally, the shining of the sun in the atmosphere brings color to the sky and to the world. In outer space, only objects have a color. All else is black. On this earth, we live in a world of shifting colors, lights and shadows, by means of the slow cold flame of the sky.

Floating

Darwin's Dust

I used to ride a quarter horse named Rita on a broad dirt field in the mountains of central California. The field was a red-brown table with blue, chaparral-covered mountains to the north and east and the long green trough of a valley to the west. The field had only two modes: muddy or dusty. When it was muddy, the land sucked at our feet. When it was dusty, the horses left a wake as they ran their courses: a braid in the pole bending as the horses wove a line around six poles and back; a triangle on the barrels, as they made a large equilateral triangle, pivoting at the nodes. Forty years later, I still have color pictures of Rita and me running the poles, with the risen dust streaming out behind us.

Sometimes, when the wind was up, there would be dust devils. Standing, waiting our turn for the poles, we would see a tan-brown helical funnel arise and weave across the field. Mainly, it would suddenly appear and as suddenly disappear, as though it had climbed after itself into some invisible chamber of the upper air, shutting the door on us below. Occasionally, the dust devil would come right at us, exploding in our faces with a burst of grit. I sometimes imagined it would pick us up, but it didn't. Quite the contrary, we ended its life.

I knew very well that the dust devil was cousin to the tornado, a turbulence that really could have picked us up and thrown us down a quarter mile away. I knew too, from the study of American history, that in the 1930s, huge dust storms had arisen, carrying off whole farms into the air and dropping their soil hundreds of miles away, driving it under doors and window sills, forcing a mass migration that had brought many people to California in desperation. I had seen the photos of advancing dust; I had seen the newsreels. From the study of natural history, I knew too that the great productive soils of the grain belts had not always been there. They had been blown there at the end of the last ice age. Later, I heard that the edges of the drying Aral Sea and of the Mongolian steppes suffer dust storms that pick up pesticide residues and industrial pollutants and carry them aloft hundreds of miles downwind, where they cause disease and poison the breast milk of Inuit women in the Arctic. Nevertheless, I supposed that these dramatic dust events were (1) local, (2) exceptional, (3) ancient, or (4) criminal. It never occurred to me that they are not only as common as dirt but also as important.

Charles Darwin began to realize this on January 16, 1832, aboard the HMS *Beagle* just off Porto Praya of the Cape Verde Islands, about 310 miles west of the coast of Africa. Whenever Darwin was at sea, he looked for things to understand. He threw nets overboard to see what was living near the surface of the sea. (To his delight, he sometimes caught swimming beetles.) He watched spiders that rode a filament of web onto the masts. He had himself towed in a dinghy astern of the *Beagle* to net and observe what he caught. He watched balls of light appear underwater and judged their depths by whether or not the passage of the ship's keel disturbed them.

On that January morning, the wind was out of the east-northeast. The ship stood about ten miles northwest of Santiago, the largest of the Cape Verde Islands. It had been hazy since dawn, the visibility less than a mile. (This condition would continue for most of the ship's three-week stay at the Cape Verdes.) It was not very good weather to observe anything.

The restless Darwin—not the graybeard sage but a nervous, beardless young man not quite twenty-three years old—paced the deck. He kept looking up at the weathervane pennant on the masthead to see if it had shifted even a few degrees. It had not shifted, but the fabric seemed a little dirty. Intrigued, Darwin asked to see it. He later reported that the gauze of the vane had filtered from the hazy air a "dust . . . excessively fine grained, and of a reddish brown color." Not content with mere collecting, he dripped acid onto one sample and set another sample in front of a flame. The dust bubbled under the acid and fused into a black bead when flamed.

A little later, when ashore on Santiago, Darwin would note that certain scraggly acacia trees on a promontory had their crowns twisted and bent so that the branches all faced northeast to southwest. "These natural vanes," he wrote, "must indicate the prevailing direction of the force of the trade-wind."

From the persistent direction of the wind and the character of the dust, Darwin decided that the dust must have come from the African coast, more than three hundred miles away. Not to be underestimated, the wind brought him yet another gift. With the *Beagle* west of the Cape Verdes and about 370 miles from the nearest landfall in mainland Africa, the northeast trade wind blew a large, live grasshopper aboard.

These small observations occurred at the beginning of the eventful five-year voyage. They occupy a paragraph or two in *The Voyage of the Beagle*. But six years after its publication, nine years after the *Beagle's* return to England, and fourteen years after the original observation, Darwin had not forgotten the dust.

Indeed, he had sent samples of his dust to the famous German microbiologist C. H. Ehrenberg, and had rounded up every other account he could find of dust observed or collected at sea. Ehrenberg reported to Darwin that the red dust contained not only soil minerals but also quantities of infusoria, vibrios, and phytoliths—that is, spores, bacteria, pollen grains, and silica. And Darwin found reports

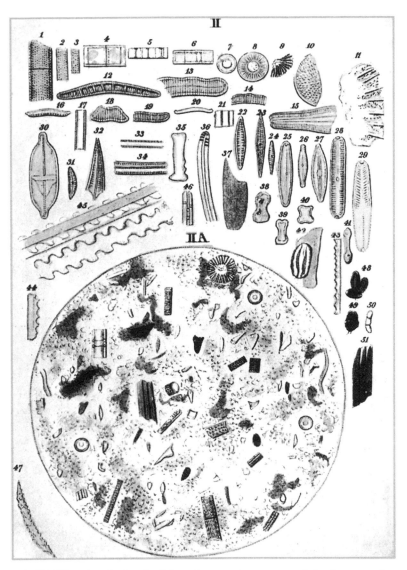

C. H. Ehrenberg's sketch of the microscopic contents of the dust sample that Charles Darwin had sent him. (Courtesy of Bob Brandys)

of seaborne dust from captains scattered over sixteen hundred miles of latitude (from 10 to 28 degrees North). At the time of their observations, the ships in question were on the open ocean from 450 to 1,030 miles west of the coast of Africa.

Darwin threw his mind out into that space like a spider shooting out a strand of web on which it might take flight. "I may remark," wrote the dust collector, "that the circumstance of such quantities of dust being periodically blown, year after year, over so immense an area in the Atlantic Ocean, is interesting, as showing by how apparently inefficient a cause a widely extended deposit may be in process of formation."

Always seeking the concert, Darwin's imagination was on the right track, and well beyond the reach of what he knew. He was just at the limit of knowledge, imagining what effect this widespread dust would have falling into the ocean. As we have since learned, this dust supplies much of the iron and calcium and more than half of the phosphorus that the ocean's plankton need to live. But not all of the dust falls at sea.

It reaches Brazil. It reaches the Caribbean Islands. It reaches Florida, Georgia, Alabama, and the Carolinas. It comes not just in dribs and drabs but by the ton, about a billion metric tons each year. This is how it gets there:

The Sahara and Sahel—the first a desert and the second a savannah that seems on its way to becoming a desert—lie in the subtropical belt north of the Intertropical Convergence Zone (ITCZ). They comprise parts of North Africa from Morocco, Mauritania, and Senegal in the west to Egypt, Ethiopia, and Sudan in the east. The regions on and around the ITCZ are very wet. Most of the world's rain forests lie in this zone. Here the globe's warmest and wettest air rises, creating clouds as it cools and forming huge, successive rainstorms. Once the air is done rising, cooling, and dumping its load, it subsides again, both northward and southward, in the subtropical zones, creating very high pressure, little rain, and almost all of the world's great deserts, including the Sahara and the Gobi.

Throughout the dry Sahara and Sahel, small-scale dry convection—caused by heating of the ground—raises the dust into the troposphere, literally the "sphere of changes," where all weather takes place. In other words, a lot of little windstorms—not rainstorms because the air is starved of moisture—lift fine soil and microbes and their spores into the upper air. In winter, when the ITCZ is farther to the south, the storms push the dust into the Atlantic trade winds. On the trades, the dust blows straight across the ocean from northeast to southwest, arriving after five to ten days in northeastern Brazil. There, the massy, dust-laden air collides with large-scale convective storms, entraining the dust and increasing the scope and power of the storms. As summer approaches the Northern Hemisphere, the ITCZ moves north, shunting the lifted dust into the expanding cyclonic wind of the Bermuda Azores High. The dust floats northwest in that clockwise flow, arriving in the Caribbean and the American Southeast.

When scientists first surmised this during the late 1960s, they worked on the basis of chemical analysis of soils and the occasional appearance in the West Indies of the African desert locust, *Schistocerca gregaria*, the same species that visited Darwin aboard the *Beagle*. More recently, satellites such as Terra, with its Moderate Resolution Imaging Spectroradiometer (MODIS), regularly take dramatic pictures of the dust—a yellow-green stain on the blue and white seascape—as it crosses oceans and occasionally even circles the earth.

Without this airborne dust, there would be no rain forests in Brazil. The dust has been blowing in equal or greater quantities since at least the last ice age. Between that time and our time, there were periods when Africa was 90 percent arid, making the volume of dust transported exponentially higher than it is now. Calcium, iron, nitrogen, potassium all blow in with the dust, but the most important nutrient it brings is phosphorus.

The soils of the rain forests are old, very old. The rainfall leaches the nutrients through them very quickly. Phosphorus—always the first of the major plant nutrients to be exhausted—is virtually unavailable in the soils. Only the annual transport of the dust from Africa brings

A cloud of dust leaving North Africa bounds for the Americas.
(Courtesy of NASA)

this crucial mineral and so permits the great trees and their colonies of epiphytes to grow.

Darwin would have been delighted to learn how his dust completed the worldwide concert of processes. Later scientists are scarcely less so. "We believe the dependence of one large ecosystem upon another separated by an ocean and coupled by the atmosphere to be fundamentally important to any view of how the global system functions," wrote Robert Swap and his colleagues in 1992. "Any strategy designed to preserve the Amazonian rain forest or any part thereof should equally concern itself with the inter-relationship between the rain forest, global climates and arid zones well removed from Amazonia."

When that dust shifts north and reaches the Caribbean instead of the Amazon, it is the ultimate source of the island soils themselves. Based on formations of calcium carbonate, the islands have only a few of the resources needed for productive soils. The establishment of plant life and the encroachment of the oceans slowly bring organic matter and minerals necessary for a soil, but the main provider of clay minerals and of phosphorus are windborne dusts. Without these dusts, the islands would not have had enough clay for the native peoples to make pottery. As summer approaches, the cyclonic wind flow brings the dust to the southeastern United States. There, once more, the old soils are poor in phosphorus. The rich dust settling there sustains the forests of the south. North Africa feeds the pine forests, making the Sahara a source of our two-by-fours.

Half the desert dust that blows around the world comes from Africa. Another quarter comes from the Gobi and the Taklamakan deserts, which lie side by side in northern China and Mongolia. These dusts ride the winds that blow clockwise around the Pacific basin in the spring. They reach the Hawaiian Islands, California, and the slopes of the Rockies. A few exceptionally large dust storms out of the Gobi have circled the globe.

The Hawaiian Islands present what soil scientists call a chronosequence. The islands were spawned from west to east by the activity of basaltic volcanoes in deep sea vents. The newest island—Hawaii, the big island—is farthest east. Its volcanoes are 20,000 to about 150,000 years old. The oldest island—Kauai—is farthest west. Its volcano is about 41,000,000 years old. Hawaii, then, possesses young soils, where recently weathered basaltic rock provides all the necessary nutrients. We would expect to see the lush tropical forests that indeed exist there. Kauai, on the other hand, should have old, deeply leached soils, poor in minerals and particularly in phosphorus. By rights, it should have a far different flora, comprising either stunted, endemic versions of Hawaii's flora or different plants altogether. In fact, Kauai has a rain forest just as flourishing as Hawaii's.

You have guessed the reason. The Gobi and its phosphorus-rich dust renew the soils of Kauai. "It is input from the atmosphere," wrote Oliver Chadwick and his colleagues in their study on the development of the Hawaiian ecosystem, "that sustains biological activity in the long run."

The air then plays a large part in the concert of processes that sustains not only the oceans but also the forests of the world. It lifts the dust, it carries the dust, it spreads the dust, and its rainstorms deposit the dust in new lands. How delighted Darwin would have been to know it, for he certainly intuited it. Moreover, it was Darwin who taught us to think in this way. His travels aboard the *Beagle* confirmed his hunch that the world is not an aggregate of stable individuals but a network of processes out of which individuals arise and into which they return. The world is a concert that brings forth its own instruments.

On the seashore in Northern Patagonia, he found a colony of sea pens, invertebrate worms that arise in groups of hundreds or thousands, each on a central stem. The polyps attached to each stem rise together, and draw back together when touched, and yet each separate polyp seeks its own food. The reproductive organs of the creature are located neither in the polyps nor on the central stem. Reflecting on the creature, Darwin was moved to write, "Well may one be allowed to ask, what is an individual?"

This is the contrary of the Darwin that we mainly receive from the Darwinists. The survival of the fittest is supposed to represent the conflict of sovereign individuals, among which the strongest wins and so gets to go on to the next round of the conflict. But in Darwin's day—at least when he was writing *The Voyage of the Beagle*—"fittest" did not mean strongest. It meant the one that fit best into the network of mutual need.

The world borne of this dust is one that survives both from strength and from weakness. The fitness of the winds is that they are strong enough to carry fertile dust three thousand miles and farther. The fitness of the rain forests is that they are able to receive it and transform it into trees.

The Spore Sucker

There is far more life in this world than we are accustomed to believe. Under the winter buds on every tree, next year's stems, leaves, and flowers are already formed and waiting. In our guts, descendants of the earth's first organism help us to digest our food. More bacteria live on one tiny flake of skin than people in the city of Pittsburgh. And the air is alive with invisible travelers: the spores of the fungi, rafts carrying bacteria, and in the right season, drifts and rivers of pollen grains.

The only reason that the world is not awash in the dead is that the fungi return them to the earth. Animals, plants, leaves, twigs, rope, jeans, hair, fingernails, chicken bones, shit, paper, rags, leather shoes, feathers, grape skins, olive oil, cotton cloth, gunpowder, pages of books, fish skin, spiders, clotted blood on bandages—all are digested and dissolved by a kingdom of creatures that fly invisible through the air. We see them only when they settle, ramify, and fruit, making mushrooms, scablike scales or round-edged shelves, or pimples on old logs.

The fungi were once classed with the lower plants, but now they have a taxonomic kingdom to themselves. If anything, they are a lot more like us than they are like plants. They live on the flesh of others, and they are cosmopolitan, spreading to every habitable niche in the globe. We breathe the spores of fungi in and out all day every day, but we seldom sense them and do not know they are there. Unless we learn to look.

I am the proud possessor of a spore sucker, thanks largely to the help of John Haines, who for thirty-four years was the New York State mycologist, that is, the fungus man. It may sound like the oddest of state jobs, but in fact John's predecessor, Charles Horton Peck, was the first great student of the fungi in the United States.

I had asked John if there were always fungal spores in the air. "Always," he replied, with a smile. "And everywhere. The only air that has no spores is the clean room where they make semiconductors." There are ten to fifteen thousand spores in the average cubic yard of air, John said. After a good summer rain, that number might rise to something between a quarter million and a million. Per cubic yard!

To prove the point, John invited me to his house in the Helderbergs, a range of hills about thirty miles from Albany. Set in thick second-growth forest near a pond and built in part with logs and wood from those same woods, his place has everything a fungus could want. The woods are cool and damp—very damp near the pond and less damp on the slope above—and there is no shortage of the things delicious to fungi: twigs and branches, leaves and stems, grass and scat, dead animals, and, of course, other fungi and other soil dwellers.

I have walked these woods with John and come upon everything from stinkhorns—the phallic fungi that are spread by flies, whom they attract with an odor more pungent than any steaming pile of dog poop—to green-stain fungi, the beautiful blue-green ascomycetes that hang like tiny scalloped eaves along the edge of fallen rotting logs, sometimes staining the whole piece an iridescent spectral color, neither really blue nor green, but something like what the Japanese mean by *aoiro*, a color that is both blue and green at once.

But on this occasion, we took no walk. We were instead to find our fungi in the air. He brought out of the garage a small vacuum pump with a tube protruding from its top. He took from a plastic bag a cylindrical cassette about two inches in diameter and an inch and a half thick. The cassette unscrewed into two halves. Cutting a piece of ordinary double-sided tape to fit inside the cassette, he carefully affixed the tape inside one half, then closed up the device again. On one face, the cylinder's central axis contains a hollow raised nipple. On the other face, there is a long narrow slit. The nipple is attached to a suction device that draws in air through the slit, passing it over the double-sided tape and exhausting it through the nipple end. The idea is that the area covered by the slit will leave a long slender trace on the tape, parallel to the slit, containing a sample of what was traveling by air.

He hooked up the nipple to the hose coming from the vacuum pump and turned it on. "Okay," he said, "let's go look in the microscope. We'll come back for this in fifteen minutes." It was a warm summer afternoon, the cicadas just beginning to sing. A great day for *Ganoderma* as it turned out.

John brought out books to pass the time. Philip Gregory's seminal *Microbiology of the Atmosphere* and R. W. G. Dennis's *British Ascomycetes*. The latter is a famous compendium of all the fungi whose fruiting bodies are not mushrooms—except for the morel—but usually little pimples that appear on the wood or in the lenticels of a twig. Almost every one of the approximately forty-five thousand known species of ascomycetes sends its spores through the air, often firing them from fleshy cannons.

There has perhaps never been a book at once so arcane and so delightful as *British Ascomycetes*. "Apothecia superficial from the first . . . ," we read, as part of one of the several-thousand exhaustive descriptions of species. "Spores with conspicuous oil drops." But the back of the book is stuffed full of color plates, showing the fruiting body in detail and sometimes in cross section, often growing on whatever it feeds on. While accurate, the renderings are amazingly evocative of a whole world that is too small for us to see. In ghostly

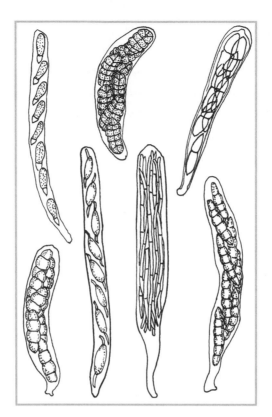

Ascospores are borne in groups of eight in structures called asci.
Sometimes the ascospores are scattered by splashing or blowing.
Sometimes they are discharged from the fruiting body.
(Illustration by Nora H. Logan)

outline, beside each color illustration, is a picture of the species's ascus—the sack that holds the spores—with its eight fruit, ready to be discharged. Even with all this, I was not quite prepared to believe that even one of these thousands would appear on our sample from the Helderberg air.

We went back to the pump, switched it off, and removed the cassette. Gingerly opening the cassette, John carefully transferred the double-sided tape to a microscope slide. After putting a drop of the mounting agent lactophenol on the tape, he gingerly set a coverslip over the top and pressed with the eraser end of a pencil. He worked very gently to remove air bubbles from beneath the cover glass. To keep it in place, he used a special adhesive placed at the four corners of the coverslip.

"This is a very important chemical in science," he said solemnly. "Generally, you must steal it from your wife." The adhesive was nail polish remover, made tacky by leaving its cap ajar for a week or two.

John put the fresh-made slide under the microscope, all the while telling me how easy it was to buy good microscopes online at very low cost. His was a Nikon Labophot with four different objective lenses and a precisely moving stage whose gears worked smoothly and with just a touch of your fingers.

We began to examine the slide. Dead ahead was a spore that looked like an Easter basket or a half-inflated hot-air balloon. It was clearly a living organism, distinct from the bits of black and the glassy fragments around it. The black lumps were carbon from tailpipes or tires. The glassy bits were silica from the soil. They were pretty, but their organization was crystalline and quadrilateral—that is, they were clearly mineral. The spore—*Polythrincium trifolii*, which feeds on dying clover—had the distinctive rounded, symmetrical shape of a living thing.

Nearby was a daisy chain of *Cladosporium* spores, which resembled a linked string of sausages with dark open pores at each end. One of the most common spores found in the air, its parent fungus eats almost any kind of sugar or starch, such as our common yeast, in whose company it is sometimes found.

Here was a piece of mycelium—not a fruiting body but a bit of the living tissue of a fungal branch. It looked like part of a tiny leg, jointed with a kind of knee in the middle. A wind had taken it from the dead leaf where it was feeding and launched it into the air. This shard was quite capable of germinating again if it settled on a likely host.

As we scrolled through the slide—side to side and up and down, following the trace made on the slide by the air drawn through the slit and against the tape—we found that it was dense with the invisible elements of the mineral and organic worlds. There was a shiny, folded starch grain; several-dozen piles of green, brown, orange, and yellow organic matter from the dirt; and spore after spore of the living.

There was an *Epicoccum* spore, which starts out as a double globe and ends up a deflated soccer ball or a globe with continents. The fungus decays everything from dying stems to wood chips, to canvas and cotton. It sometimes spoils stored food. Scrolling along, we found some clear basidiomycete spores, appearing like transparent bags of loot. When they grow out, these spores eventually make mushroom or shelf-shaped fruiting bodies. They recycle wood and leaves, not to mention unprotected lumber. Then came one after another the spores from *Ganoderma* species, much like the other basidiomycete spores but with a kind of double ring outlining each one, reinforced with little red-brown cross pieces. *Ganoderma* spores are everywhere in the summer air, a plume of tiny golden eggs on the wind. One species, the artist's conk, can put out four and a half trillion spores in a six-month season.

Most of the spores will fall where they cannot live. Some will land on dead wood and decay it. Some will land on wounded parts of living trees and infect them. *Ganoderma* fungus can degrade the wood of living trees quite slowly, but sometimes it spreads rapidly. I have seen oaks whose whole base is abloom with the copper-red and cream-colored brackets of *Ganoderma lucidum*. When there is that much infection, it is time to remove the tree. The Chinese love *Ganoderma* and have used it as a medicine for more than two millennia, prescribing it to treat asthma, hypertension, arthritis, and ulcers.

Turning the knobs of the microscope—one to cross the trace, another to ride up and down along it—we passed over the record of that moment in the air's life. Big, dark, and round, one smut appeared, and then another. The smuts are fungi that often decompose grass, both living and dead. Most of our major crop plants—wheat, barley, corn, oats, sugar cane, and pasture grass—can be attacked by smuts. The ergot of rye (see page 59) is a smut whose fruiting body is a poison. One corn smut, on the other hand, is regarded as a delicacy in Mexico.

Here was a spore with connecting points at both ends, either a broken ascomycete or a mitospore separated from its daisy chain. And then the spores of *Alternaria* fungi, resembling a cross between a hot water bottle and a crocodile, crosshatched, with a slender snout. (This genus is responsible for spoilage of vegetables, such as tomatoes, carrots, and potatoes, and in sensitive people it can lead to asthma. It also decays dead plant tissue.) And over there by the salt grains, we could see *Fomes fomentarius*, a wood decay organism, and another congregation of anonymous clear basidiomycetes looking like an order of ghostly Italian sausages.

"You could get lost in this world," I said with delight.

"Yes, you can get lost in it for forty years," John answered. "I did."

Suddenly he stopped spinning the knobs and moved his eyes carefully to get the best view through the twin eyepieces. "This jellybean thing with an eye in the middle and flat on one side, and a slightly pigmented slit on one side," he said with pleasure, "is a member of Xylariaceae, one of the few ascomycetes that gets into large wood and decays it. Most ascospores work in leaves and twigs. This is probably in the genus *Hypoxylon*. It is what makes spalted maple."

Spalted maple brings a lot of money. The lovely black lines in spalted maple are nothing but the mycelia of *Hypoxylon* fungus, called the endostroma. Spalted maple is so popular and expensive that people now cut maple and stack it green, and then watch for the *Hypoxylon* fungus, hoping they will catch it at the right moment before the board is too rotten to make fancy spalted boards.

Then we found another ascospore, with the look of brass knuckles. "I have been trying to figure out what this is for a long time," said John, "but I still haven't got it."

In my view, this was better than crab fishing. It was better than tide pooling. It was better than trout fishing. It was one of those rare and startling events in life when creatures from another world come to meet us.

John saw the shine in my eyes. "You know," he said slyly, his short white beard wagging, "that vacuum pump of mine costs a few hundred bucks, and you can't really carry it around. But I bet if we found a good little vacuum—a detailer, the kind you use to clean your car seat or to take the dust off the computer keyboard—we could make a spore sucker for about twenty dollars."

I did not need much urging. We immediately repaired to the Internet. Someone was selling a lovely cheap battery-operated detailing vacuum. It was an elegant shiny black cylinder—it looked like a piece of cop equipment—and it even came with a rubber neck that seemed perfect for attaching the cassette. It arrived by mail a few days later.

Alas, it did not suck at all well. I risked arrest by carrying it up to the observation deck of the Empire State Building, and leaving it on for fifteen minutes with its neck protruding from my backpack, but when we mounted the slide and looked through the scope, there was no trace at all. Not enough power. *Very* disappointing.

In the meantime, I had ordered a klunky but serviceable old university student microscope, an Olympus CH. Its action is a little sticky, and there are some odd blobs in the optics, but it is good enough. But what was I going to look at? Even if I could borrow John's vacuum pump, how would I set it up in the middle of the Brooklyn Bridge? Then, I really would get arrested.

Dirt Devil to the rescue. The company listed online a detailing vacuum cleaner with a charging dock. It was about the size of a robin's body, *sans* tail and with the wings folded. I bought it. A single piece of rubber tubing affixed to its snout and secured with electrician's tape made it ready to receive the cassettes. But would it suck?

I ambled out onto the Brooklyn Bridge, my spore sucker hidden in my day pack. It was six o'clock on a July morning. Partly cloudy. A little breezy. I tried not to look suspicious. When I reached the first stone tower, I looked out over the water. I was about a third of the way across the bridge. I figured that even if I didn't end up in a prison without a key, I would likely catch nothing but car exhaust and salt air from the East River, which is really a section of the Hudson River estuary. I leaned my backpack against the stones, opened the top slightly, adjusted the spore sucker so that the cassette hung about two inches out of the bag and into the air. I turned it on. I looked around. Nobody stopped or questioned me. I returned to my close examination of nearby Governors Island, then shifted my gaze to Wall Street, then over to Brooklyn Heights.

The fifteen minutes were over sooner than I thought possible, and the sucker was still humming strongly. Its battery had staying power! Now if only it sucked strongly enough . . . and if only there were something there!

With difficulty, I mounted the tape on a slide. It was hard to get the air bubbles out of the lactophenol. I put it under the low-magnifying 10× objective, I ran up and down, back and forth, looking for a sign of the trace. There it was! A slender line of schmutz that I could follow left to right, right to left, across the slide. And though the magnification was low, I could distinguish at least some spores in it. Powering up to my 40× objective, I could see much more clearly.

I was right about the exhaust. There was plenty of black carbon along the trace, but look, here were four different *Alternaria* spores, each resembling a cross between an alligator and an enema bag. And three or four gatherings of *Ganoderma* spores. The slender two-ended squeeze tubes of *Cladosporium* species were there by ones, by threes, by the dozen, in piles, in squadrons, and in sausage links. Two round grains of grass pollen stuck together between the points of a six-spined plant hair. (Many leaves have microscopic hairs that serve as glands to release moisture.) There were two-celled *Xylaria* spores, and the plaid of a *Torula* yeast. (This yeast eats paper, leaves, and wood. It is cultivated and used to flavor packaged foods. It tastes meaty.) And there on the edge of the trace was a grain of pine pollen, with its Mickey Mouse ears. What was that doing here? There were bits of organic tissue, a jointed insect antenna, a few hunks of fungal mycelia, and a single beautiful pale-purple scale from a moth's wing, looking like the most impossibly delicate of whisk brooms. Here and there were translucent blobs, some with bits of carbon or silica adhering, others just shiny blobs. These were the aerosols of fat. This spore sucker was worth its weight in gold!

I decided to see how far afield and in what varied habitats I could find these invisible travelers in the air. I carried my spore sucker to sample the air in a transect that went from a high meadow in the Sierra Nevada of California, to Death Valley and beyond, into the arid Mojave Desert. Many different habitats—more and less heat, more and less wind, more and less water, more and less vegetation, some of them places where few creatures of any kind can stay alive.

The meadow on the Cottonwood Creek at about 10,300 feet in the High Sierra, with the massive wedge of Mount Langley north in the distance, is perhaps the most beautiful place I have ever been. I was here many times as a teenager, and it is so strong in my memory that by thinking of its bare granite trails, I can smell them. It turns out that this is for a very good reason. A great deal of the dusty trail isn't on the ground. It's in the air.

I extracted my spore-sucker sample along the side of the meadow, through which the oxbows of the Cottonwood Creek meander. A lodgepole pine forest stood behind me. There were pussy willows along the meadow's edge, and shooting stars and small yellow buttercup-like flowers blooming. Much of the ground was too wet to walk on, and I knew that out toward the middle it turned into a deep bog. Beyond the cordon of forest, to west and east, rose steep broken

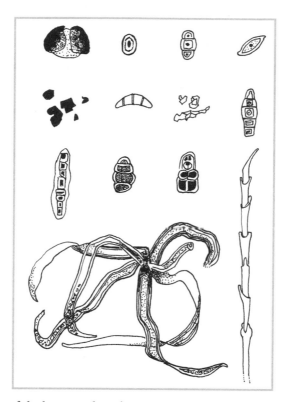

A selection of the living and nonliving microscopic contents collected from my spore sucker on the Brooklyn Bridge. The spearlike process is an insect's hairlike seta; the Medusa-like object a plant hair, possibly from the underside of an oak leaf. Note the resemblance between the spores in this group and those drawn by C. H. Ehrenberg. See page 27.
(Illustration by Nora H. Logan)

granite cliff, with great hunks of shiny granite talus punctuated by slides of smaller scree.

It was a sunny morning in June. The wind was light and variable. But the slide I made from the sample was a paradise of silica glass, flaked from the bones of the mountain: clear glass, gray glass, brown glass, sea-green glass, in oblongs and polygons, large and small. This is exactly the smell of the place: dry and sharp, with a whiff of dung and water.

Amid the glass was a spore and pollen world of astonishing diversity. There were dozens of dark dusky round smut spores, feeding on the meadow grass. There were jointed strands of yellow tubules that were fragments of fungal mycelia, ripped from their substrates perhaps in the last big blow or sandpapered up by the glass dust. They seemed to be the visible parts of an invisible network that wove through the valley. There were many of the banana-shaped spores of ascomycetes and deuteromycetes, some whole and some divided by septa into multiple cells: *Leptosphaeria*, *Xylaria*, and *Venturia* spores, some feeding on dead or dying tissue, some causing cankers on living leaves and stems. There were rust spores, looking like little sea urchins, fungi that require two different host plants in order to stay alive. There were the sinuous pollen grains of the willows and the grass pollens, some of them with round, single-nippled grains and some with what resembled lines and loops of green thread on their round faces. There were a few three-pored tree pollen grains from some broad-leaf tree that I could not see or identify. There were a number of *Cladosporium* spores, pale-yellow flasks with their narrow ends, looking much like those I had found in the air on the Brooklyn Bridge. I was beginning to understand how John could have spent the better part of his life in this world of surprise and delight.

Back down the east side of the Sierra is Walt's Point, at about nine thousand feet. It is a little parking spot pasted on the side of a mountain, with a five-thousand-foot drop just off the edge. You can see Owens Dry Lake stretching out way below and the White Mountains beyond, on the edge of Nevada. The granite here looks eaten by the wind. (It is also one of the scariest hang-glider launches in the entire world.) The flora is a kind of thin chaparral, with sage and juniper clinging to the dry land.

I took my sample on a hot day. There was, for a change, little wind, but I did not expect to catch much in such desolation. Just as in the sample taken at Cottonwood Creek—thirteen hundred feet above and a world away—there was a solid curtain of glass, but here the glass was ground finer. The silica had the same colors, but the polygons were small and scrambled. The living were here too, and in numbers. There was the three-pored triangular pollen of the sage, a few grains of pine pollen, and a grain of juniper pollen with its polygonal inner sculpturing. There was a little black carbon in this sample, while there had been none at all in the high meadow, three miles from the nearest road. And look, here were a few *Ganoderma* spores, just as on the Brooklyn Bridge thirty-five hundred miles away, and over there, a number of smuts, a few *Ulocladium* spores, looking like spume, or perhaps rather these were grasses being devoured by a committee of smuts. Here was a *Torula* resembling a chain of bubbles, and a coffee klatch of brown *Coprinus* spores. (This fungus will digest all kinds of herbaceous plant parts.) The fungi and the pollen were bravely residing in a place I could not wait to leave.

At the bottom of the hill, in the little town of Lone Pine, elevation thirty-seven hundred feet, I took a sample on a side street at six o'clock in the morning. There were cirrus clouds high overhead, with a long mare's tale indicating a high wind way aloft. There were grass and juniper nearby. I wedged the spore sucker in a chain link fence in front of a rundown house, in the shade of a cottonwood poplar. There was little wind at the surface.

Glass was present in this sample, but much less. It didn't carpet the trace. There was a lot more black carbon and a lot more of the green-brown lumps of organic dirt. I saw lots of *Cladosporium* and lots of *Leptosphaeria* spores with a diamond-shaped internal sculpture. There were still many dark smuts, and round pale pollen from the cottonwood. There were *Coprinus* spores and two-celled ascospores. A slender strand of grass had the circle of a smut affixed to it at one end. There were the jointed setae of insects, the crosshatch cells of a bit of bark, and the fat multi-septate spores of *Alternaria* and *Ulocladium*, as well as some lovely *Ganoderma* specimens. Running through the whole slide were two long twisted strands of fiber: one blue, most likely from blue jeans, and one red, perhaps from a shirt or a bandana. This was my Wild West slide.

High and low, and even on the windswept dry Sierra scarp at Walt's Point, there was no shortage of fungi to recycle what could live in each place. The grains of pollen showed what else could live there.

I carried the spore sucker with me up the other side of Owens Valley to the Bristlecone Pine Forest, and then down into the Mojave Desert. Most of the same fungi appeared in all the samples. It was obvious that the lightness of the spores made it possible for them to travel anywhere on the wind. Indeed, most genera of fungi are cosmopolitan around the world. Some of the spores that Darwin had collected on the *Beagle* were the same spores I found at Cottonwood Creek and in the middle of the Mojave Desert.

Even at Furnace Creek in Death Valley, one of the lowest and hottest spots in the world, the same creatures were active. I set the sucker up the next morning around eleven o'clock, when the mercury in the thermometer was passing through 101 degrees Fahrenheit. What could live in this? I thought.

Evidently, fungi care little about heat. There were *Coprinus* and *Bipolaris* spores, and a knot of small black smuts, along with *Leptosphaeria* or other banana-shaped multi-celled ascospores. The surprise was a wonderful piece of plant tissue. In it, I could see the sheet of quadrangular cells, with two-celled ascospores settled on them. Black lines coming from the spores had broken through the walls of the cells and filled them, exiting into the next cells through the far side. This is what a spore does. It releases long strands of hyphae that colonize the plant for a day or a year. They hydrolyze the tissues, breaking down the cellulose and lignin, returning the plant to the soil and the air. The largest organism on earth is a fungus of the common genus *Armillaria*. It occupies the forest duff and the roots and butts of trees over an area of almost twenty-four hundred acres in eastern

Oregon. How many thousands of miles of hyphae are part of this immense network?

I have become like a fisherman. I carry my spore sucker everywhere, just in case. On New Year's Eve in upstate New York, I set the sucker out at 12:03 a.m., just into the New Year, when the temperature outside was about 23 degrees Fahrenheit. To my surprise, I caught dozens of wonderful Diatrypaceae ascospores that were practically clear and sausage shaped. They appeared in groups of eight, just as they had been inside the ascus before they were released into the air. The members of this family are champion rotters of the dead wood of deciduous trees. They are very commonly found in winter, wrote Dennis, particularly those that infect the dead wood of oaks.

I had sampled the hottest and driest place I knew. I wanted to try the coldest too. Later in January, at about nine o'clock at night, I set the sucker out on top of a stack of logs. The temperature outside was –9 degrees Fahrenheit. Eighteen inches of snow covered the ground. The sucker hummed as merrily as though it were a summer afternoon. I retreated indoors, the tips of my fingers already numb. Fifteen minutes later, I retrieved the sucker and plated and mounted the sample on a slide. There was hardly a trace at all, but there was something there: I saw shards of iridescent silica in polygons and long quadrilaterals, and two or three lumps of organic matter, with their tones of yellow, green, and brown. Look, here was the dead banana of an ascospore, its usual clear insides transformed by a thin red line. Over here were three smuts stuck tighter, little black and brown buttons, apparently alive, but without any bit of grass to infest. And wait, over here was one *Ganoderma* spore. It looked to be alive. Then, more silica. A thread of cloth, now bereft of any color, its fiber twisted like rising smoke. A jointed bit of fungal hyphae, colorless and dead.

But yes, there was something alive. Even at –9 degrees. Floating in the cold night air. Something *there*!

Where Fungi Are

Where do fungi live? Ask R. W. G. Dennis. By all accounts, he was a dour and difficult individual, but his exact account of where he finds each of the species in his volume on ascomycetes is delightful. To get an idea of the range of fungal habitats, consider this small selection:

Fallen chestnut leaves
Burnt ground
Mushroom beds
Soil between paving stones in damp cellars
Damp plaster
Fallen needles of pine
Decaying leather
Sodden wood
Cow dung
Spent hops
Droppings from rabbits and mice
Rotting sacking
Rope
Leaves of poplars
Bright golden-yellow spots on the leaves of birch

Where Fungi Are

Fallen mummified fruit
Dead raspberry canes
Willow branches in the spring
Living leaves of clover
English ivy
Dead and fallen leaves of holly
Thalli of lichens, erumpent, parasitic
Flies
Bees in autumn
Small spiders among debris of marsh plants
Boletus mushrooms
Shed horns
Rotting hooves

Splash, Fire, Blow, Fling

A good-sized example of the horseshoe-shaped fruiting body of *Fomes fomentarius* brought into a lab in Denmark sent out white clouds of spores at a rate of 250 million per day for ten days. They drifted around the lab on its breezes. The air just above a wheat field moderately infected with smut may contain twenty-five million spores per square yard.

Rhizopus stolonifer puts up a tiny round head full of ascospores. When it is ripe, the top collapses, turning the ball into what C. T. Ingold, the author of *Spore Liberation*, aptly called a "pudding bowl." The shards of the spore-bearing cell walls, and the individual spore masses themselves, collapse into the bowl. In the first wind, they are scoured out and carried away, making the species a laboratory pest because it turns up in every petri dish.

The spores of fungi may travel a few feet or ten thousand miles. In 1934, plant pathologist Fred Meier at the U.S. Department of Agriculture convinced Charles and Anne Lindbergh to carry a sampling device of his own design on a flight from Maine to Denmark. Called the Sky Hook, the device allowed the Lindberghs to expose oil-treated microscope slides to the atmosphere at an altitude of about three thousand feet as they flew over Labrador, then over the Davis Strait, then over East Greenland.

Ascomycetes propel their spores up from the still layer into turbulent air.
Basidiomycetes drop their spores from mushrooms or shelflike bodies into
turbulent air. (Illustration by Nora H. Logan, after C. T. Ingold)

Though there were more and denser collections made over Labrador, the Lindberghs collected large numbers of spores in every location. Among them were many common kinds that showed up in pioneer aerobiologist Pierre Miquel's samples from nineteenth-century Paris, in Darwin's sample from the open Atlantic, and in my spore sucker when I used it in New York and California. Particularly abundant were spores from *Cladosporium, Leptosphaeria, Mycosphaerella, Uromyces,* and *Venturia* fungi.

And spores are not limited to the boundary layer, below an altitude of eight thousand feet. A living spore of a common penicillium has been collected from an altitude of 253,000 feet in the exosphere.

The fungi travel for their work. They decompose, derange, destroy, decay the dead. They also infect living plants. The potato murrain that starved Ireland, the bunt and the rust that destroyed whole crops of wheat, the phylloxera that decimated the old vineyards of France, the defoliation of apple trees and the rotting of fruit on the stem, the virtual elimination of American chestnut and American elm from the landscape—all are consequences of the spread of fungal pathogens.

Sometimes fungi cooperate with insects to the destruction of living plants. The death in the last three decades of more than thirty billion trees in the conifer forests of North America, caused by a variety of pine beetles that bore into the wood, could not have been as effective as it was, had the beetles not been carrying fungi that infect the wood while the beetles infest it. A few species feed on the fungus gardens that grow in the woody tissue.

On the positive side, fungi are also the most prolific and important symbionts in nature. Individuals of most of the world's woody plant families must be infected by mycorrhizal fungi in order to thrive. These fungi infect but do not kill root tissue. The hyphae that elsewhere would penetrate and digest the tissue, cell by cell, deriving their food from the breakdown of the wood, here penetrate but do not digest. By creating a bridge between the soil and the roots, they help the roots to take up water and nutrients, particularly phosphorus, without which the energy molecule ATP cannot be made. In exchange, the roots feed the fungi with sugars created by photosynthesis in the leaves.

Likewise, a huge number of species of the ascopores never occur alone, but instead in association with algae. Together, the two form the lichens that are pioneers in slowly making soil from rock. Again, the fungi provide a network of hyphal threads on which the algae grow, and the algae provide the fungi with food to do its job.

But how do the spores get into the air and go where they need to go? Fungi that grow on the trunk or twigs or branches of a tree or shrub are already in the air, so they have little problem with entering the turbulent lower layers of the wind. Fungi that grow on the ground are another matter. There is a very thin but powerful, still layer of air that lies right against the ground and against every pebble, rock, trunk, or branch that rises from the ground. Beyond this layer, the air quickly turns active and turbulent. If a spore wants to do anything but fall instantly to the ground, it must get past this thin motionless layer.

The three main groups of spore makers—the ascomycetes, the deuteromycetes, and the basidiomycetes—differ mainly in the way they have approached this problem. The ascomycetes are also known as the cup or the flask fungi, for the shape of their fruiting bodies. The cup or flask points from the ground up into the air. To get the spores off the ground, the ascomycetes often fire them like balls from a cannon. The deuteromycetes instead hold a single spore at the end of a flexible strand of tissue. They find ways to fling that spore from the strand tip into the air. The fruit of the basidiomycetes is usually a mushroom, a toadstool, or a shelf on the trunk of a tree. The fruit itself lifts the spores up above the still layer of air, and its overarching shape protects them from excess water.

Consider *Pilobolus*, a genus of fungi that grow on dung. You can't get much lower than that. One of the hyphae that will bear the spore grows upward toward the light. A clear spore begins to develop at its end. That spore acts like a simple eye, focusing light into an oil-filled chamber rich in orange carotene that lies beneath the spore body. The pressure rises to greater than seven atmospheres, about the same as that inside a high-pressure truck tire. The spore separates from its hypha, and as it does so, the chamber bursts, squirting out a gout of sap and shooting the spore up to ten feet away. (Notice that because the spore orients to the light, it is also likely to launch toward open space.) The spore is in a sticky gelatinous mass. If it hits a bit of grass, it is likely to stay there, until the grass is eaten by some passing deer or vole, which excretes the digested grass with the spore in it. And the cycle begins anew.

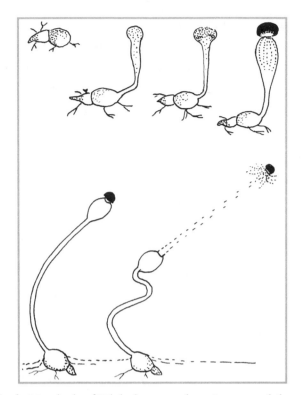

The fruiting body of Pilobolus *extends, points toward the sun,*
and fires its spores. (Illustration by Nora H. Logan, after C. T. Ingold)

The *Sordaria* fungi are ascomycetes that also live on dung. Their
gun is a repeater. The structure that carries the ascospores—eight at
a time—is shaped like a flask with a very narrow neck. Similar to the
spore hypha of *Pilobolus*, it turns toward the light, so aiming the gun.
As the structure matures, the spores work their way up the long neck
of the flask. Only a single spore will fit through the narrow passage.
When the spore punctures the thin membrane that covers the passage, pressure is released, and the spore shoots into the air. Then, the
flask contracts. Again, a single spore creeps up to the top of the flask,
and again it breaches the end and is fired away. One by one, the firing
continues, until all eight spores are gone.

Many of the ground-living ascomycetes have some such device.

The comparatively large *Peziza* fungi—the cup may be an inch or more across, growing on dead wood or on sawdust—not only aim but also emit an audible hiss when they fire.

Some of the ascomycetes use rainfall to help them time their shots. Apple scab—the ascomycete that causes cankers and premature leaf drop on apples and crabapples—spends the winter maturing on the ground in last year's infected leaves. As the weather begins to warm in the spring, the fruiting body matures and waits for rain. Dew will not do. It has to rain. When the rain stops and the relative humidity suddenly declines, the swollen fruiting bodies force the asci out through their slender tips, and for the next two or three hours millions of spores are shot up into the air, just in time to infect the new crops of flowers and leaves.

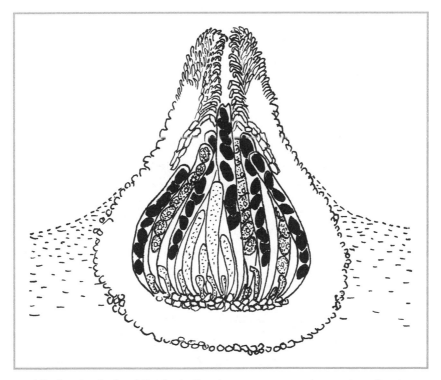

The fruiting body of Sordaria *fires its ascospores one by one into the air. (Illustration by Nora H. Logan, after C. T. Ingold)*

The ascomycetes often use a drop in humidity to set off their spores. So do the deuteromycetes. (Technically, the deuteromycetes are merely the vegetative reproductive forms of other kinds of fungi.) They are the flingers. They swell up at night, when the relative humidity is highest, then release their spores at daybreak, when the humidity drops. The blue mold of tobacco, for instance, holds its spores very insecurely on the gossamer tips of slim branched hyphae. When the humidity drops at morning, the main stalk of the hypha dries and twists violently, spinning the spores off into the breeze. On others, the spores may be born on an inflated hyphal tip. As the day dawns, the temperature rises, and the humidity declines, the sensitive, water-filled tip collapses on itself. For a time, the structure remains like this, but it is under pressure. When it ruptures, water pours out and the tip springs back into its original shape, flinging off its spore.

The basidiomycetes, toadstools and bracket fungi, on the other hand, like to release their spores when water is plentiful. For this reason, some of them preferentially release the spores at night, though some fungi—such as *Fomes fomentarius* and the ever-present *Ganoderma* species—draw water from the trees whose tissues they are digesting, making them able to release all day and all night.

Compared to the other fungi, the basidiomycetes are elaborately constructed. Their mushrooms or brackets are high enough above ground to escape the thin layer of still air. Underneath each fruiting body is a network of pores or of radial files of gills. Within these are millions of club-shaped organs called basidia, a word that means "club" in Latin. Four spores are attached to each basidium. When the fruit is mature and conditions are right, the basidia eject their spores one by one from their perches at the tips. The spores fall into the air. When the basidia are done, they deflate and decay. In many basidiomycetes, the mushroom shoots its wad in a matter of a few hours and the whole fruiting body collapses. In others, like *Ganoderma* species,

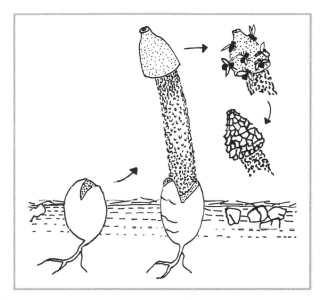

Phallus impudicus erects its fruiting body into the air. The putrid odor attracts flies, which carry off the spores. (Illustration by Nora H. Logan, after C. T. Ingold)

the fruit can last for many years, each year forming a new set of active pores and basidia.

You could fill an amusement park with the many ways in which fungi liberate their spores. Of course, some that are already growing higher on a plant—including many of the molds, smuts, and rusts— simply form a cup structure that encourages scouring by the wind. When the spores are ripe, the wind just takes them away. Others, like *Verticillium* fungi, which cause troublesome wilts on maples and other garden trees, hold an open cup too, but only the passing mist can scavenge the spores.

A few are simply wild cards. The aptly named puffballs contain their spores within a thin waterproof spherical wall. They sit on the ground. If you find one, you can make it work just by pressing on the ball. A cloud of spores shoots out the narrow opening, like smoke from a chimney. In nature, animals occasionally do the puffball the service of expelling its spores, but in most cases, raindrops likely do the job.

And what about the even more aptly named *Phallus impudicus*? Like the salacious words among the epigrams of Martial that were typically left untranslated in prudent, nineteenth-century Englished versions of the book, the common name of this fungus—stinkhorn—gives only a small clue to its way of life. But you get the point without translation. For most of its life, the fruiting body of *Phallus* is an egglike thing that lies just below the soil surface, filling with water that it holds in a sort of jelly. When the spores are mature, the egg suddenly begins to erect into a phallus, carrying its stinking mass of sticky spores up four or five inches into the air. There, the putrid scent attracts flies, which carry the spores away with them.

The wonderful amateur mycologist Mary Banning—whose astonishing watercolors of the fungi of Maryland were discovered in a manuscript in a drawer at the New York State Museum—told the story of a collecting trip during which she found a fine example of *Phallus* that she needed to bring home so she could paint it. She was obliged to travel in a public streetcar, and although she had her find wrapped closely in paper, it made its presence known. "When the car halted at the station to change horses," she wrote, "the flies rushed in in myriads, nearly devouring the few passengers, yet no one but myself knew the cause."

The Ergot of the Rye

The fungi, when they are not decaying the dead, are mostly responsible for diseases of plants. The names are expressive of their effects: scabs and rusts, smuts and leaf spots, wilts and blasts, stunts and yellows, bunts and scorches. Admittedly, sometimes flying insects—leaf hoppers, beetles, or the like—help the fungal organism around, and anything that hops on or off plants—insects, birds, squirrels, bats—helps the wind distribute spores, and some spores move through the earth or the water. But mainly it is the wind that spreads plant pathogens.

Occasionally, fungal disease attacks people. Most today are annoyances: candidiasis, ringworm, athlete's foot. Occasionally they are more serious, such as the liver disease caused by inhaling *Aspergillus* spores and the lung disease caused by *Cryptococcus* infection. In the Middle Ages, however, one fungal disease was a scourge.

For more than a millennium in middle and northern Europe, the black banana-shaped fruiting bodies of *Claviceps purpurea*—growing just as though they were a part of the rye—were ground up in the mill and eaten in bread and cereal. It was not until 1853, in fact, that it was finally proved that those black shoots among the golden ones on a mature head of rye were not simply a form of the cereal, but rather a healthy mature colony of the fungus.

Claviceps purpurea is an ascomycete, so we have R. W. G. Dennis's wonderful description of the apparent black fruit of the rye: "sclerotia elongated, more or less cylindrical with rounded ends but usually with slight longitudinal grooves and ridges, formed beneath the ovary of a grass flower and growing out to replace it . . . , black externally with hard white flesh." It sounds delicious, but it is not meant to be eaten. Yes, it causes the plant to put out a sticky honeydew that attracts insects, which get the conidial spores of the fungus on their feet and carry them to other rye flowers, infecting more. Its next vocation is to fall to the earth, where it ripens, where the tiny narrow-necked fruiting bodies form and in July shoot into the air the long crystal-clear needle spores. They float there, and just as though they were pollen grains, they are caught on the out-thrust stigmas of the rye flowers. Just like pollen, they send a tube to penetrate the ovary, but they are parasites, not fertilizing males. Another black banana is ready to form.

When people ate bread or cereal made with ergoted rye, strange things happened to them. Some suffered convulsions; some lost the feeling in their extremities and eventually lost fingers, toes, earlobes, and even larger parts to gangrene; some saw colors, lights, and things that were not there. Some suffered all three fates. The loss of feeling—caused by an alkaloid in the ergot that constricts blood vessels, reducing flow—was often followed by a reddening or blistering of the skin and by an intense, intolerable burning. For this reason, the disease was first called *ignis sacra*, or "sacred fire." When the monks of Saint Anthony were founded to care for its sufferers, the disease came to be named Saint Anthony's fire.

It was one of the most deadly diseases during the Middle Ages in Europe. It had not become an epidemic earlier because prior to about the fifth century AD, rye had been tolerated simply as a weed in wheat fields. Even if it was eaten, it was only as an occasional contaminant. It was learned, however, that rye could survive bad weather and tough climates, where wheat might not, and so rye gradually became the staple crop of the poor in colder temperate zones.

Thousands upon thousands became sick and died, particularly in what is now Germany and France. The monks of Saint Anthony—who at their height ran more than 350 hospitals—could often effect a cure because they did not serve rye bread or rye porridge to their patients. When the cured returned home, however, and went back to their ordinary diet, they often suffered another bout of the disease. It was said that the disease became worse with each onset.

As early as 1670, a French physician, Dr. Louis Thuillier, intuited the cause of Saint Anthony's fire. He observed that the disease was not infectious. One family member might get it but not another; a person totally isolated from contact with others might get it; it was more prevalent in the country than in the city, though sanitary conditions were worse in the latter. He decided that the cause must have to do with diet. Because the rich almost never got the disease, he wondered what was different between the diet of the rich and the poor. The answer was rye bread.

Everyone knew about the black cockspurs—the name "ergot" means spur that grew in the rye, but no one thought they were harmful. Indeed, they were just one of the things associated with growing rye. But there were many more spurs in some years—chiefly when the spring was cool and damp—than in others. The heavy cockspur years, Dr. Thuillier realized, coincided with outbreaks of Saint Anthony's fire. It would be almost two hundred more years before one of the great Tulasne brothers—among the founding fathers of mycology—actually explained the life cycle of *C. purpurea*, but the French country doctor had correctly diagnosed the disease.

Rye seed is now routinely treated to prevent ergot, except in rye fields that are grown not for the grain but for the fungus. Medieval midwives had recognized that small doses of a drink prepared from the cockspurs could sometimes help a woman in labor. (This had been another of Dr. Thuillier's clues.) The drink brought on contractions and seemed to reduce bleeding. The alkaloid responsible for this reaction is now isolated from the sclerotia and regularly used in medicine. Another ergot alkaloid—the one that constricts blood flow—is the basis of a drug to control migraine headaches. As for the alkaloid that caused hallucinations, it was the base chemical from which the psychotropic drug LSD was first synthesized.

Lifted, Lofted, and Living

Fungi shoot their spores, or splash or blow or drop them. Wind-pollinated trees and grasses hold their pollen up into the wind. Bacteria do nothing. In fact, a gale will do very little to carry a single bacterial cell into the air if that cell is not otherwise attached.

From the point of view of bacteria—and of everything alive—the good news is that they always are attached: to soil particles, to mineral and organic dusts, to bits of leaves or bark, to skin cells, to fibers, to oil drops, to saliva, to hair, to spores, to bursting bubbles on the surface of the sea. When these rafts are lifted into the air, they carry the bacteria with them, and so circulate these tiny indispensable creatures around the globe.

Consider your bedroom. The dust there is rich in bits of human skin, several thousand of them per cubic yard. These make wonderful bacterial rafts. When you make the bed—fluffing the sheets, plumping the pillow, smoothing the covers, or settling the spread—the number of cells lofted into the air jumps exponentially, and with it the number of bacteria in the air. During an average bed-making—if there is such a thing—there are almost four hundred thousand skin cells wafting through the air, each carrying about two hundred different species of bacteria.

Lifted and lofted on every kind of substrate, indoors and outdoors, huge numbers of bacteria end up in the air. An estimate of the total number of cells in the air around the globe each year is the number 1 with twenty-four zeros after it. That makes between one thousand and ten thousand single-celled creatures per cubic yard.

There is no shortage of bacteria, but why? Like the fungi, many bacteria fall into the soil, where they keep us from being overwhelmed by the sour dead. Where fungi sometimes specialize in breaking down resistant materials such as lignin and cellulose, bacteria preferentially digest fresh green materials high in nitrogen. They are also attracted to the root zones of plants. The roots specifically emit materials palatable to bacteria in the hope of attracting them. A root sheathed with bacteria is protected from infection by pathogenic fungi.

More important still, it is only through the work of certain bacteria that the relatively inert nitrogen of the atmosphere can be captured for use by living beings. Some of these bacteria in fact live as symbionts on the roots of plants in the legume family. The plants provide the bacteria with the energy to live, and in exchange the bacteria, called rhizobia, convert atmospheric dinitrogen into ammonium, a compound that can be used by plants and animals.

Other bacteria—even some photosynthesizing cyanobacteria—convert nitrogen without the symbiotic association, but all must do so by creating a peculiar intracellular air. The process stalls if oxygen is present, so the cells must specifically exclude that gas in order to fix nitrogen. This is a particularly difficult trick for the cyanobacteria, since they actually make oxygen, but they have developed cells that are oxygen proof for the purpose.

Though it takes place on a scale so tiny it may seem inconsiderable, the fixation of nitrogen by bacteria is as crucial as the liberation of oxygen in photosynthesis. These bacteria make a hundred million metric tons of usable nitrogen compounds each year. All amino acids, proteins, and nucleic acids depend on nitrogen as a crucial chemical constituent. No plant or animal except these few species of bacteria can take nitrogen from the air. So without them, there are no behavior, no reproduction, no plants, and no animals.

The vocation of many bacteria is to live in the soil, but unlike fungi and pollens, some bacteria not only travel but also live in the air. A bacterial cell can stay in the air for a few hours to a few weeks, depending in part on when and where it rains. (Most cells are removed from the air by rain and snow, not just by running into a tree or a building or a rock.) While there, some feed on the sulfur, nitrogen, and carbon compounds that exist as other aerosols aloft, and even reproduce in cloud water every four to twenty days or so. Some of the bacteria are also autotrophs, like plants, living on sunlight.

Viable bacteria have been found thirty-five miles up in the atmosphere. High up in clouds, some bacteria help generate the ice nuclei that lead to rain and snow. Researchers in one study were puzzled to find that leaf fragments were apparently serving as ice nuclei for raindrops. Typically, ice nuclei must form on a specific matrix that matches the structure of an ice crystal. Even a tiny shard of leaf is too large for this. The researchers learned that the ice was forming on a protein found in a species of bacteria that had been lofted on the leaf. If bacteria are feeding and reproducing in the clouds, they might also affect the number of aerosols of other kinds in the air—sulfates, nitrates, carbons.

Bacteria, then, do double work in the great terraqueous machine. While underground, they compost the dead, protect roots, and fix from the air the nitrogen without which not a single amino or nucleic acid can be made. Aloft in the clouds, they create condensation nuclei, and thus affect the amount and frequency of rain and snow.

The Pollen Rain

Bacteria are the smallest airborne creatures, needing help to get aloft. Pollens are the giants of the invisible world of air. When they appear in an air sample, they are often the largest things on the slide. And because they carry the male gametes of wind-pollinated plants, they usually appear at a certain time of year in great numbers. Pollen is tough on the outside but tender on the inside. The outer layer of the pollen shell is one of nature's most durable coatings. You can cook it in a five-hundred-degree oven, or bathe it in acid or lye, and it will come out looking just the same as it did when it went in. The insides, on the other hand, live as briefly as a few hours and never more than a few days, no matter how you protect them. They contain a male nucleus that fuses with a female to make the embryo, as well as two additional nuclei that fuse with another nucleus in the female to make food reserves for the embryo. Finally, the insides contain hormone shots that tell the female it is time to make fruit.

In the course of eons, nature seems to have thought better of wind pollination, designing numerous plants that attract insects to carry their pollen for them. The insects know what flower they came from and what flower they are going to—hence, the chances of marriage are much, much better. The anthers that make pollen for an insect-pollinated plant can produce as few as one thousand grains of pollen,

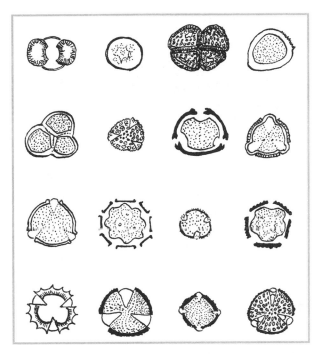

A selection of pollen grains, from wind-pollinated trees and grasses.
(Illustration by Nora H. Logan)

while a wind-pollinated birch anther churns out ten thousand and a hemp anther seventy thousand.

Were natural selection a simple matter of efficiency, one would anticipate the withering away of the wasteful wind-pollinated plants, but they remain the anchors of the world's flora, as they have been since the advent of trees and grasses. The boreal forests, the temperate forests, and the great grasslands and savannahs are all based on wind-pollinated plants. So much for efficiency.

The term pollen "rain" is an understatement. For the plants whose pollen is carried on the wind, pollination is a numbers game. For the hazelnut, for instance, the chance of a given grain of pollen reaching a pistil that it can fertilize is about 2.8 million to 1. Pollen "deluge" is more to the point. A ten-year-old beech branch liberates thirty million grains of pollen at a shot; a ten-year-old birch branch, one hundred million. A pine sends out two million grains from a single cone, and a spruce anywhere from half a million to two million. The spruce forests of Sweden put out seventy-five million tons of pollen in a season. Five hundred million grains float off from a single shoot of hemp; fourteen million, from one corn plant. Ragweed spirits away into the air over a billion pollen grains per plant. Every year, the United States sinks beneath the weight of a million tons of ragweed pollen.

Mostly, the pollen falls within twenty-five to fifty miles of its point of origin. Pollen is very much larger and heavier than a fungal spore. Pollen doesn't usually make up more than 5 percent of the sample by number, but it takes up room. A big updraft is needed to keep pollen in the air for very long.

Occasionally, a storm does carry pollen far. On the evening of the 24 June 1914, a Norwegian Arctic expedition ran into a pine pollen storm at sea, more than fifty miles from the nearest pine forest. The pollen fell at a rate of 150 grains per cubic inch, turning the decks yellow, as though they had been doused with a very fine corn flour. Even stranger, on the island of Tristan de Cunha, lost in the South Atlantic, cores taken in peat bogs revealed the pollen grains of *Nothofagus* trees and *Ephedra* plants, which must have blown from their nearest habitats, twenty-five hundred miles to the west in South America.

But most pollen falls pretty close to home. A storm wind may blow it to the east one day, and another to the northwest on another day, but averaged over a few decades, the amount of pollen that has fallen would give you a pretty good idea of what grew in the vicinity, even if every tree had since been removed. Palynology is built around this fact. If you take sediment cores from areas that are relatively undisturbed and if you date those cores—the deeper they are, the older—you can tell what plants were on the site at what time, and so you can tell a great deal about the landscape and sometimes the people who inhabited it. The best place to get undisturbed cores is a lake bottom or a peat bog. If you see earnest-looking people out drilling in a pond or on a bog, they may well be palynologists.

It was palynologists who established the rhythm of the ice ages by determining when the ground in a given locale was covered with the pollen of steppe grasses or of boreal forest. They recorded the retreat of the glaciers by noting when the grasses gave way to forests of juniper, birch, and willow, and later when birch and pine gave way to oak, alder, linden, and elm.

They can map when a place was first devoted to agriculture or another human practice by studying the pollen in the sediments. The first appearance of weeds in the pollen record often marks when agriculture came to a place, as does the presence of the pollen grains of the cereals. Pollen accounts reveal that the Romans brought walnuts north into their colonies about two thousand years ago. The heath pollen of Scotland appeared after forests were cleared and large-scale grazing began. When the Maori population exploded six hundred years ago, it was recorded in the disappearance of the pollen of the native conifer, the appearance of a layer of broken charcoal, and the subsequent spread of the pollen of a weedy fern. It was the palynologists who told us that in a Neanderthal burial of fifty thousand years ago, the dead woman had been placed on a bed of flowers.

Sometimes the pollen record gives us surprises, good and bad. It turns out the heyday for pollen in some places during the Holocene—one name for the era in which we live—is not now. Rather, it was about two thousand years ago. The pollen record of the White Mountains in New Hampshire, for instance, shows that white pine and hemlock were able to thrive then at elevations five or six hundred feet higher than they do now. It was warmer there then than it is now. We are perhaps on the downhill slope of this age, although some palynologists are skeptical of the existence of any such modern age at all. "It is premature," one remarked, "to say that the Pleistocene has ended." Looking with a long lens, palynologists are as concerned about a return to the ice ages as about global warming in the near term.

Pollen records in the eastern United States map the virtual disappearance of the chestnut tree with the coming of the chestnut blight. They also map a similar precipitous decline for hemlock pollen in the period four thousand to five thousand years before the present. That is doubly bad news, but the hopeful sign is that hemlock came back. It was the best shade conifer in the United States for decades until the advent of the insect pest hemlock woolly adelgid, which has decimated hemlock populations once again. Perhaps once more the tree will recover? But how and when?

Invisible Cities

Paris was called the capital of the nineteenth century. It was a focal point of the Industrial Revolution, a term that had been coined by a Parisian a century prior. In 1879, the third Paris World's Fair had just closed, marking the recovery of France from the disastrous Franco-Prussian War and the equally disastrous suppression of the Communards. Painter Édouard Manet was in his prime. Expatriates like Alfred Sisley and John Singer Sargent were hard at work. Paul Gauguin was still painting dark-toned Paris scenes; he had yet to find the bright colors of the South Seas.

The royalists who had run the Third Republic up to that time were in disgrace, and were replaced by moderates, who relaxed the iron hand that had suppressed the poor. Paul Lafargue, the son-in-law of Karl Marx, had just founded the Partie Ouvrier Française (POF), the first Marxist party in France. Emile Zola was writing about the life of the streets, and Jules Verne had recently published a novel about microbial warfare. Paris had just become the first city in the world to be connected by telephone, and a French company had published its first plans to build a canal across the Isthmus of Panama.

Pierre Miquel was not so interested in what could be seen in Paris as in what could not be seen. From his base in a converted castle at the Parc Montsouris in the fourteenth Arrondissement, he wandered through the sewers and the hospitals, and down the central streets of Paris. He took with him the grandfather of all spore suckers, a machine that passed air over a slide coated with a sticky paste. It was slow but sure. In forty-eight hours, it collected about 264 gallons worth of air. (The modern Hirst collector will take about 6,340 gallons of air in that time.) In more than thirty-four years of collecting and deciphering, he mapped the invisible streets of Paris, the ones inhabited by the fungi, the bacteria, the tiny crystals of silica, the brown organic soil, the red iron, the hairs of plants (what makes leaves fuzzy), the occasional thread from a garment, and the scales of butterfly wings.

He wanted to map invisible Paris, the city that flowed in the air around and through its citizens, potentially bringing them health or disease. He did not care if he could identify each species. Rather, he wanted to count the kinds of creatures and measure their flux. Miquel was the first person to devise an accurate means of counting his catch, so it was from him that we got our first picture of how the contents of the air differ from time to time in one place or from place to place in one time.

His Montsouris Observatory was on the southern edge of Paris. Miguel measured the influx of bacteria and how it varied according to the direction of the wind and the character of the weather. He noticed that during a hard rainstorm the catch of fungi decidedly declined—only to jump fivefold to tenfold when the rain ended—but the catch of bacteria did not decline nearly so much. He reasoned that if that rain had washed most of the bacteria in the air out of it, then the only way that the count could still be high is if there were bacteria reproducing in the clouds and falling in the rain. A perfectly absurd idea, it was thought at the time, but in the last decade we have learned that he was right.

The best catch of bacteria came when it was moderately dry out-side. The bacteria—at least ten times smaller than fungal spores—would be lifted by the million on bits of dust, organic matter, and mineral matter, and would gradually be drawn onto his glycerin-coated slide. He noticed, however, that the catch depended greatly on which direction the wind was blowing. He got much more when the wind was blowing out of the north, northeast, or northwest than he did when it was blowing out of the south, southeast, or southwest.

After decades of measurement and calculation, Miquel was able to say that the bacterial load increased ninefold or tenfold when the air was coming to Montsouris after passing over Paris. When he went up onto Mount-Saint-Genevieve to the south, the count was sixteen times less than the average for Montsouris. Evidently, Paris was a bacterial paradise.

Paris at the time was about sixteen miles square. Miquel estimated that on an average day in Paris, forty trillion bacteria were produced, of which about five trillion would end up in the air. He learned that at Montsouris the bacteria had two daily maxima, at 7:00 a.m. and 7:00 p.m. There were two maxima downtown as well, though these were influenced by rush hour and the times of street sweeping. Also, the minimum in central Paris was equal to the maximum at the observatory.

The opposite was true for fungi. On an average summer day at Montsouris he got about 23,076 spores per cubic yard. (On a good day, right after a rain, the number might jump sevenfold or eightfold.) Even in midwinter, he could find about 770 per cubic yard though with snow and cold, there might be even fewer. Hardly ever were there none. Downtown and indoors, however, the number of fungal spores was far less. There were only 4,000 per cubic yard inside the Hôtel-Dieu, the downtown hospital. And in the sewers beneath the rue de Rivoli, there were forty or fifty times fewer than that.

The large flux of bacteria came from the city; the biggest flux of fungi, from the country. He inferred that human disease would most likely be caused by bacteria, and plant disease by fungi. He was right in this as well.

In the wake of Louis Pasteur's work on microbes, Miquel focused on the living agents of disease. He did not count the nonliving particles that, as industrial production and machine-driven transport increased, became major invisible constituents of urban air. In the industrial era, neither bacteria nor fungi have been the primary source of airborne contaminants that damage the lungs and other organs. Rather, particles small enough to lodge in the upper or lower airway and in the lungs themselves more often have caused disease.

Through millennia, the human body evolved to face its primary enemies: bleeding to death or dying from the consequent infection. We had to fight bites, cuts, compound fractures, burns, and other types of wounds. To protect itself, the body became expert at making scars. When a wound occurred, the body first stopped the bleeding by producing clots at the site, then inflamed the site with antibodies to resist the spread of infection, then formed scars over the wound, allowing the tissue to regenerate and heal. Clot, inflame, scar. It was a good program for that kind of wound.

As industrial processes—factories, steamboats, railroads, cars, electric generator plants—rose in number and intensity, a new kind of wound began to occur. A person breathes hundreds of gallons of air per hour into the lungs, which have more exposed surface area than any other part of the body except the skin. Sulfates, nitrogen compounds, tiny particles of earth or metal, volatile organic compounds such as polycyclic aromatic hydrocarbons (PAHs) and polychlorinated biphenyls (PCBs), thin aerodynamic particles like those of asbestos—all can be inhaled, and all might be small enough to get stuck in the respiratory system.

Just as with a cut or burn on the skin, the body perceives these internal intrusions as if they were wounds. Its response? Clot, inflame, scar. This might be an appropriate response were the attacker a bacterium, but not when it is a nonliving particle. The inflammation brought about by macrophages, antibodies, and antioxidants cannot dissolve the particle, so the inflammation continues, becoming chronic. At the same time, the wound response brings collagen to the site and begins to build a fibrous scar.

The lung tissues change. They are, in pulmonologist Dr. Jesse Roman's word, remodeled. If the lodged particles are large—say 2.5 to 5.0 microns in diameter—they will stay in the airways, and this is where scarring will occur. Asthma can be the result. A buildup of mucus and spasmodic narrowing of the airways will cause periodic trouble breathing. If the particles are smaller—2.5 microns in diameter or less—they will travel into the lungs proper, among the alveoli, which actually transmit oxygen to the bloodstream. Scarring there can cause fibrosis, a buildup of nonfunctional scar tissue that permanently impairs breathing, or it can cause a hollowing out of the tissues, as occurs in emphysema.

But a small particle inhaled into the lungs might not stay there. It might instead be absorbed and transported to other organs in the body, such as the heart, the stomach, the liver. Air pollution is associated not only with an increased incidence of lung disease, but also with an increase in other inflammatory diseases that are common in the industrial world.

Hospital admissions in cities around the globe are directly correlated with the amount of pollutants in the air. In Atlanta, Georgia, in 1996, there was a successful effort to keep cars out of the downtown area during the Summer Olympics. During this time, the number of emergency room visits dropped precipitously. The moment the Olympics ended and the cars came back, the number jumped up again.

Is the Furniture Poison?

I once met a gray-haired black man in New York's Central Park. He was fishing in the Harlem Meer, a very shallow body of water at the northeast corner of the park. He was catching sunnies—sunfish—and because the water was so shallow, I could see the fish clearing their circular nests on the bottom. I could also see, scattered across the bottom, old bottle caps, crushed cans, condoms, small crack vials, knots of decaying yellow and black leaves, a wheel from a roller skate, a part of a bag of Wise potato chips, some of the hub of an old bicycle wheel, a few spokes still attached like the spines of anemone. He told me he had once caught a five-pound catfish in this same lake. I made appreciative remarks, as any fisherman would, with just a skeptical glance at the shallow meer and the thought that maybe a two-pound fish, if that, would be more like it. I noticed that the sunnies he had caught were swimming around in a five-gallon compound bucket.

"What are you going to do with them?" I asked.

"What do you *think* I'm going to do with them?" he answered.

"Not eat them!" I exclaimed. "You can't eat something you catch in the Harlem Meer!"

"Sure I can," he said with a smile. "I always do."

"But you could die of that."

"Well," he reflected. "You gotta die of something."

Is the Furniture Poison?

We both laughed, as did the half-dozen other fishermen who had overheard our talk.

Ever since then, I have had that observation ready when I see people going into apoplexy at the sight of a smoker within fifty yards of them, or covering their mouths in horror when a bus goes by. All our lives are a continual dying, the fisherman reminded me, and no matter how well I protect myself, I am still bound for that end. A better approach to life is to live it in the face of its absolute uncertainty as fully as I can.

Perhaps I would not go so far as to eat fish from the Harlem Meer, but on the other hand, I do go into the office every day, and at home, I sit on the sofa, sleep in the bed, and put up new vinyl wallpaper in the bathroom. Arguably, it would be far better to eat sunnies from the Meer than to live at home or work in the office.

Toxic fogs, smog-producing inversions, and noondays that were black as night alerted those of us who live in the so-called developed world to the dangers of outdoor pollution as long ago as the 1920s and 1930s. (Indeed, King Edward I had complained of the soot in London as early as 1307!) By the 1970s, laws began to control the emissions from these constant burnings, and today the amounts—particularly of black carbon—are well below the levels they once reached. Still, although the outdoor pollutants are less visible than they once were, they continue to be harmful.

In the developing world, the situation is worse. China has created a system for rating air pollution. The minimum acceptable level is grade 2. In 2009, of 500 Chinese cities assessed, 290 did not make this level, and of those, 119 were not even up to the unacceptable grade 3. Under such circumstances, there is strong motive to stay indoors and to make houses into breathing units, isolated from the outdoor air.

In the West, there is less need to hide indoors—though Americans now spend 92 percent of their time inside—but we and everyone else have another reason to make our houses and offices airtight. The costs of heating and cooling encourage conservation by means of better insulation and more tightly sealed doors and windows.

But the indoors is a poor refuge, for the Chinese and for Westerners, because the same distempered technologies that have loaded the air outside with excess carbon, with particulates, sulfates, nitrous oxides, ozone, and volatile organic compounds, have gassed the inside too. The new furniture in my house may resemble the blue easy chair I had from my father and he from his, but they are similar only in the way they look. Inside my father's chair are cotton batting, iron springs, and a cherry frame. It is held together with mortise and tenon joints, and pegged with pine. The upholstery is cotton. The new chair has a plywood seat base, laminated frame, and polyurethane foam. And the chair is held together with formaldehyde-based adhesives. The upholstery is a stain-resistant synthetic.

Recently, when my wife and I went to buy a new bed, we found that only the most expensive ones bragged of their content of cotton and wool. As for the rest, the sales copy was silent on their make-up, emphasizing instead their softness and coziness. It would cost us about two thousand dollars to get a queen-size mattress whose contents we could account for! Comparably cozy beds of mysterious composition cost under seven hundred dollars.

The mystery materials often give off gas. They are the adhesives that glue pieces together or that bind the layers of plywood or the shreds of particleboard. They are the foams and insulators. They are the acoustic tiles, the floor tiles, the subfloor fiberboard, the seat bases, the treated upholsteries, the frames of cabinetry. They continually give off a wide variety of volatile organic compounds into the indoor air, chief among them formaldehyde.

It used to be thought that 0.1 part per million (ppm) of formaldehyde was a safe level, but since then a wide range of different sensitivities to the gas have been found in different people. Some are troubled by as little as 0.01 ppm; others tolerate more than 31 ppm without complaint. Symptoms range from watery eyes, sniffling, and sneezing, to constriction of the airway, difficulty breathing, nausea, chronic asthma and rhinitis, and inflammatory damage to the kidneys, liver, and bloodstream. Rats exposed to a steady dose of 15 ppm develop cancer of the nose.

In response to such data, the California Air Resources Board decided to lower the acceptable level for off-gassing of formaldehyde from indoor products to 0.027 ppm, effective July 2010. As the deadline approached, industry journals were full of hand-wringing and complaints. More time was needed to offload the old product, they complained. One major retailer lamented that it would have to discontinue its most popular bedroom set because it could not comply with the new standard. (A bedroom set! Where people sleep!) Many remarked that they did not trust their Asian suppliers and did not even know if they would perform reliable tests.

In Atlanta, a pulmonologist got a visit from a couple who had just moved into a new house. The house was wonderful, and they were very happy, but the husband had begun to cough and wheeze continuously. They all puzzled as to what could be the cause. Nothing in the house appeared to be responsible. The symptoms continued.

One day at the doctor's office, the wife asked, "What about the sofa?" It turned out that her husband snored. He was frequently exiled from the connubial bed and had to snore away the night in the living room. They had just bought a new sofa.

The wife said, "You know, come to think of it, I get the sniffles around that sofa."

· They removed the sofa. The symptoms disappeared.

About the same time, the Federal Emergency Management Agency (FEMA) quietly began to sell off the travel trailers that had been given to victims of Hurricane Katrina as temporary housing. The prodigious off-gassing of formaldehyde in these trailers had sickened thousands of the recipients of government aid. FEMA officials put warning labels on the trailers, saying they were unsafe for habitation, and sold them anyway. (A label is easily torn off or effaced.) The officials reasoned that the trailers would likely not cause symptoms if they were used only for a weekend trip! Perhaps they should have proudly proclaimed that these trailers were wonderful examples of modern architecture because they "reject the demands of inhabitability," to quote Jorge Luis Borges and Adolfo Bioy-Casares's hoax architecture critic H. Bustos Domecq.

Now up will rise the defenders of our civilization to proclaim that we are far better off in our indoor air than are the benighted 50 percent of the world's population that lives in rural areas, cooking and heating their homes by burning wood, leaves, dung, bones, or whatever organic material they can light.

The defenders are indeed right. The open burning of biomass fuels is responsible for a huge mortality among the rural poor. A World Bank study estimated that 1.9 million deaths per year are due to the inflammatory diseases caused by breathing the smoky indoor air. Particulates released into the home by this burning affect particularly women and children—who spend most of their time there. Asthma is the least of the problems. More damaging are serious lung disorders such as emphysema, although hardly a single one of the dying has ever smoked. Perhaps three billion people are affected.

But there is a ready and reliable solution: improve the stoves and vent them through a tight chimney. The problem goes up in smoke. Dr. Roberto Accinelli Tanaka instituted a stove replacement program in two rural towns in Peru and studied the results. With the new stoves, the proportion of women in the study group reporting daily morning coughs declined from 80 percent to 35 percent; the proportion of those reporting dizziness from moderate exercise, from 80 percent to 40 percent. The incidence of pneumonia dropped from 17 percent to 2 percent. The problem of biomass fuels is serious indeed, but it is tractable. An individual's change of mind and a relatively cheap new stove are all that is required.

Our problems in the industrialized world are less immediately life-threatening, but also far less tractable. It is not just a question of buying our bedroom set from a different craftsman, since most of our buildings and our furniture are not made by craftsmen. They are rather assembled on production lines in far parts of the world and transported to our sites, or they are assembled locally out of parts sourced from such production lines.

Our problem then is not just about a new stove and a chimney. It is about a different way of making things. In the developed West, only the affluent can afford craft products, and indeed they flaunt their ability to get such products. The Amish have an idea that goes under the rubric of "No unequal yoke." They will not become involved in a transaction that includes an entity far larger in scale and scope, an entity that they cannot engage as an equal in the transaction. Our civilization suffers from a yoke so unequal that we can no longer identify the partners in it. The retailer buys from the jobber who buys from the broker who buys from the factory in China whose parts come from a manufacturer in Vietnam, who ships to a port of entry and trucks to the local area, and at last with great good luck and just in the nick of time, the perfect-looking shiny product arrives to be sold in the showroom. It looks as perfect as modern marketing and finishing can make it look.

But underneath is chaos. Not the play chaos of scientists, but the denaturing, disfiguring, morbid, depauperating, deranging, body-and-soul-decomposing chaos of a badly made thing that barely keeps alive the people who have made it and shipped it, while ill serving the customer who receives it. The only ones who do well in the transaction are the managers who conceived and executed the scheme. And they do well only financially. And where do *they* go to buy furniture? They go down to that fine local maker who can tell them where every piece of wood in the dining room table was cut, and by whom, and who joints his table with the care of a Shaker craftsman and finishes it with beeswax.

The Air after 9/11

On September 11, 2001, two planes struck the twin towers of the World Trade Center in lower Manhattan. Within an hour and a half, both buildings had collapsed, pulverizing and expelling into the air cement, wallboard, plastic, cellulose, mineral wool, fiberglass, cement dust, asbestos, microscopic shards of glass, silica, heavy metals, and organic compounds, as well as carcinogenic benzene and other combustion products from the burning 23,775 gallons of jet fuel. This was neither a brick and mortar building nor a stone or wooden one. It was a curtain wall of glass, behind which were interior walls of sheet rock and mountains of plastic for the furniture and housings of the computers. The fires continued unabated until 14 September, when the first postattack rain diminished them somewhat and washed some of the dust out of the air and into the Hudson and the East River. The fires were not finally extinguished until weeks later, but they again diminished in strength after a second rainfall on September 25.

Nevertheless, on September 13, New York Mayor Rudolph Giuliani reported that "the air is safe as far as we can tell, with respect to chemical and biological agents." On September 18, Christine Whitman, administrator of the Environmental Protection Agency (EPA), reported that she was "glad to reassure the people of New York . . . that their air is safe to breathe and the water is safe to drink."

On September 27, a crew from my small tree company and I wended our way through the mountainous traffic, and through a checkpoint at Brooklyn Bridge followed by one at Canal Street in lower Manhattan, to a client located on Broadway, about a block and a half from the burning pile. It took us about two hours to get from the office in Red Hook, Brooklyn, to the site approximately one and a half miles away. We needed to care for a long line of big upright hollies planted in raised containers at a building there. We were concerned they had been damaged, and wanted to assess the soil condition, since we had reason to believe there had been a massive influx of burned junk.

On 9/11, my crew had been working a little east of there at a memorial park in lower Manhattan, pruning trees, when my foreman heard a loud sound and noticed paper falling through the air and settling in the tree. He picked up a piece with the end of his pole saw. It seemed to have blood on it. He came down from the tree and called me. The crew shouldered their gear and walked out of Manhattan over the Brooklyn Bridge. By the time I saw them—I was standing at the Brooklyn end of the bridge because no one was being allowed to cross into Manhattan—they were completely covered in a gray dust that was like silt in a matrix of cotton. The hollies must have been covered too, then.

Sixteen days later, four of us arrived at the site on Broadway. We had been told the air was safe, and we saw what looked reassuringly like an air sampler attached to a light pole near the hollies. Nonetheless, because I apply pesticides, I have a good selection of masks and respirators. I had asked the men to bring these, just in case. We got out of the truck. The wind was blowing what remained of the smoke plume from the towers to the south, so it did not pass right over us.

From a distance, the trees looked relatively undamaged. I walked about fifty yards to the raised containers. The soil surface was six to eight inches deep in each container. The whole space between the top of the soil and the lip of the containers was filled with that same cotton silt that had come out of Manhattan with my men on September 11.

My foreman appeared opposite me on the other side of the container. I was starting to feel a little dizzy and my throat was burning. "Get out the masks," I said. He already had them in his hands. We decided to clean out and discard the detritus that had settled in the containers. Whatever it was, I figured it could not be good for the plants. As is our standard practice, we took a sample of the material to have it tested for pH and nutrients. We applied a root stimulant with water, to help the trees recover.

On our way out, I looked with suspicion at what I imagined was the EPA monitoring device. It was a sort of stainless-steel slide whistle elegantly strapped to the light post. We knew the air was not right just by breathing it. We took our sample of the detritus with an old trowel. When the sample came back from the lab, our suspicions were confirmed. The pH was a little over 10, almost a million times more alkaline than what a holly likes, and who knows what it would do to a human lung. The pH of caustic lye is only 13, and that of ammonia is 11.

As it turns out, however, the EPA had been in there way ahead of us. On September 12 and 13, they swooped in and took samples at a number of sites within a half-mile radius of the World Trade Center footprint. To refine their samples, they first used a 53-micron sieve to take out the bigger particles. They stirred up what remained and sieved again to sort out particles larger than 10.0 microns. They then used something called a 2.5-micron cut cyclone to get down to particles that were 2.5 microns or smaller. They collected the 2.5-micron fraction on Teflon filters. Only about 2.2 to 4.0 percent of the total sample was that small. They reasoned that particles larger than 5 microns seldom are successfully deposited in the lungs of lab animals, and there was generally very little material at all in the 2.5- to 10.0-micron category.

Then they extracted it, wetted it, pipetted it, shook it, sonicated it, extracted it, desiccated it, took the pH, froze it, lyophilized it, and finally analyzed the contents, reserving a little for use in toxicology studies on mice. To tell what was in it, they used X-ray fluorescence, neutron activation analysis, and inductively coupled plasma spectrometry. What a lot of astonishing care they lavished on this woolly dust! There was only one problem: they got the wrong samples.

Instead of taking air samples, they sampled the dust on the ground. Not that that would not give them interesting and useful results. A lot of the fallen dust could be and was resuspended by the wind. And it was certainly interesting to us with regard to plants, which take up most of their nutrients through the soil. But most of the internal exposure in humans would come through the air entering the lungs. What was now on the ground had recently been in the air, but why not also sample what was still in the air? Pierre Miquel could certainly have helped the EPA here, even with his primitive spore sucker.

The particles that remain longest in the air are typically the smallest ones. Heavier, larger particles settle first. So if the EPA scientists were looking for the fraction 2.5 microns or smaller, they were looking in the wrong place. Likewise, 2.5- to 10.0-micron particles still might more likely be found in the air than on the ground. The EPA did not start taking actual *air* samples until September 25. Yet by September 18, the EPA administrator was assuring the citizens of New York that all was well.

Even with the ground samples, however, all was not well. Like us, the EPA scientists got pH readings of 9 to 11 for the materials they scooped up. And they found that calcium carbonate and calcium sulfate—both major ingredients of wallboard as well as cement and concrete aggregate—were major parts of the dust, as they had been of the building. The scientists noted without comment that fibers approximately 1.0 micron in diameter were found in most of the samples. They did not mention other glass fibers because they are typically longer than 2.5 microns, although their diameter is less than 2.5 microns. So, the pH was high; the calcium materials were known irritants to the eyes, nose, and throat; and although the scientists did not note it, the presence of longer, slender fibers might result in materials that could lodge and persist in the lungs.

Yet both the mayor of New York and the head of the EPA had already assured us that the air was safe to breathe. Perhaps they were depending on the resilience of the human lung. It is a fact that people typically consume at least two tablespoons of mixed dust per day, yet the lungs do not fill up. Why? Because the lungs are an organ that makes all the EPA's fancy testing look like a kid playing with Tinkertoys.

There are three parts to our breathing apparatus: the trachea; the bronchial tubes that lead into the lungs proper; and the masses of the lungs, full of a dense network of alveoli, where the actual gas exchange takes place. The first two are lined with mucus-impregnated cilia. The larger particles of dust—whether they be fungal spores or silica—tend to get caught on the cilia in the trachea or the bronchial tubes. From there, the cilia try to pass the particle, hair over hair, back up to the place where it is dumped into the glottis and then routed to our digestive system. So we eat that dust, but we do not necessarily breathe it.

Smaller particles may actually get down into the alveoli, thus the source of the EPA's worry about the dust smaller than 2.5 microns. Even here, however, the organ has an answer. Cells called phagocytes—that is, eating cells—swallow up the offending particle and again deliver it back to the bronchial tubes, where it takes the cilial elevator to the glottis, and so on through the digestive system and out again. Particles that escape the phagocytes may instead reach the lymph and be carried off through the bloodstream.

The EPA officials depended on the resilience of the human lung. Perhaps they should also have read a little more classical literature, or remembered the sayings of their youth. When I was a boy, if we were being sent to what we regarded as hard and hopeless labor, we said that they were sending us to the salt mines. People have been saying something like this for two millennia, because in classical times the worst thing that could happen to them was to be sent into a mine. Whether they mined salt or copper or iron, their doom was certain. In most cultures, only criminals were sent into the mines, and for the most heinous crimes. It was expected that they would die there, and they usually did, within eight years at the most. No one was measuring to see if the particles they knocked off with their picks were greater or less than 2.5 microns in diameter. The point was that the air was full of dust, enough to overwhelm the elegant design of the lungs. The air at the World Trade Center after 9/11 was more like that in a mine rather than the air after a mere release of dust.

It is interesting to note that a day after he had assured everyone there was no danger, Mayor Giuliani contacted his law department, instructing the lawyers to seek to limit the amount of damages that could be extracted for injuries suffered on the site.

Ten years later, the number of people who have sought medical advice as a result of their exposure at the site amounts to forty-three thousand of the sixty to seventy thousand people who worked there. They complain of everything from persistent cough, wheezing, breathlessness, asthma, sinusitis, and laryngitis, to serious diseases including forms of pneumonia, sarcoidosis, and bronchiolitis, to acid reflux and loss of the sense of smell, to posttraumatic stress disorder.

Seven of the worst-affected patients had biopsies done in 2007 at Mount Sinai Hospital, as part of the World Trade Center Medical Monitoring and Treatment Program. Six of the seven showed significant quantities of aluminum and magnesium silicates in the lungs. Four of the seven showed chrysolite asbestos. Surprisingly—and potentially more dangerous—four of the seven showed carbon nanotubes in the lungs. These spider webs of carbon, only two to two hundred nanometers in diameter but often long enough to look tangled in the biopsy specimens, were likely products of the fire, the transformed residues of plastics. It appeared in each patient that these tubes were persistent, caused inflammation and fibrosis, and potentially were the nuclei for nodules that formed, reducing lung volume.

The nanotubes are similar to another long thin contaminant in the postattack air. Although fiberglass fibers may be well over 2.5 microns in length, they may be less than 1.0 micron in diameter. In some cases, these shards became lodged in the lungs of responders, where they can shed smaller attached particles, creating a sort of glass grenade in the lungs.

Among the worst features of the continuing reports of lung and other health problems is that they are increasing, not decreasing, as the human bodies continue to react and modify tissues in response to internal irritants that will not decompose or go away.

When Christine Whitman was severely criticized in congressional hearings for her comment about the air after 9/11, she defended herself vigorously. People, she explained, needed to be reassured that everything would get back to normal. What was she to tell them? That we would know nothing for weeks?

I find it very odd that in a democracy we should assert that a reassuring statement is better than a true one. It is the totalitarian state that asserts that its higher-ups know all the answers which they will dispense to us as needed. (That is why the German weather forecast for D-day was so poor, as you will see on page 144.) In a democracy, we are meant to know, to debate, to find out together. This ought particularly to be the case when the air we all breathe is in question.

Spinning

Weaving

The air is a weaving. Like a piece of cloth, it shows a beautiful pattern. But you have to look very closely to see the colors and forms beneath its surface, the weave by which it is made. The air is the weaving of gases and ground. When rain or snow falls, it is seldom just water that comes down. Rather, it is a solution of water with all the dusts, the liquids, the smokes, and the microscopic organisms that have risen from the surface of the earth.

Each stir of the wind lofts particles of blue jean threads, plant hairs, skin cells, spores, yeast, algae, plankton, bacteria, pollen, soil, silica, soot, dead bugs, the scales of moth wings into it. Each cough or sigh or song releases more into the air. The fungi fire their spores into it, and the wind-pollinated plants open their flowers and shake out their pollen into the air. What smells in a flower, a forest, or a fart rises into it and condenses into liquid particles. Forest fires and volcanoes add to it. So do power plants, car and truck exhaust, the smokestacks of ships, and the contrails of planes. All of these particles are called by the general name "aerosols," that is, things dissolved in air.

Imagine you are holding a basketball in front of you, one hand on top and one on the bottom. Now, move your hands as though they were feeling all around the surface of the ball. In that volume of air, there are at least fifteen thousand bacteria. You might also find ten thousand grains of silicate dirt, a material that looks like tiny shards of cracked glass under the microscope; and another ten thousand black spots of carbon, whether from exhaust pipes, barbecue fires, forest burning, tire rubber, or all of them at once. Maybe there are another few thousand particles of brown dirt, mainly humic acids. In spring, you might find fifty thousand pollen grains, maybe all or most of them from the two or three species shedding at that moment, and another thirty-five hundred fungal spores. (If you happen to be standing near a happy and productive shelf mushroom of the genus *Ganoderma*, on the other hand, you might get a dose of more than a million, since the fruit can put out thirty billion spores each day.) Aerosols of carbon, sulfate, and nitrate, and drops derived from the defensive chemicals, terpenes and isoprenes, emitted by trees, flowers, and grasses—depending on just how full the air is that day— number between 74 million and 299 billion. Among that number too will figure droplets of fat, the most common aerosol in New York City, emitted by restaurant chimneys and by thousands of food carts.

By no means is the air empty. There might be many fewer aerosols on a calm day in midwinter in a cold infertile place, but never none. You breathe all of them in and out. Some cause allergies, some cause worse; most do nothing at all.

Around the world, there are one billion metric tons of organic aerosols in the air each year, with another five billion metric tons of mineral dust, and 3.3 billion metric tons of sea salt. There are likely between 10^{22} and 10^{24} bacterial cells in the air at any one time. More than fifty million tons of fungal spores travel by air each year. Of reflective sulfates, there are perhaps a hundred million metric tons— from coal burning, from the oceans, from aircraft, and from fires. Of organic carbon, there are another fifty million metric tons, from the burning of fossil fuels and from fires, as well as another twenty million metric tons of black carbon, the soot that you can see coming from the tailpipes or from dirty coal. Soils, people, animals, and fertilizers emit nitrous oxides that turn to nitrate aerosols, at a rate of about eighty million metric tons each year.

It is possible for rain or snow to fall without the intervention of any of these aerosols. When pure water is lifted high into the atmosphere and reaches temperatures below −40 degrees Fahrenheit, ice forms spontaneously, and being heavy, it begins to fall, entraining more ice and more water to fall with it. In warm clouds, where the air is super-saturated to two or three times the theoretical maximum amount of vapor it can contain, small cloud droplets begin to aggregate, gain mass, and fall, all by themselves. In this case, the falling water smacks into aerosols, carrying them to the ground, but it does not otherwise combine with them.

However, in most of the temperate world, cloud droplets and cloud crystals—the precursors of rain and snow—happen because water and aerosols become one. Each cloud drop is a solution of an aerosol with water. Each cloud crystal is an ice cube formed on the lattice provided by an aerosol. Every time this rain or snow falls, then, it is not made of just water but is a soup that might contain everything from nitrates and sulfates to humin and silica and phosphorus, to bacteria and fungal spores.

How does the weaving of gases and ground work? Consider the sky above one of the most remote places on earth, the Amazon rain forest north of Manaus in Brazil. The trade winds out of the northeast must travel more than eight hundred miles over the rain forest to reach this area. In the rainy season, the frequent cloudbursts over the forest deplete the air of pollutants. Here, if anywhere, the weaving must work as it did before people filled the air with pollutants.

By far the greatest number of aerosols in this sky are those that come from what the trees and other plants give off—not what their leaves or the fungi that live on them give off, but the gases that the plants themselves emit. These are mainly terpenes and isoprenes. We detect the terpenes in the air as the forest smell, or the odor of a flower. The plants use them as attractants and repellants. The isoprenes help plants resist damage from intense light. These substances are volatile gases when we sniff them, but as they rise through the air they condense into tiny liquid aerosols—mainly smaller than one micron. At this size they make excellent cloud condensation nuclei. The blue of the Blue Ridge Mountains and the great smoke of the Great Smoky Mountains are entirely due to water that has condensed on aerosols of this kind, creating the characteristic haze.

Next most common in the sky over the rain forest are the composite particles. Their cores are sulfates or chlorides that blow in from the oceans. These particles acquire a veneer of the liquefied exudations from the forest, so they are a mixture of inorganic and organic materials.

Far fewer in number but greater in mass are the primary particles that blow up into the air. These include leaf hairs, bits of cellular matter of leaves or skin, fungal spores, bacteria, and viruses. All the way across the Atlantic and over eight hundred miles of forest, the wind, as Darwin conceived, brings mineral dusts—chiefly clay minerals—from the Sahara. And even deep in the Amazon there are particles of carbon—both black and clear—from the burning of wood, of coal, and of oil. Many of these particles also take on a coating of the other organic aerosols, whose origin is the gases given off by the trees.

The larger bits contribute only 1 percent of the particles in this air, but they make up 70 percent of their mass. There may be only two or three of the big particles in a given gallon of air aloft, but their effects are crucial.

The tiny particles are good at making cloud droplets but are poor at making rain. The smallest updraft is enough to keep these droplets suspended in the air. The big particles are most often the ones to start cloud formation and rain. At temperatures above −13 degrees Fahrenheit, it is the spores, the leaf cells, the skin fragments that first allow ice to form, clouds to swell, and rain to fall. When the temperature falls below –13 degrees, then the clay particles that have come all the way from the Sahara become effective ice nuclei and so lead to rain. The residues of the desert make the rain of the rain forest.

When these large particles are coated with organic aerosol, they might instead act as immense cloud condensation nuclei. Because the surface area and mass of the impregnated particle is so much greater than that of an ordinary isoprene-derived aerosol, it is already almost heavy enough to fall. When its organic coating soaks up water, it begins to fall, and even without ice nuclei, rain begins.

The weaving of the air brings the rain. The rain maintains the forest, but what allows the forest to rain is partly emitted by the forest itself—the organic aerosols, the microscopic plant hairs, the spores, the bacteria—and partly imported from across the seas.

In this faraway and relatively pristine environment, the number of aerosols is what determines how many droplets will form and how much rain will fall. The situation is different where people live and constant burning, growing, and harvesting occur. In more polluted parts of Amazonia, the number of human-made aerosols is vast. When clouds form in such a region, and in most of the rest of the world, it is not the number of aerosols that determines the clouds and the precipitation. There are always more aerosols available than there is water to mix with them. Rather, it is the strength of the updrafts that determines the strength of clouds and storms.

There have always been more aerosols over land than over the open ocean. Before humans became city dwellers, there were perhaps twice as many aerosols on average over land as over the sea. As humans gathered in large groups, the difference began to accelerate. Even before the industrial era, the burning of wood, turves, and dung—to heat houses, to fire clay, to forge iron—put large amounts of soot and other carbon compounds into the air, along with a few sulfates and nitrates. From these came the pea-soup fogs that could make noonday London as dark as dusk.

In the twentieth century, much of the industrial world began to ban open burning, reducing the amount of black carbon in the air. At the same time, however, there was a rapid and sustained rise in the burning of coal and oil, for heating and cooling, for industrial processes, and for transportation. Ocean spray, once the chief source of sulfate aerosols, now runs a distant second to the sulfates produced by burning coal. At least five times as much sulfate comes from coal as from the seas. The amount of nitrate has also increased dramatically, some from tailpipes and a great deal from fertilizer-based agriculture.

There is now likely to be an order of magnitude more aerosols over land than over the remote oceans. In other words, if prior to urbanization there were a thousand aerosols in a packet of sea air, there might have been two thousand in the same-sized packet over land. Today, by contrast, if there are a thousand aerosols over the ocean, there are ten thousand or more in the same-sized air parcel over land.

Each tiny aerosol attracts water. Because the amount of water is limited and the number of aerosols large, each aerosol creates a smaller water droplet. The result may be plenty of cloud, but little immediate rain, because the cloud droplets are too small and light to fall. Indeed, scientists studying pollution in the mid-twentieth century theorized that polluted air would cause droughts because the small droplets would never coalesce and fall. And indeed, when you give the air unlimited aerosols all at once—as in a wildfire—rainfall is suppressed.

But this is not our experience. If anything, the last part of the twentieth and the first part of the twenty-first century have seen an increase in storms, particularly violent storms with large amounts of rain and snow. The large number of aerosols plays a part in this change.

In places like Beijing, China, where there is still a great deal of open burning and where poor-grade coal is a common industrial fuel, there is a great deal of soot in the air. Soot is black. It absorbs sunlight, and as it does so, it warms. A large number of black-carbon aerosols, therefore, will tend to create a warm layer of air aloft. The warm layer creates a temperature inversion that inhibits the rising of water-laden air. Still, the sun heats both the sooty air and the land and water beneath. When solar heating finally makes the wet air warmer than the inversion layer, the lower air punches up through the inversion. The fast-rising moisture condenses and falls with terrific force.

But *we*, in the Western world, are not like that. No indeed. We have long ago banned open burning, and we promote the use of cleaner coal. There is less black carbon in our air. So why do we too experience a larger number of severe storms? Even though few of the aerosols in our air are black, there are still huge numbers of them, and so there are large numbers of tiny cloud droplets. One consequence is that the clouds made from such aerosols live longer. They do not "rain out" as quickly, as the saying goes. The amount of water vapor in the air on average has increased by 5 percent in the years since World War II. The vapor represents a lot more fuel to make bigger storms.

Compare the air to a forest. When forest fires occur regularly, there is less fuel for any one fire, so the burns don't become conflagrations. If you prevent forest fires and build up a huge mass of living and dead wood in the forest, when a burn at last occurs, it is likely to be serious and large. When increased atmospheric carbon warms the air and when more vapor is available, conflagrational storms become more likely.

Not only is there more water in the air, but as the air is in constant motion, it is possible for the laden air to move to places where mountains or fronts force it to rise, or where the updrafts are strong enough to carry it far aloft. Once it reaches high elevations, where the temperature is less than −49 degrees Fahrenheit, the water will spontaneously form ice and heavy precipitation will begin.

When there is more water vapor in the air, heating and spinning produce dramatic effects. The year 2011 was a banner year for storms in the eastern United States. Twice in April—from the fourteenth to the sixteenth and again from the twenty-fifth to the twenty-eighth—large tornado outbreaks occurred across the Southeast and into the Northeast and Canada. In the second outbreak, 353 tornadoes touched down, the largest number ever recorded. Solid brick homes were pulverized, pick-up trucks ripped to pieces, cars wrapped around tree trunks, and a Wrangler jeans plant blew away. Blue jeans fell from the sky across three counties.

On August 28, a storm named Irene made landfall in New Jersey and moved north across New York, Connecticut, and Vermont. In New York City, the authorities closed subways and trains and enforced mandatory evacuation zones, in anticipation of a major hurricane. Little damage occurred, and the local media sounded almost disappointed as they noted that the hurricane had been downgraded to a tropical storm.

The winds disappointed, but in upstate New York and Vermont, the rain did not. It began on the evening of August 27 and continued throughout the next day. A light rain turned to a steady rain, and a steady rain to a pounding rain. I went to sleep to the sound of it on the roof, woke to the same sound twice during the night, and got up in the morning to find the rain still falling. I have always loved the sound of rain on the roof. Not anymore. It would not stop, not for the whole night, not until the afternoon of the following day.

The waterfall outside my house is usually loud. Now I could not talk over it. Standing by the roadside on an ordinary day, I would look down about thirty feet into the gorge to see the falls. This morning the water had risen to within five feet of where I was standing. As I watched, a red footbridge from up the hill came caroming down the chute of water and rushed away toward the Hudson. Water started to leak through the stone walls of our house.

A classic nor'easter spin brought the storm. Forecasters at the National Weather Service in Albany tracked it the best they could. Up until August 27, they were still not sure if the vortex would hug the coast or spin away offshore. A parcel of upper air energy from

Alaska made its way across the country. By the evening of the twenty-seventh, they could see that the trough from Alaska would run into a ridge offshore, squeezing Irene in between them.

The forecasters knew then that it would be a historic storm, not for its wind but for its water. They figured on eight to twelve inches of rain in some parts of the local area. Instead, they got twelve to eighteen inches. Bridges that had stood for two hundred years were washed out. Towns that had not flooded since the American Revolution found themselves underwater. Now, when I hear rain on the roof, I look toward the waterfall. It had come very close to breaking its banks.

Almost exactly two months later, another anomalous storm hit the Northeast. Again, it was propelled by the cyclonic spin of a nor'easter. Squeezed between a high-pressure anticyclone to the west and a spinning low-pressure cyclone just offshore, moisture-laden air spun up from New Jersey, into New York and New England. More than a foot of heavy wet snow fell in some places.

During Irene, the rains saturated the ground, causing tree root systems to loosen, so whole trees often failed from their base. In the autumn snowstorm, the leaves were still on the trees, and branches and limbs broke under the load wherever they were weakly attached or wounded. The landscape looked as though a heavy hand had simply folded the trees over, leaving large limbs and leaders hanging aloft. As it was happening, the reports of cracking limbs made the forest sound as though an army of hunters were firing at fleeing deer. The date was October 29. The last date on which more than an inch of snow had fallen in New York in the autumn had been November 1, 1879.

Will this pattern of storms be seen in the future as an anomaly? Or with so much more water vapor in the air, is it now normal? "Everyone talks about global warming," said Gavin Schmidt, head of the NASA climate models at the Goddard Institute for Space Studies, "but changes in rainfall often have a bigger impact. We're forcing the climate into a state we have not seen for millions of years."

Vortices

Spin drives the power of storms. The spin might be as small as the twist that a passing jack rabbit starts in hot dry desert air. It might be a dust devil that spins up and lifts a kangaroo rat fifty feet into the air before dropping him. (The rat is angry, but unhurt.) Or it might be as large as the one-thousand-mile-diameter, counterclockwise spinning cyclone of a nor'easter that crosses whole continents, dropping rain and snow and bringing damaging winds. It might be as strong as the three-hundred-mile-per-hour tornado in Tell, Texas, that drove a wisp of straw straight through a telephone pole. Or it might be as devastating as the hurricane whose storm surge washed over Galveston, Texas, in 1900, knocking most of the town's buildings off their foundations and killing eight thousand people.

Spinning storms represent the freedom of the air. What happens in their wake is unpredictable. A tornado can open the ground allowing prairie grass to grow stronger. It can cause one town to give up and its citizens to move away. Another town might find a civic purpose that it had lacked for a century. A hurricane can do likewise. It can help to topple the party of an American president, for example, as the disastrous response to Hurricane Katrina did to the Republican Party during George W. Bush's presidency. But it can also bring a boon to fishermen. In the Far East, fishing fleets sail into the water where a typhoon has passed, knowing that it is likely to have stirred up nutrients from the bottom. The nutrients cause a bloom of plankton, and the bloom brings schools of fish to feed. The fishermen prosper. Global warming also is marginally slowed, because as they die, the plankton sink out of sight, carrying their carbon with them. For millions of years, that carbon may remain buried in deep sea sediments.

The largest spins—the great thousand-mile vortices of the cyclones that cross the Northern Hemisphere continents from west to east— do more than bring bad weather. The cyclones damp the winds. Max Margules, who in 1903 wrote his seminal study "On the Energy of Storms," noted that every storm transforms heat energy into mechanical energy. The warm rising air and the cold sinking air acquire a spinning motion. To conserve energy, that motion must be spent. If it were all spent as wind, we would live with average winter wind speeds above a hundred miles an hour. But the spins lift vapor, condense it into water, and spill it again. The evaporation uses some of the mechanical energy, and more is dissipated in the friction of falling rain and snow. We get big winds, all right, but we do not blow away.

More important, the counterclockwise cyclones keep the whole atmosphere in motion. Aloft in the Northern Hemisphere, the air moves in general from west to east. Clockwise-spinning anticyclones have high pressure at their center. They bring sinking air and clear weather. Counterclockwise-spinning cyclones have low pressure at their center. They bring precipitation and wind. The anticyclones make ridges in the moving air, and the cyclones make troughs.

The cyclones work against the flow of the atmosphere because their flow turns back from east to west. You might think that the whole worldwide circulation of the air, blocked by these vortices, would slow to a crawl, then stop. Whatever weather you were having at that moment, you would have eternally. But the contrary is the case. Think of three logs placed next to each other, in contact along their whole length. If you spin the two outside logs, the inside log will turn also, apparently all by itself. The relative motion of the other two logs is what guides and directs the motion of the middle log. Just so, the spin of the cyclones is in fact what keeps both cyclones and anticyclones heading from west to east, bringing their succession of storms and sunny days. The weather is steered along the pattern of ridges and troughs that forms as the contrary spins roll.

The cyclones are the big weather-makers for the temperate world. (In what follows, we will consider the Northern Hemisphere only. The same rules apply to the Southern Hemisphere, only there the spins are reversed.) The air of the middle latitudes is warmer than the air at the poles, so the warmer air rises and moves northward. The spinning of the earth turns that northward flow to the east. Hence, the general path of air around the north temperate sector of the globe is from west to east—that is, westerly. The very cold air from the polar region sags southward and turns westward. The two flows might simply pass one another, or they might ride over and under. Sometimes, however, the warm air digs north and east into the flow of the cold air, while the cold air digs south and west into the flow of the warm air. In that case, a counterclockwise rotation begins. It is like the eddies at the edge of a creek, where the water spins back on itself instead of simply flowing downhill. Both masses of air begin to spin around an empty center. This center creates a centrifugal force that empties air out, while a contrariwise pressure-gradient force—the tendency of winds to blow from high to low pressure—pushes back in. A spinning vortex forms, with low pressure at its center. This vortex shape is responsible for the power of storms.

Stronger in winter than summer, these cyclones are not rare events. There are more than six hundred each year in the Northern Hemisphere. When they come along the eastern seaboard of the United States, we expect a period of steady rain (the warm front lifting), then a clearing, then a shot of heavy rain (the cold front passing) followed by gradual clearing. Pilots are so familiar with these cyclones that they have mnemonics to help them remember what to do. One goes, "Look for the worst weather in the northeast corner of a low."

~

The spins that lead to the big winds—tornadoes and hurricanes— are infrequent, because only very particular combinations of temperature, pressure, and wind create these spins. We know more or less where and when they will occur, but their number, strength, time, and location are mysteries until they appear.

The strongest winds naturally occurring on the surface of the earth—almost three hundred miles per hour—are found in the biggest tornadoes. They come from a vortex with runaway tightening, where the inward- and outward-tending forces of the spin collapse toward the center point, dramatically accelerating the motion. There are only two regions in the world where tornadoes are common. One encompasses Bangladesh and northeastern India. The other is the American Midwest. Both regions lie east of a major mountain range (Rocky Mountains for the Midwest) and north of a warm ocean (the Gulf of Mexico). The combined influence of the two is what drives these intense and slender spins.

In the spring as the world is warming, the prevailing westerly winds force air up the west side of the Rockies. The air cools as it rises, and precipitation may fall. The air loses much of its moisture, and therefore is dry when it passes the summits of the range. On the east side, the air flows back down the slopes. When air flows down a slope, it compresses and warms. This warm air spreads out like a blanket over the Midwest. Meanwhile, southerly winds bring the very moist air of the Gulf of Mexico northward into the region. This air is cooler than the air that flows down from the mountains. It filters in beneath the warmer layer.

The stage is set for what the fine student of tornadoes Howard Bluestein lovingly calls "severe weather." Forty years ago, when he was graduating from the Massachusetts Institute of Technology in Cambridge, Bluestein was invited to visit the University of Oklahoma at Norman. Perhaps, the inviter reasoned, he will stay with us to study these terrific storms. Bluestein replied that he wouldn't go there unless it was the last place on earth, but somehow he was talked into it. Once he got there, he never left.

The first ingredient you need for a tornado, Bluestein explained, is a lot of energy in the air. When the warming mountain air lies over the slightly cooler wet Gulf air, the situation is more or less stable as each day begins. As the day warms, however, the sun heats the ground, and the moist air near the surface gets warmer—not everywhere, but where the ground is warmest. There, the low-level air heats and begins to rise. It pushes up against the still slightly warmer dry mountain air above it, rising to the level where the temperature of the two layers is equal.

Imagine you are pushing against a web that resists you. You push harder and harder. There is more and more potential energy in your pushing, but it is still butting up against the stretching web. Suddenly, the web breaks. The potential energy is released as kinetic energy, and you seem to fly through the shredded web into the air beyond. That is what happens as the rising wet air warms. When it is warm enough, it bursts through the cap of mountain air and sails upward all the way into the stratosphere. As it rises, the water condenses, releasing more energy. Towering cumulonimbus clouds form. The energy contained in the storm is now tremendous. Thunderstorms with torrential rains and heavy winds are the result.

When such storms occur close together, they tend to cancel one another out. When the rain falls, part of it evaporates as it enters into unsaturated air. The evaporation cools the air. This cold air shuts off the temperature gradient that is driving wet air upward. When the storms occur in widely enough separated locations, however, the cold pools do not prevent other storms from forming.

Multiple large thunderstorms are what tornadoes need in order to form. And they need two more things. There has to be spin up high in the storm, whether caused by a low-level jet of air or by a new converging weather front. And that high spin needs to meet a low one. Sometimes, the low spin is caused when friction with the ground shifts the low-level wind direction. More often, it comes from the meeting of cold air and warm air at the edge of a major thunderstorm.

Whenever they appear, tornadoes usually occupy the same part of an intense thunderstorm, right in front of a sharply delineated protuberance at the base of the storm's leading edge, called a wall cloud. This is the place in the storm where maximum updrafts and maximum downdrafts meet. The air coming into the cloud and rising is very warm. The air where rain is falling is cooling as the raindrops evaporate, soaking up energy. Where the cooling air meets the warm air, spin begins. It is like the air above a radiator in a cool room. Sometimes, you can even see the waves form in the air where the two temperatures meet, just above the radiator top. Fortunately, this combination of ingredients happens comparatively rarely. The great atmosphere scientist Edward Lorenz calculated that the chance of any random gram of air having been part of a tornado as one in one trillion.

Though even a very large tornado is no more than two miles in diameter, the power of the storm in that small area is tremendous. The mechanical power of wind to move standing objects increases as the square of the wind speed. The Fujita Scale of tornado intensity counts F5 tornados as the strongest, with winds of about 260 to over 300 miles per hour. An F5 tornado is characterized in the scale with unscientific candor as "Incredible." You will know if you are in one because "strong frame houses [are] lifted off foundations and carried considerable distances to disintegrate; automobile-sized missiles fly through the air in excess of 100 meters; trees [are] debarked; steel re-enforced concrete structures [are] badly damaged."

Though less than 1 percent of all tornados are this intense, the possibility of such damage makes a good argument for the Plains Indian way of life: travel light and be ready to move. It is interesting to note that of the described symptoms of an F5 tornado, not one of the damaged items is native to the plains. Trees are rare, and when they occur, they are usually found in the canyons made by streams. Grass is the rule, a plant that has 70 percent of its biomass underground. Frame-like structures—forests, for example—do not occur. Most animals live in burrows where they can ride out storms, or in the air where they can soar away. And buffalo, though they slightly resemble automobiles—are specialists in running. Cowboys will tell you that if a bison charges you, do not try to run. Not even the fastest horse can outrun it.

∼

A hurricane, like a tornado, is produced by a very peculiar spin, but one unlike a tornado's. The peak wind speeds are a third slower than those of a tornado, but the hurricane spin covers a lot more territory and lasts days instead of minutes or hours. The diameter of the spin in a big tornado can range from a hundred yards to two miles. In a hurricane, the spin covers fifty miles or more.

To get the whorl of a hurricane, with its eyewall towering from the ocean to the stratosphere, you need the same thing you need for a tornado: rising moist air and something to give it spin. But there the resemblance stops. Most Atlantic hurricanes begin with the warm dry air of desert Africa flowing over the cool wet air of the Atlantic. The meeting of the two makes a kink in the air. The convergence of the two flows pushes the moist air upward. Its vapor condenses, creating more energy from the latent heat of cooling and increasing its buoyancy, resulting in a whopping thunderstorm. Most of these thunderstorms peter out. A few do not.

Where the storm travels over very warm water, the ocean water evaporates into the unsaturated air above it. The kink in flow initiates uplift, so the evaporated water in the air rises. It reaches its dew point and condenses, releasing more energy and increasing buoyancy. The air continues to rise, just as it would in an ordinary thunderstorm. At the top of the troposphere, it spills and begins to descend and warm. The falling air that overflows the storm at the top creates lower pressure beneath it, so more moist air is drawn into the center of the storm and rises.

As long as the seawater on the surface stays very warm, it feeds more evaporating water into the growing storm. The kinked wave, twisted by the turning of the earth, begins to spin. The pressure in the center of the spin drops. Winds near the surface rise. The clouds and the rain will spin in a gyre that grows in speed and intensity from the sea surface all the way to the stratosphere.

The stadium effect of the swirling clouds in the eyewall of a hurricane.
(Courtesy of National Oceanic and Atmospheric Administration)

Pilots who penetrate the eyewall and fly into the central low-pressure eye of the storm see a memorable sight. All around them swirls a coliseum of cloud, sloping outward as it rises, like the stands in an immense stadium. The clouds show colored striation where even stronger convective winds are mixing in. The pilots can see blue sky above them at the top of the storm. Often, they can also see all the way down, ten thousand feet or more, to the whitecaps on the ocean waves.

The process by which the eyewall forms and maintains its spin is so intense and so efficient that it cuts off the normal mixing of warm moist air with cool dry air, the process that usually helps a storm to dissipate. Thus, energy that would otherwise be spent in evaporating water and cooling the air instead must be dissipated by the wind alone.

Spinning air accounts for the power of storms, so weather forecasting focuses on the kinks, the waves, and the vortices that turn vapor-laden air to cloud, precipitation, and wind. All of these are represented on weather maps as ridges, troughs, and cyclonic and anticyclonic gyres. The struggles of the warm, the wet, the cool, and the dry determine the shape and intensity of the spins. When during World War I, Jacob and Vilhelm Bjerknes and Tor Bergeron, of the Bergen School of Meteorology, first drew the weather maps that now every forecast shows, they envisioned the air as a battlefield. Hence, they named the edges where warm air and cold air collided "fronts," like the western front in the war.

Ground Truth

The instrument is about the size of a quart of milk. It is a cardboard box with a water-activated battery inside, along with a pressure sensor. Protruding from the top, maybe four inches, is a thin wire topped by miniature goalposts about the size of a child's thumbnail. Midway between the two posts is a dimple. This little drop of metal is the thermistor, a sensitive thermometer. Printed in large letters along one side of the carton is the legend "HARMLESS WEATHER INSTRUMENT."

Kimberly McMahon, a young woman with long black hair and cinnamon skin, laughed as she explained the words. "Once we had one of these things land in somebody's driveway in Massachusetts," she said. "They called the bomb squad, and *they* got their remote control robot out to look at it." She turned the carton over in her hands, smiling mischievously. "Heck, it was just a harmless radiosonde." Ever since then, every radiosonde launched, which happens twice a day from ninety-three sites around the United States and from another roughly eight hundred places around the world, carries a legend to distinguish it from a terrorist bomb or an alien invasion.

"Ground truth," she said, with reverence. "The radiosondes give us ground truth."

It is a funny name for a truth obtained by releasing a balloon-borne instrument that immediately leaves the earth and climbs to over a hundred thousand feet in altitude, before its helium-filled balloon expands to its breaking point and bursts, dropping the sonde back to earth under a bright-orange plastic parachute. While it is broadcasting data, in fact, a radiosonde is never on the ground. And the facts that it gives are not extrapolations or approximations. They are reliable, undeniable data collected by an instrument that actually was where it said it was, and measured things as they were at that place and at that moment in time. A great deal of weather data comes from satellites looking down from space. They can tell a lot by the color, emissions, and path of the clouds, but they cannot see through the clouds to the surface of the earth. Only the radiosondes—as well as sondes attached to airplanes—climb up from the ground through the atmosphere, measuring the temperature, the dew point, the pressure, and the wind speed and direction as they go. They tell the unvarnished truth.

Everything that happens in the air has to do with only whether the air is rising, what the pressure is, how the wind is blowing, what the temperature of the air mass is, and how much water vapor is in it. The radiosonde measures all these things.

It is a gray day just before dawn near the turn of the year when I arrive at the building housing the National Weather Service in Albany, New York. There is six to eight inches of snow on the ground, and the frost has gone down about a foot into the dirt. Unlike most National Weather Service offices, this one is located not in a cookie-cutter building, but on the third floor of a glass-and-steel academic structure on the campus at the State University at Albany.

Kimberly is already at her desk, the instrument resting gently on a piece of foam beside her. We exchange pleasantries. "Ready to go?" she asked. "Don't take off your coat."

She gives me the quart-sized box. "Don't set it down on anything," she said. "We might damage the instruments."

We climb the stairs to the roof, edge out the door, and round the corner, watching for ice on the walkway. In front of us is a small building that resembles a metal box with a large pimple attached at one end. The pimple is the launch dome.

Inside the building, there is enough heat to run the computer, but in the launch dome there is no heat. The latex balloon fabric is slumped on a raised platform, a yellow hose beside it. Kimberly fixes the hose to the balloon and starts to inflate it with helium, reading off the pressure until she has what she wants. The balloon sways like a drunk trying to rise from the ground, then takes its full shape and rises into the air, bumping the closed roof of the launch dome. She ties off a double knot to seal the end, then ties a second knot to make sure there will be no leak. The knot is attached to one hundred feet of string. At the far end of it, we affix the radiosonde. The instrument needs to hang far enough below the balloon that it does not read the heat the balloon itself radiates.

After a call to the Albany airport to get clearance from air traffic control—we have to wait for a 757 to pass—she opens the dome. The balloon jostles and sidles, like a big dog eager for a walk. When the dome is fully open, she releases the balloon. It rises quickly into the air, then sets off at a forty-five-degree angle to the south-southeast, rising quickly toward the low stratus clouds.

Kimberly grabs the sonde as the one hundred feet of line plays out. Just before it reaches the end, she gives the instrument a toss upward so it clears the edge of the dome. For a moment she remains poised like a modern dancer, her right arm upraised in arabesque.

We leave the little building just in time to see the pale balloon fade and disappear in the stratus, and then retire to the warm office back on the third floor, where the data are already flowing in. The data are automatically plotted on a weather chart called a SkewT diagram. On this graph, the vertical axis shows air pressure and altitude. (The one decreases as the other increases.) The horizontal axis is marked with the temperature in Celsius and Fahrenheit, but the temperature lines in fact tilt to the right of the vertical. (The temperature readings are skewed diagonally to the right, hence, the name "SkewT.") Wind speed and direction are indicated with a system of fletched and barbed arrows, located at the right of the diagram.

There are other forms of thermodynamic diagrams, but this is the easiest to read and interpret. On the left is a green line, indicating the dew point. Slightly to the right is a red line, indicating the temperature. The dew point is the temperature at which this air would be fully saturated with water. When temperature and dew point meet, clouds form and it is a good bet that rain or snow will fall. At the surface this morning, the temperature is 31 degrees Fahrenheit, or just below 0 degrees Celsius, and the dew point is 26 degrees Fahrenheit, or about –5 degrees Celsius.

As the balloon rises, however, the two colored lines change their relative position. At about (one kilometer) (0.6 miles) aloft, the two lines meet. That meeting marks the layer of low stratus through which the sonde left our sight. It also marks the source of the freezing rain that stuck to my window on my drive here.

Just above that, however, the two lines separate widely. The temperature—which had been declining with height—suddenly rises instead. Here is an inversion. Cold air will not rise through warmer air above it. An approaching warm front has ridden in above the stratus layer, capping it at just over a kilometer in altitude. You can read the thickness of the cloud layer right off the chart.

The sonde keeps rising. At about two kilometers (1.9 miles), both the temperature and the dew point begin to decline again, though the lines remain widely separated. There is no cloud layer aloft then, all the way up. At a height of around ten kilometers (6.2 miles), the temperature once again begins to rise and keeps rising until it reaches the end of the chart, when the balloon bursts and the sonde begins its parachute ride back to the surface. This zone of rising temperature

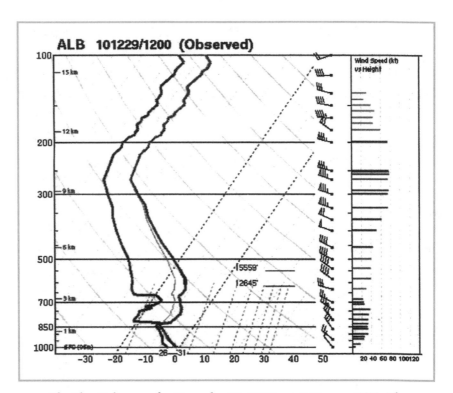

The SkewT diagram for December 29, 2010, at 6:00 a.m. EST. The barbed arrows at right represent direction and speed of the wind. Where temperature and dewpoint meet, precipitation occurs. (Courtesy of National Oceanic and Atmospheric Administration)

aloft marks the stratosphere, where the absorption of ultraviolet radiation by the upper air makes it warmer than the troposphere below it.

Throughout the ascent, the wind speed has risen and fallen at different altitudes, but all of it has come from the northwest. There is no rotation, no suggestion of a forming vortex.

The main questions that our launch raises this morning are the following: Will it snow, sleet, or rain? And will the precipitation freeze when it hits the ground, making black ice? The surface temperature is just below freezing, and the cloud forms aloft at a temperature of about –14 degrees Fahrenheit (–10 degrees Celsius). Water can remain in a liquid, supercool state, down to right about −10 degrees Celsius so whether rain or snow will fall is an open question. In fact, one forecaster coming into the office from the east said he had sleet and snow on his way in. Another, coming in from the north, said he had rain. Because it is already about 32 degrees Fahrenheit (0 degrees Celsius) and the sun has yet to rise, any black ice that forms is liable to be short-lived.

This vintage postcard shows the launch of a German military weather balloon. (Author's collection)

It is amazing to be able to learn so much from an instrument that simply rises through the air. In summer, the radiosonde is key to predicting thunderstorms. It takes wet, fast-rising air to make a powerful thunderstorm. The biggest cells reach all the way up to the stratosphere. Were this August 29, not December 29, the skewed temperatures would likely be over toward 68 degrees Fahrenheit (20 degrees Celsius) or more. If during the afternoon, big wind shifts were to occur, the temperature and dew point lines would almost be joined, and if the two lines were to lean steeply to the left—showing a dramatic decline of temperature with height and so suggesting that the warm wet air would rise rapidly—then the forecaster would be ready to issue warnings for a severe thunderstorm.

Kimberly quality-corrects her data and sends it off to the national Storm Prediction Center. Somewhere up in the air, the radiosonde is probably still descending, perhaps to land in a tree in the southern Catskills or to fall into the Mohawk River. Sometimes, the instruments are recovered and reused. Often, they are not. Still, the budget for the whole national radiosonde program is only about $3 million a year. Compare that to the $200 million it costs to launch a single weather satellite, and the program begins to look pretty cheap, even if three or four times as many balloons were launched.

El Greco's Clouds

When wet air rises, clouds come. Twenty percent of the solar energy that reaches the earth bounces back into the atmosphere. This is the largest transfer of heat on the planet. When the air warms, it vaporizes water and carries the gaseous water high aloft. As it rises, it cools. When the gas has cooled to its dew point, the vapor turns to droplets again, and the clouds appear, looking like wisps, or ragged gray blankets showing shards of blue, or like piles of pillows or stacks of straw, or like white lenses or rolling seas.

Only over the last century have scientists been able to map and describe the life and death of clouds, but over the last half millennium, painters have been giving us clouds for contemplation. Through their work, we have come to know the power of the air to create and to destroy, both in the world and in our hearts. "The sky," wrote the nineteenth-century English painter John Constable, "is the chief organ of sentiment." And he added that the most important thing a painter needed to know about the sky was that it never stands still.

Aristotle agreed, but while Constable celebrated the power of clouds, Aristotle thought the atmosphere a puzzle and a terror. To him it was the most changeable and inconstant thing on earth, but it was also that through which he saw aloft to the perfect, eternal regularity of the heavens. Augustine was of the same opinion. He gave the demons bodies made of air, subject to storms of passion, unlike the unmoving, never-changing real God. The demons, in Augustine, are imaged by weather: storm, tempest, turbulence.

The impulse of the ancients was to exorcise the air. Even where landscapes are seen—whether on vases or in frescoes—they do not picture clouds. The medieval paintings of gardens or of hunts focus in the foreground, sometimes even tilting the picture plane to exclude the sky or filling the frame with trees or flowering plants. Where there is a sky, it is often done in gold.

Weather creeps into paintings when artists begin to value and to show daily life in this world, for it is in the *course* of our lives—not in the great moments, the occasions of the fruition of our busy plans—that we understand the air and our place in it.

Even then, however, clouds are slow to enter the picture. In the wonderful Book of Hours *Les Très Riches Heures du Duc de Berry*, painted by the Limbourg brothers between 1410 and 1416, at least the sky is blue. And in its accurate depiction of the tasks of life, it shows the occasional cloud. In the illustration of February, there is really a cover of stratus, for example. But in the illustrations for the rest of the year, clouds are just fit in to balance the otherwise cobalt blue sky. The human landscape takes up the bulk of the page. Each painting is crowned with a tympanum, a golden semicircular arch, showing the sun upheld by a man riding a horse-drawn court, along with the constellations of the season, and the calendar of the days.

Like Aristotle and Augustine, the painters of the book seemed to regard the sky as an interposition between daily lives on earth and the perfect, geometrical motions of the heavens. Their blues and their wisps of cloud are a shorthand for the atmosphere. The real interest takes place below in human actions and above in the golden tympanum of the eternal zodiac.

How different is the atmosphere of Giovanni Bellini's *Madonna of the Meadow*, painted about a century later. There is no overarching gold. The Madonna and baby sit in the foreground of a worn agricultural landscape. The pair are front and center in the canvas, so large they seem almost like natural features themselves, a kind of double mountain. But Jesus is lying with arms akimbo on Mary's lap, and he is fast asleep. You can feel her hips adjusting gently to make sure she does not wake the sleeping child, even though she is seated on a gravel bank.

Above the scene float cumulus clouds, of middle height, just such as would be thrown up by a little warmth and by the lift provided by a wind sloping up the hill on which sits the town, or perhaps by the convergence of two air masses.

But for some reason, the figure of the child seems almost weightless, and the connection of the pair to the scene behind them is tenuous. The posture of the babe is said to prefigure the posture of the Pietà, when the crucified Jesus is laid again in his mother's lap. The whole picture asks, "What have I to do with Thee?" or more generally, "What has all this to do with God?"

The scene appears to be at the cusp of spring. A stork—whose migration marks the beginning of spring in southern Europe—is fighting with a snake. Old leaves still hang on the hornbeams, while new leaves appear on other trees. In the background on one side is a heavily cloaked shepherd. On the other side, a man lies against a bank, either exhausted or asleep. The cumulus clouds—typically clouds of spring and summer when abundant warmth starts the convection that sends them rising into the heights and making thunderheads—look ahead to full spring and promise the beginning of warmth.

Front and center in this scene sleeps the naked baby. This is as bald an assertion of the Christians' revolutionary idea as has been painted. The idea is that this sleeping baby without a stitch of clothing on in this barren barnyard will resolve the melancholy of human life in joy. And he will do it not by fiat from above, but by living this same rough tilting painful life. He will somehow redeem the moods of the skies that frame our daily lives.

Pieter Bruegel the Elder saw as well as anyone the influence that clouds have over us. He came from a tradition that valued the landscapes of everyday life, and one that was blessed with a large and active sky by the relatively flat topography of the Low Countries. In his five paintings of the months, made in 1565—each showing a task of daily life—the sky and its clouds govern the mood. The early-summer painting, *Haymaking*, shows a sky hazy in the distance but bright blue overhead, with high broken cirrus clouds. More than two-dozen people move through the scene with energy and purpose, each doing something: scything, carrying, raking, walking, sharpening a scythe.

In the late-summer painting, *The Harvesters*, the whole sky is covered with a warm haze that intensifies the yellow of the ripened wheat. Here, some people are scything, some binding the sheaves, but the principal group is seated, eating and drinking, while one mower lies flat beneath a tree, asleep.

In *The Return of the Herd*, men and cattle are all in motion, but crowded, lumbering, heading from right to left and into the background. The cattle are being driven down from their summer pastures as autumn advances. The herders are using their goads. Behind them, to the right, a front is advancing, dark nimbostratus clouds overspreading the land. As the herders goad the cattle, the clouds goad the men.

The sky in *Hunters in the Snow* has the blue-gray color of winter haze. It reflects the almost equal tones of the frozen ponds. Finally, *The Gloomy Day* is a painting that, like the beginning of Lent, stands at the hinge of the year. Winter is not yet gone, but spring is not far off. The dawn sun lights the earth and fields like a fire. But the sky above is still dark with the retreating clouds of what must have been a violent storm, as it has capsized ships in the harbor. Branches and trees are down, likely broken by the storm. Men begin to harvest the wood, both to heat their still-cold homes and to make wattles for the fencing that will be needed with the advance of spring.

In Bruegel, the needs of daily life rhyme with the skies of the season. In Peter Paul Rubens's *Stormy Landscape with Philemon and Baucis* (1620), the sky governs the land. The painting shows the moment in Ovid's story of the old couple Philemon and Baucis, when Zeus and Mercury draw the pair aside to witness the destruction of a land given over to evil. The whole painting is organized in convective whorls. Hardly a single line is straight up and down. Rather, the background clouds crowd forward and to the left, with driving rain slanting downward. Where the rain strikes land, the scene shows a torrent that bends back from left to right. Trees, road, water, foam—all participate in this general swirling.

It would be hard to more accurately portray the violence of a supercell thunderstorm and its effect on a landscape, yet that is not half of what is going on in this painting. Four tiny figures—the old couple and the gods—stand in the corner. Their smallness against this tumult gives the viewer a visceral sense of the power of the weather in human life. Everyone is taught ad nauseam that the Greco-Roman gods were personifications of natural forces, the chief of the gods a thunder god. Here, without any preaching, one sees why people might have felt this to be so. The weather rules the Rubens. Even the gods—admittedly disguised as humans—seem small.

The Limbourg brothers gloss the sky in *Les Très Riches Heures* to get right to the heavens. To them heaven is a place of calm, regular, perfect, never-changing motion. Bellini suggests that perhaps the changeable skies are not unheavenly. Bruegel and Rubens celebrate the changing sky and the power of storms. But it is Doménikos Theotokópoulos, known as El Greco, who translates the clouds into the foundation of heaven and ultimately people into weather, who rise convective into the ever-active, never-resting sky.

El Greco's heaven is not the stolid, geometrical golden tympanum of the Limbourg brothers. It is the heaven of a new cosmology. God in this view is the fullness of being. Every thought of this God is an act. El Greco's clouds celebrate a heaven that is in constant motion. It is rather the world on earth that is slow, feeble, and dark.

In *Burial of the Conde de Orgaz*, the many human figures below the clouds are dressed in black, backed by guttering candles, and in dozens of states of contemplation, sadness, and hope, but all quite still. Only a young boy is seen in full figure, and he is still, pointing to the one place on earth that is bright and active. The colorful figures are Saints Augustine and Stephen, clad in figured cloth of gold. (Augustine, as we saw, feared the changeable sky, but here El Greco has made him give the body of the count to a massive thunderstorm.) They lift the limp body of the count, who is dressed in shining gilded armor. The dead man looks much more lively than the living. His body has the S-curved shape of a rising flame.

Above their heads are ranks and folds of towering cumulus. An angel appears to wrest open a hole in the clouds with his wings, carrying with him the infant soul of the dead man. Above, the heavenly world is active. Angels are moving clouds, while Christ sits enthroned in white robes that themselves are almost clouds. The saints in joy inhabit ranks of cloud. It is exciting to know that El Greco could imagine this cloud landscape, for it resembles very closely the landscape of clouds that we discovered three centuries later, when humans learned to fly.

Here is the pattern of most of the painter's later great works: an earthly world of darkness, angularity, and doubt, with a heavenly world of color and rapid change above it. My favorite example is a relatively simple large canvas that shows Christ as a boy clinging to Joseph. It is rare that Jesus is shown as a boy at all. They are high on a hill near Toledo (indeed near the very view of Toledo that El Greco will later paint without figures). It is darkening, and both of their faces show concern. But above their heads spin three completely joyous angels. The angels are bright in color. Two seem to be cherubim, with cheeky faces and little clothing; the third wears a robe that is flowing with the direction of her flight. None of the three is resting or standing. From the point of view of the observer, all are akimbo, out of balance. And it is they—these cloudlike beings—who bring the color to the scene, dropping red roses onto the head of father and child.

The Big Mistake

El Greco's sky is active, alive, and mysterious. It cannot be described or predicted. It is the world as God knows it, a world of pure act. But the painter only suggested that this was how the sky behaved. In 1947, more than two centuries later, Dave Fultz showed with his dishpan (see page 12) that indeed the patterns in the air might never repeat, that they were perhaps ever creative and new. About a decade later than Fultz, Edward Lorenz proved it. It seems right and proper that he did so by accident.

The young Lorenz had been trained as a mathematician, under the great student of dynamic systems George Birkhoff, but before Lorenz could get his PhD, he was drafted into the air force as a meteorologist for the Pacific theater of World War II. When he returned to school at the end of the war, he decided to use his mathematics to study the weather. In theory, he considered, if he could solve the equations that should govern the weather—equations of temperature, pressure, density, motion, thermodynamics—he could predict the weather as far into the future as he wished.

This Promethean dream had not originated with Lorenz. In 1895, the Norwegian meteorologist Vilhelm Bjerknes had first suggested it might be possible to make accurate and far-reaching weather forecasts by solving the dynamic equations. Bjerknes was disappointed.

He came up with the equations, all right, but as written, they were not linear and could not be solved. Twenty years later, the wonderful polymath Lewis Fry Richardson figured out a way to do good-enough, approximate solutions, and thought he could actually make accurate forecasts. Unfortunately, to make them he would have needed more forecasters than there were people alive on earth. (For Richardson's weather theater, see page 134.)

Like Bjerknes, Lorenz felt strongly that the dynamic equations, if they could be solved, would predict what the air would do. Like Richardson, he thought he could massage and approximate the equations so that they *could* be solved. Unlike either of them, Lorenz had a computer.

With the Royal McBee LGP-30—an early computer about the size of the average desk—Lorenz thought he could make up for the lack of several billion people to do the calculations. He needed only one thing: the right job.

Lorenz had indeed just been hired at his alma mater, the Massachusetts Institute of Technology, a good place to be for this kind of work, but he had been hired to replace Thomas Malone. Malone was a statistician. He had wanted to use the new computing power to compile vast lists of the weather as it had occurred at different locations in the past, and to crunch these numbers to predict what the weather would do tomorrow, next week, and so on. It was a kind of mathematical formalization of the pattern-recognition work that most weather forecasters already used informally. With the new computers, huge amounts of data could be gathered, analogues found, and equations created. The high temperature today in Tokyo, for example, would be calculated as 0.7 times yesterday's temperature at Kyoto plus 0.3 times today's temperature at Kagoshima. No less a figure than the mathematician and polymath Norbert Wiener had declared that this method would prove more useful than anything that might be done with the dynamic equations.

Lorenz doubted it, but his new job was to assess and if possible to extend Malone's method of linear regression. Lorenz decided to test the method against a simple weather system that he could create by using the dynamic equations. If it could accurately predict weather for this simplified system, perhaps it could do likewise for the real weather.

Lorenz used twelve equations. They gave winds that flowed from west to east, with irregular waves in them. They allowed warm and cold air to move from place to place, bringing more or less convection and changing the shape of the waves. This model was certainly not anywhere near as complex as the real weather, but it gave results that looked very much like the complex patterns in Fultz's fourth dishpan regime.

Using the Royal McBee, Lorenz created twenty years' worth of simulated weather by solving the equations for that time period, in six-hour increments. All twelve equations were solved for each increment, and the results of each calculation became the input data for the next calculation, and so on, 29,200 times.

The Royal McBee took about forty seconds to make its four sets— one set for every six hours—of twelve calculations for each day. Then it took another ten seconds to print the resultant numbers for that day. (It gave a printout only for each day's results, not for each six-hour increment.) When all was said and done, it took about a minute to calculate and print the data for each day. So the twenty-year run took a little more than five days.

In order to get all twelve output numbers for each day on one line of the printout, Lorenz made a compromise. He instructed the computer to round off the numbers from six figures to the right of the decimal point to three figures, before it printed the result. In other words, the numbers printed on the sheets represented actual results rounded off to the nearest thousandth. This way, it would be easy to read and compare the numbers for each day, since they would form a regular grid across and down the page and could be scanned with the naked eye. He figured that the difference between what the computer calculated and what it printed out would be negligible, since it remained accurate down to one part in one thousand for each number.

As Lorenz had expected, when he tried out the linear-regression equations on this simulated twenty years' worth of weather, the equations did not work well. They did okay for the first twenty-four hours, a lot less well for the next twenty-four, and beyond that, they were as good as useless. In short, they were not even as good as experienced forecasters looking at weather maps and applying their knowledge and intuition. Just as Lorenz had expected.

But in the midst of the experiment, something strange had happened. He had wanted the machine to repeat a set of calculations that had already been done. He found the place in the overall forecast where he wanted the repeat to begin. He typed in the results for that day as the initial conditions for calculating subsequent days. The results he typed in, then, because they came from the printout, were rounded off to the thousandths. He wanted about two months' worth of data from that point forward. At a rate of one minute of computer time per day of weather, he had an hour to get coffee and maybe drop in on a colleague while the Royal McBee hummed onward.

On his return, he tore off the new printout and laid it down next to the original printout to make sure the two matched. Sure enough, the first day was spot on, but for the next day, the results differed in the last decimal place. By the fourth day, the error had doubled in size. After sixty days, the results bore no resemblance to one another. It was as though he had simply chosen two different forecasts at random.

The Royal McBee had a habit of malfunctioning . . . but not *this* time. A check showed that it had worked perfectly.

"At this point," Lorenz remembered, "I became rather excited." He realized that the difference came from the two sets of input numbers. Those that the computer had generated in its twenty-year odyssey were accurate to six places to the right of the decimal point, while those he had input for his sixty-day repeat were the figures that had been rounded to three places in order to keep all twelve numbers on a single line of paper. This was a difference of less than one one-thousandth for each of the values. Yet it had been enough to skew the results so far that after sixty days, no one could have told that the two forecasts came from virtually identical original conditions.

If this were as true for the real world as for this simulated one, then the tiniest difference between two initial states of the weather—far too small for us ever to observe—would result in two future states that bore no resemblance at all to one another. No matter how carefully we observed. No matter how accurate the integrated equations. No matter how powerful the computer.

Lorenz first described his unexpected results in a paper in 1963. When he had previously suggested that cyclones and anticyclones might be generated by imperceptible disturbances in the normal flow of air, another meteorologist had scoffed that if this were true, then just one flap of a seagull's wing might change the weather forever. "The controversy had not yet been settled," Lorenz reported in 1963, "but the most recent evidence seems to favor the seagulls."

Many years later, after a career spent proving that it will never be possible to make long-term weather predictions, Lorenz was to reflect, "There is no way of knowing whether or not I would ever have become involved with predictability at all, had it not been for that minute or so when I typed in the wrong numbers." This is not just a gee-whiz remark. It is a fundamental statement about our response to what the air brings. Lorenz was prepared. He was exquisitely trained to do what he did, and he deeply loved the mathematics he employed. (He was one of those people who occasionally dreamed of equations and woke up to write them down.) Lorenz was alert. Another person might have been content just to prove that he was right in his thesis, that Malone was wrong, and toss the errant calculation into the trash as an anomaly. That would have been a common enough reaction, but not very memorable drama. It became very interesting when, instead of crowing about his victory and retiring from the stage—pushing the inconvenient discrepancy behind him—Lorenz brought the unexpected result into the light of day, turned it over in his mind, and asked, "How come?"

The theater of the air often brings us what we do not expect. Malone was wrong, all right, but so was Lorenz. Neither Malone's statistics nor Lorenz's equations will ever make long-term predictions about the air. Lorenz hung in there for the sake of what was true. To do so, he had to change both his mind and the course of his life.

The Forecasters

William Cobbett spent the years 1822 to 1826 traveling the countryside of England by horse, observing (and lamenting) the states of farming and rural life. Once, riding toward the top of a hill to get a view of the Isle of Wight, he met a pair of turnip-hoers coming along in the opposite direction. They exchanged pleasantries and, as is common, traded views on the weather. The turnip-hoers assured him that they had lived in this country for many years, and that the day would stay fine and clear. Yes, indeed.

"Soon after the two turnip-hoers had assured me that there would be no rain," reported Cobbett, "I saw, beginning to poke up over the South Downs (then right before me) several parcels of those white curled clouds, that we call *Judges' Wigs*. And they are just like Judges' wigs. Not the *parson-like* things which the Judges wear, when they have to listen to the dull wrangling and duller jests of the lawyers; but, those *big* wigs which hang down about their shoulders, when they are about to tell you a little of *their intentions*, and when their very looks say, '*Stand clear!*' These clouds (if arising from the South-West) hold precisely the same language to the greatcoatless traveler. Rain is *sure* to follow them. The sun was shining very beautifully when I first saw the Judges' Wigs rising over the hills. At the sight of them he soon began to hide his face and, before I got to the top of the hill of

Donton, the white clouds had become black, had spread themselves all around, and a pretty decent and sturdy rain began to fall."

The rural rider ends up soaked to the skin. He saw the weather coming, but only a few minutes before it came. And the natives who had known the country their whole lives were dead wrong about it.

Forecasting the weather is not about familiarity. If, as Fultz demonstrated and Lorenz proved, the exact same weather conditions have never recurred in the history of the planet, weather forecasting may seem a hopeless task. We are immersed in a world where the smallest unobserved change could make the difference between a sunny day and a massive storm. The tide tables seem so perfect and regular to us because we do not live in tide pools. As outsiders, all that really matters to us are high and low tides, and toward which tide the sea is presently tending. However, to a tide pool creature, the state of the tide—like our day and night—is only a background against which their lives take place. The specific height of a wave, what predator it might bring in, what companion might wash away, what food gets deposited—all these matter to the tide pool creature, just as the events of our days matter to us.

Still, precisely because it matters so much, we wish to know what the weather will be. More ingenuity and more computing power have been expended on weather forecasting than on any other problem. ENIAC, the very first computer, was quickly used for weather forecasts, and each time computing power improves, the new machine is used to forecast weather. If we can predict the weather with some confidence one, two, or even three days ahead, a driver can avoid the black ice that sends his truck skidding into the car carrying a family of four. A fisherman might stay in port rather than set sail when the day after tomorrow all hell will break loose.

The first man to publish a weather forecast was Admiral Robert Fitzroy, the erstwhile captain of the HMS *Beagle* and Darwin's friend, companion, and sometimes antagonist on that voyage.

Fitzroy had been appointed in 1854 to begin to collect and organize meteorological data gathered at sea by British ships. After the loss of the ship *Royal Charter* to a sudden storm in 1859, Fitzroy decided that he must find a way to use his data to forecast the weather. Among the information he collected was pressure data derived from barometric observations. The barometer was the legitimate predecessor to all the forecasting tools in use today, and it still provides the first sign that the weather is changing. Rising pressure usually indicates the arrival of air that will subside, suppressing clouds and providing fair weather. Falling pressure usually indicates the coming of air that will allow vapor to rise, producing wind and precipitation. Relying primarily on this type of data, the admiral began to publish his forecasts in *The Times* in 1860.

Fitzroy's newspaper reports represent the first time that the term "forecast" was used, and his colleagues in the Royal Society strongly objected to it. How dare he, they intoned, publish uncertain results! Rather, he should wait to see what happened and then assess the accuracy of his predictions. They suspected him of aeromancy, a kind of divination based on the properties of the air.

Fitzroy patiently pointed out that his purpose was not to be right all the time, but to be right enough of the time and also *in time* to prevent the loss of life. He had ship captains carry barometers aboard, regularly recording pressure measurements that he compiled and studied, seeking patterns that would presage rain, wind, frost, squall, gale, and fog. He had barometers installed at ports, complete with "special remarks" that suggested what different patterns of barometric readings might mean for the weather. He created a system of warning flags to be hoisted in the event that his barometers foresaw bad weather approaching.

This was in essence the beginning of what is called synoptic meteorology, that is, the study of past patterns in the weather to suggest what future course the weather might take. Even today, a good part of the skill of weather forecasters is to apply their experience of pattern to all the numerical analyses available to them. On Fitzroy's death, however, the daily publication of weather forecasts was discontinued. The scientists were embarrassed that their colleague was sometimes wrong, and the ship owners were distressed that his reports might slow the march of their commerce by delaying sailing.

Four decades later, Jacob and Vilhelm Bjerknes, and their student Tor Bergeron, were the first to make weather maps that we would recognize. They acknowledged the importance of rising and falling pressure, but they saw it in the context of weather systems. They were the first to describe the spin of the cyclones and their procession around the globe. Use of "L" to indicate low pressure, "H" for high pressure, half circles to signal a warm front, and triangles to signal a cold front was their invention.

They saw the weather as a struggle among warring forces of temperature, pressure, and humidity. It occurred to Vilhelm that if he could write and solve the equations that governed the play of heat and cold, wet and dry, up and down, stasis and motion, he ought to be able to predict the weather accurately. But he could not solve the equations he created.

The first to actually use mathematics to predict the weather was Lewis Fry Richardson, a Scots Quaker. He had taken a first in physics at Cambridge, but he ended up in charge of a remote observation station located on a high wet moor in the Scottish highlands called Eskdalemuir, population 265. Wet is perhaps an understatement. The British record for rainfall—better than three inches in less than half an hour—was recorded at this station.

In his lonely sodden outpost, Richardson was assigned not only to keep track of magnetic and seismic data but also to collect measurements of temperature, pressure, wind, and rain. Though he had not originally been trained as a meteorologist, he saw quickly what Bjerknes had seen: that it should be possible to apply the equations of motion and thermodynamics to predict future weather. During his three years at the station, he wrote the first draft of a book that adapted the equations so that they could be solved and the weather thus authoritatively predicted.

As a Quaker, he was a conscientious objector during World War I, but from 1916 he served with the Friends' Ambulance Unit in the French Fourth Army. When not carefully steering the wounded around shell craters, from the front to the hospital through the north of France, he worked on the manuscript of "Weather Prediction by Numerical Process." Somewhere near Rheims he lost the manuscript, only to discover it a month later under a pile of coal in a rest billet. Had he not found the paper, he would have lost more than paragraphs and equations. In fact, armed only with slide rule and logarithm tables, Richardson had been laboring week after week trying to make a valid weather prediction using his mathematical method. The prediction was for only six hours of weather over central Europe for the early morning of May 20, 1910.

He had chosen this date and time for two reasons. First, on this date, Vilhelm Bjerknes had recorded the data from coordinated weather balloon launches that had taken place all over Europe as part of International Balloon Day. So Richardson had comprehensive data to work with. Second, since the date was in the past, he could compare his results with what had actually happened. He would know in short order whether his forecast had been accurate. (Fitzroy's critics would have been pleased.)

He divided his area of Europe into twenty-five squares, each two hundred kilometers (125 miles) on a side, and he vertically divided the air into five layers. Thus he created a grid of 125 compartments. Figuring weather data for each compartment and calculating the change in parameters from one compartment to all the compartments adjoining it, he expected to predict the weather six hours in advance.

His results? The stratospheric wind increased tenfold, and the sea-level barometric pressure shot up by 145 millibars to a new world record of 1,108 millibars!

What had really happened that morning? Little had changed in the surface or the stratosphere. The day had continued cool and calm, the pressure almost steady.

Richardson readily acknowledged the failure. In his book, he attributed it to the poor quality of the observations. The Irish meteorologist Peter Lynch—who repeated Richardson's experiment using computers in 1994—agreed. Richardson's observations were subject to serious errors, in part because they were based on small differences in large numbers. Thus, if the difference were off by only a few units, it might make a hundredfold distinction in the results. Lynch employed modern methods of smoothing out what he called the "high frequency noise," and succeeded in getting a fairly accurate prediction, using Richardson's equations.

Undaunted, Richardson envisioned a future theater of prediction in which cooperating humans might actually predict the weather before it occurred. It was a vision worthy of the seventeenth-century mystic Giordano Bruno. Richardson's weather theater consisted of a vast globe, with all the regions of the earth depicted on its inner surfaces. Individuals would be seated in row after row and rank after rank in galleries located around the inner surface of this globe—both around the globe and up and down. Each of these individuals would be in charge of computing the weather data for that particular spot on the globe. A system of signals would show each person the results of the calculations just made by the people in the adjoining seats above and below, left and right. These results would then be the input data for the person's next calculation. Regional directors would ensure that each area was keeping pace with the developing forecast, while a single overall conductor stood on a tall pillar that positioned him at

*A graphic representation of Lewis Fry Richardson's weather theater, with
the director at the center and the "computers" lining the inner surface
of the globe. (L. Bengtsson)*

the center point of the globe. He would shine a rose-colored lamp on
anyone who was getting ahead of the overall prediction, and a blue-
colored lamp on anyone falling behind.

Richardson called his vision a "fantasy," but he figured it would
take about sixty-four thousand people to make it work. Never mind
that he would certainly have needed backup for bathroom breaks,
meals, and sheer exhaustion, the number was dramatically low.
Other meteorologists have since estimated that to accomplish what
he intended, Richardson would have needed at least two hundred
thousand people and at most a number of individuals greater than
the total number of people alive on earth. However many people it
might take, it is interesting to note what Richardson called each of his
workers: a "computer."

Although his prediction theater never was populated by human computers, electronic computers would come to serve the same purpose. And they would do so using exactly the strategy first presented in Richardson's theater. The most robust weather models in use in the early twenty-first century are constructed as an immense grid of boxes that divide the air into thousands of compartments, just as in Richardson's theater. Predictions are made by measuring the energy that flows among all the grid's boxes, using suites of equations that measure the motion and the heat flow of the air.

The beauty of this forecasting is not only in the complexity of the weather models, but especially in the modesty of its ends. Given what Lorenz discovered, no one expects to make a skillful weather forecast *ever* beyond about two weeks into the future, and highest probabilities reside in the one- to two-day range. Perhaps someday they will reach three days. Such astonishing means for such modest ends! Almost every nation with a weather service has its own global weather model. Most forecasters use their national model, along with a selection of those made by neighbors, as well as finer-scale, more local models. Each model comprises more than a million lines of computer code. Most also regularly compare their forecasts to what actually occurs, using the real data to amend future predictions.

One limitation on accuracy was thought to be the lack of small-scale measurement. If your grid boxes measure fifty miles on a side, they will be far too large to record the rise and dissipation of a few thunderstorms or even of a good-sized squall line, which can be twenty miles in breadth or less. If this were the case, then forecasts should improve as the boxes were made smaller to include these "forgotten" data.

Paradoxically, when you make the boxes smaller, you create even greater challenges to accuracy. Including the small-scale storms increases the complexity of the model, so that now it must take into account the real fact that small storms and even passing dust devils feed their energy into the larger-scale movement of the air, thus changing the forecast. To take these little processes into account requires even more physics and even more lines of computer code. There is likely to be a benefit for the accuracy of predictions, but on the scale of hours not days. Not only that, the more detail you put in, the slower your program will run, until you are making a very good prediction some time after the events have occurred.

The greater possible improvements come not from more precision, but from less. If tiny differences in observations make large differences in the forecast down the road, then we can improve the accuracy of forecasts by making many different forecasts at the same moment based on slightly differing initial conditions. Intentionally tweaking the observations a large number of times—making them apparently less accurate—yields better results. Comparing the results of these many different forecasts and finding their common ground provide a higher degree of confidence that the common results are actually going to happen. All major models—the Global Forecast System (GFS), its embedded North American Mesoscale (NAM) model, and the much-used European Centre for Medium-Range Weather Forecast (ECMWF) model—are often now run not only with one assumed beginning but also with twenty or more slightly different ones. Learning where the multiple forecasts coincide narrows the range of possibilities.

This ensemble forecasting is regularly used by people for whom the results really matter. Utility companies, for example, need to know as accurately as possible whether rain, snow, freezing rain, or an ice storm is likely to occur. An ensemble forecast gives the whole curve of probabilities. Based on it, the companies can call in two hundred trucks from out of state to help in case of a probable ice storm, or decide to rely on their own crews.

The best forecasting tools also reflect on their own errors. At MIT, the atmospheric sciences professors regularly gather large groups of talented forecasters to predict the same weather at the same time. They then rank the different forecasters based on the accuracy of their predictions. MOS, the ringer in the group because it is not a person, is very often the winner. Model Output Statistics as a forecast tool doesn't go beyond two days into the future, but it is notoriously accurate. Instead of relying exclusively on models or observations, it combines observations with model predictions and statistical methods to home in on the forecast. MOS has a long record of its forecast temperatures for a grid of points around a location of interest, say, Logan International Airport in Boston. It also has a long record of the *actual* high temperature at Logan. By creating an equation to compare those actual readings with the forecasts, it can hone the model's output and come up with a comparatively good forecast.

But MOS does not always win the game. Sometimes Ensemble does. In this case, "Ensemble" is not based on many tweaked runs of the same model, but on the combined forecasts of all the individual contestants. Although occasionally one forecaster outdoes the rest, it is usually the combined average of all their forecasts that beats any individual (sometimes including MOS). "Forecasting is one of the very few things I know in the world," said MIT atmospheric scientist Kerry Emanuel, "that is better done by committee than by an individual."

The notion applies even to an assembly of models. Say you have four good models, and you rank them for accuracy of prediction. Three are comparable, and one is considerably worse. If you average the forecasts of the three comparable models, you get a better forecast than if you have chosen only one. And if you include the fourth model in the average—even though alone it was the worst by far—you get a better forecast than the average of the other three!

Why is this so? There is more world in the ensemble forecast and less thinking. Not that both are not absolutely necessary, but the world is the indispensable ingredient for making forecasts better.

Fudging, taking errors into account, leaving blanks for what we don't know, talking it out and agreeing—all these lead to better prediction than toughing it out by the exact numbers.

It is rather like Thomas Jefferson's argument about balanced government. After the debacle of the Articles of Confederation, the Founding Fathers seldom argued about whether government should be larger or smaller—a red herring, if ever there was one—but about how its powers should be distributed. They ended up creating an impenetrable system of checks and balances, not to make government more efficient, but to ensure that it would be inefficient and imprecise enough to respond to lived experience, not theoretical demands.

The Weather on D-Day

Perhaps the most important weather forecast ever made was the one for D-day, the Allied invasion of France. It succeeded not because of the brilliant work of any solitary forecaster, but because a group of forecasters imitated the weather. They jostled, yelled, scribbled, and cast malevolent looks at one another. They fought it out and voted. And in the end, they were just right enough.

The invasion of France had been scheduled for June 5, 1944. To bring off the invasion, General Dwight D. Eisenhower needed a full moon, a low tide, little cloud cover, light winds, and low seas. (The low tide was necessary to allow soldiers to see, avoid, and disarm the mined obstacles that the Germans had placed in the surf.) He could have had the full moon and low tide on June 5, 6, or 7. He could have had the low tide without the full moon on June 19 or 20. But what about the weather?

Outside, on the morning of June 4, the weather was mostly clear, with a light breeze blowing. May had been a pleasant month on the English Channel, but June was not shaping up to be so. The Azores High, a semipermanent high-pressure zone in the mid-Atlantic that moved north during the summer and south during the winter, had not come as far north as usual. When its influence dominates the weather, Europe and the south coast of England experience dry warm summer days. Where it stood then, however, it was steering a series of low-pressure troughs across the North Atlantic and into the English Channel.

The first ships for the invasion had left Scotland, steaming south, on May 28. They were now in midcourse, forming their convoys, and the preparation to move three million armed souls from the south of England to the north of France was far advanced. Landing craft were jostling in Portsmouth Harbor, which was so crowded that you could walk from one shore to the other without touching water. Sherman tanks had been fitted with flotation skirts to help them wallow ashore. Supply vessels were following to bring in howitzers and materiel. Other ships were towing long jetty-like caissons to create temporary ports.

Into the middle of this armada came the chief meteorologist, Group Captain James Martin Stagg, a terse Scot with a long, thin, pale face, closely cropped hair, and a severe mustache, to report that his three teams of meteorologists—conferring and arguing by telephone—had grudgingly reached agreement. The weather for June 5 would be bad, very bad. Winds in the channel were likely to be force 5 on the Beaufort Scale—a stiff breeze, not yet a gale, but enough to set up a swell that would trouble ordinary ships, never mind the landing craft. Worse, the sky would be overcast, and the cloud bases at only five hundred feet, making the launching of paratroopers impossible, rendering precision bombing of the defenses out of the question, and making it too difficult for naval gunners to judge the accuracy of their salvos.

The operation was put on hold. Radio silence was in effect, so destroyers were deployed at flank speed to head off convoys, signaling them with flags or lamps or handing out cryptic messages like "Post Mike One," meaning return to harbor. That night thousands of troops remained on their landing craft in the harbor, seasick with the swells and sickened by the smell of vomit.

Would the weather improve?

Although the military commanders had routinely been asking for weather forecasts a week into the future, they were told again and again that such forecasts are uncertain. Only the team of American forecasters, led by Irving Krick, was confident that they could see that far forward. Comparing past weather systems to the current ones, they contrived to predict how the present weather would evolve. Alone among the three teams forecasting, they suggested that June 5 would be just fine.

The two British teams—one from the navy and one from the Meteorological Office (called the Met)—were far less sanguine about June 5, and they were not so sure about June 6 just yet. In the Met Office was Sverre Petterssen, a Norwegian meteorologist who had been a student of Tor Bergeron, the man who discovered how raindrops form and who was himself a student of Vilhelm and Jacob Bjerknes, the meteorologists who first described the birth, life, and death of the kind of storms now crossing the Atlantic.

For June 5, the British teams prevailed. They used methods developed by the Bergen School, gathering measurements of temperature, pressure, and humidity from stations on land, at sea, and in the air. (They were even incorporating data gathered from German U-boats, whose code had been broken so that their weather reports to Zentralwetterdienstgruppe were immediately available to the Allies.) With this data, they tried to map the systems of counterclockwise-spinning storms, finding their warm and cold fronts, the pressure drops around their lows, and the position and direction of following highs. Where the lows passed, bad weather was to be expected. When the ridges of highs moved in, fair weather should follow.

The British made no pretense at being able to see beyond twenty-four to forty-eight hours into the future. Nevertheless, they were pessimistic on the night of June 3. It looked as though the cyclone system that would be bringing bad weather on the 5th would be followed by another such system on the 6th. The American Krick was infuriated by their reticence, and would later claim that it was only the farsightedness of the American team that allowed the invasion to succeed.

Petterssen told a different story. According to him both British teams had been quite pessimistic until the afternoon of June 4, when the weather had indeed begun to deteriorate, as they had predicted. A single ship stationed six hundred miles west of Northern Ireland to record the weather, however, began to report a rising barometer. Out there in the mid-Atlantic, the pressure kept rising. Perhaps, they reasoned, the Azores High is moving north. Perhaps it will shunt the coming storm to the north, or at least stall it for a day. They detected a break in the weather.

The Met Office team still voted no for June 6, but the British navy team and the Americans carried the day. Late on the evening of June 4, Captain Stagg met again with the Allied commanders. Outside, the trees were swaying in the wind, and a hard rain fell. Stagg told Eisenhower that they thought the weather would improve. There might be winds of force 3 or 4, with a few excursions to force 5, but the sky should be clear. It might cloud later, but the cloud bases should stay high enough for the naval gunners to spot their shots. Not ideal, but good enough.

The commanders met with Stagg again at 0430 on June 5. The high pressure was holding and building in.

"Halcyon Plus Five finally and definitely confirmed," the word went out. This was the go code.

At 0900 on June 5, the convoys set out again in the face of force 5 winds. This was particularly troublesome to the landing craft and to the bellies of soldiers unused to the sea. Sea sickness continued throughout the seventeen-hour crossing.

Early on the morning of June 6, the Pathfinder planes for the paratroops ran into unexpected banks of clouds over the coast of France. They dropped their visual and radar beacons, but many fell in the wrong places. With the cloud cover, many of the visual beacons could not be seen. The paratroops themselves went in C47 transport, flying in a V of v's formation. They too hit the cloud bank. The pilots had to break formation to prevent collisions. Some tried to get above the clouds. Some tried to go below. Some took evasive action as the antiaircraft fire began. The paratroops were dropped or glided in far from their intended targets.

As the landing craft moved in, waves were five to six feet high in midchannel, higher than expected but not impossible to survive. The wind had shifted to the northwest, driving the craft into the beaches with the wind at their backs. Some were swamped; some were wrecked. Of the thirty-two tanks going into Omaha Beach, twenty-seven were lost.

But the rest got in. At the end of the day, under a partly sunny sky, 59 degrees Fahrenheit with force 4 winds, the Allies had a firm hold on the beaches. They had lost twelve thousand men, but that is a fraction of the seventy-five thousand they were estimated to lose had they not had the element of surprise.

Why were the Germans surprised? They knew as well as the Allies that 5, 6, and 7 were the only days in June with the right tides and right moon. In May, they had stood on full alert at full-moon, low-tide times. What happened? Why was General Rommel—the man in charge of the Normandy defenses—in Berlin taking a walk with his wife, who was trying out her birthday shoes? Why were half the division commanders and a fourth of the regiment commanders at a war games exercise in Brittany planning for the invasion defense? Why were the torpedo boats in the harbor? Why had so many men been relieved of the heavy tasks of building the defenses and sent for a little rest and relaxation?

The Germans believed that the weather was too bad for the Allies to invade. This was not the fault of poor forecasting. Group Captain Heinz Lettau—later a revered professor of meteorology at the University of Wisconsin—saw the same succession of fronts as did the Allied forecasters. He may or may not have noted the marginal improvement of the weather on the 6th. Even had he seen this, however, his orders were clear. The High Command had decided that an invasion was not possible if there was a risk of the winds reaching force 4 or higher. (The Germans had put off their own planned invasion of Britain, Operation Sea Lion, in 1940, in part because they could never get what they felt was a calm-enough sea for the troops to cross.) Lettau was confident—and right—that there would be a force 4 wind on June 5, 6, and 7. Ergo, there could be no invasion. What the Germans failed to find out was that the Allies thought force 4 was just fine.

Just as important, Lettau did not have the benefit of colleagues to disagree with him. As contentious and nasty as the infighting had been among the three groups of Allied forecasters, each team got a vote, so the most persuasive case was likely to prevail. The Americans were most sanguine, believing they could forecast a week or better into the future by comparing weather maps for the previous days. The Met Office forecasters, using ground and upper-air observations and seeking to map the progress of fronts, believed they could go forward only a day or two at best. The naval meteorological service focused on wave heights and their effects on the invading landing craft. Among them, they came up with an ensemble forecast that allowed the generals to make intelligent decisions.

Lettau, following specific directives from higher-ups, had to predict that the invasion would not occur, regardless of any disagreements in his team. It is also likely that he caved in to military demands for a long-range forecast. He told them that the bad weather would continue for weeks. He himself knew that such a forecast was uncertain at best, and so did his colleagues. Left to himself, Krick would have done just the same—though promising good weather, not bad—telling the generals what they wanted to hear. Only the presence of his fractious colleagues prevented him.

In the end the Allies won the day because in order to predict the weather, they acted like the weather. Competing groups jostled and maneuvered, each trying to pressure the others into accepting their point of view. In just the same way, the high- and low-pressure cells fought and spun into one another over the Atlantic. The forecasters reinforced their own ideas, and none of their ideas was the winner, just as each gyre and each center of low and high pressure pressed against the others, squeezing out the future among them. The Germans, on the other hand, believing that they could conquer uncertainty by fiat, declared that weather and people would conform to their assumptions. They were proved wrong. The Allies appeared on the beaches of Normandy, just like a surprise storm.

After the war, German Admiral Friedrich Ruge praised Eisenhower for making "one of the truly great decisions in military history." No German commander could have done so, he added, without seeking permission from higher up. The German brain was clogged and sclerotic with hierarchy. It should be remembered that Rommel was at the time part of a plot to depose Hitler. Perhaps his trip to Berlin was not just to give his wife a pair of shoes?

Forcing

Gavin Schmidt is an Englishman with a short beard and a face between round and oval. He has an engaging smile. When he talks, he sits back, leans forward, and moves around, as though he were involved in some sedentary sport. With one arm he shows how ocean density slopes, and with the other he runs a current into the slope, bending his body and explaining, all while his head is tilted at a forty-five-degree angle to the floor. He looks and acts like he would be a good pub companion, perhaps good at darts or skittles and certainly good at the pub quiz. On the large white wipe board in his office, along with the requisite equations, is a sketch of what appears to be a compound aerosol, with mischievous eyes and smiling face. Propped against the board on the pen rest is a poster presentation explaining how global warming will harm the taste of beer.

Schmidt is in charge of one of the principal computer climate models in the world. It divides the atmosphere into more than two and a half million boxes, each one hundred kilometers (sixty-two miles) on a side and stacked forty boxes deep from the surface to the stratosphere. "It's an everything-and-the-kitchen-sink kind of model," said Schmidt. The model attempts to measure all energy inputs and outputs to each of the boxes, to calculate the average state of the atmosphere at any time in the near or distant future. Schmidt insists that it is not the number of the boxes that makes a model valuable, however, but the quality of the physics that informs them. How closely do the equations in the model resemble the way in which the air actually conserves mass and energy while going through its unceasing and unpredictable changes?

A climate model is unlike a weather model. "Imagine," said Schmidt, "that you have a stream that is very turbulent. You can see things rushing down this way and that, and you think, 'If I put in a stick, I don't really know which way it will go.' But it's still being controlled by the banks. So if you change the course of the stream, you don't change the turbulence, but you can affect where the stream goes and how fast it gets there." The banks keep the chaotic water following a particular course. A weather model is interested in tracking the turbulence; a climate model is interested in the location of the banks. These are what the climate scientists call the boundary conditions.

Some changes can shift the climate's banks, that is, change the boundary conditions. The brightness of the sun, the amount of ice in the oceans, the eruption of a volcano, a change in the amount of greenhouse gases—any and all of these might shift the banks. They are called forcings, since they can force the climate into a new pattern.

When Mount Pinatubo erupted in the Philippines in 1991, global temperatures declined by half a degree for all of 1992. The volcanic plume had ejected thirty million metric tons of sulfur dioxide into the stratosphere. There, the gas oxidized to sulfate aerosols and repeatedly circled the globe. Because sulfates are essentially reflective, they lowered the amount of solar energy reaching the earth's surface. The earth cooled.

Sulfates do not remain in the air for more than about a year, so the effect was temporary. But during that year, the volcano indeed had shifted the banks of the climate stream. This was not a bad thing, since, as it turns out, photosynthesis works much better under diffuse solar radiation than under full sun. (High-intensity light actually damages the light-capturing chloroplasts, causing the plant to spend a great deal of energy on cell repair.) In the Harvard Forest in rural Massachusetts in 1992—and likely around the globe—the plants made food twice as well as they did in the average, non-volcano year.

Stronger and longer-lasting forcings come from the effluents of industrial humanity. Using the air as a global dump for exhausts of every kind, we have caused the climate banks to shift in two ways, and in opposite directions. Greenhouse-gas emissions force the climate as a whole to warm. Aerosols emissions force it to cool.

Human-induced greenhouse gases—chiefly carbon dioxide and methane, released from fossil fuel burning, from mining, from irrigation, and from stock raising—cause a persistent warming. The amount of carbon dioxide in the atmosphere has increased by more than 30 percent since 1850, and it continues to rise at a rate of one-half to a full percentage point each year. In response, the climate has warmed, likely by at least 1.5 degrees Fahrenheit.

This may not sound like much, but already the effects have been profound. As of late 2011, the sea level around the world had risen by almost seven inches. The ten-warmest years on record had occurred since 1999. The extent of Arctic sea ice was declining at more than 11 percent per year. Annually, Antarctica was losing more than twenty-six cubic miles of ice, and Greenland was losing one hundred billion tons. A new island appeared on maps of the east coast of Greenland, exposed by receding ice. In the Inuit language it was called Warming Island. Plants and animals including pests like the hemlock woolly adelgid, were extending their range into areas that once were too cold for them. Warmer winters reduced the winterkill of other pests like bark beetles, facilitating outbreaks.

If we were to stop producing aerosols tomorrow, there would soon be a dramatic decrease in aerosols in the atmosphere; the same is not true of carbon. Burning fossil fuels releases as carbon dioxide the solid or liquid carbon that had been safely sequestered underground for millions of years. Though it may be only five or ten years until that airborne carbon is photosynthesized or otherwise falls to earth, only a small amount will be buried again. The rest becomes a long-lasting part of the carbon cycle on air, sea, and land.

In burning fossil fuels, we have partly undone the millennial work of our planet in burying carbon. The only reason why oxygen is free in the air is that the dying bodies of creatures—often including their calcium carbonate or chitinous shells, both rich in carbon—sink to the ocean bottom or are buried in the earth, and are entombed there. When we exhume buried carbon as coal, natural gas, or oil, we unbury what the planet worked so hard to put away.

Greenhouse gases have already forced the climate stream to change its banks, but given the huge quantities of the gases we have put into the air, some scientists wonder why it has not changed more than it has. There are two possible explanations. One is that the earth is simply not very sensitive to the changes we are making in it, so large increases in greenhouse gases make for only small temperature changes. The other—and more likely—explanation is that while greenhouse gases force the climate to warm, the aerosols force it cool.

Sulfate, nitrates, organic carbon, dust, and sea salt—whether produced by nature or by man—are reflective aerosols. They diffuse incoming sunlight, meaning that the surface heats less than it would have. Black-carbon aerosols—the soots from bad coal or burning wood or refuse—instead absorb sunlight, but while this heats the layer of the atmosphere where the aerosols are found, it may also reduce the heat reaching the earth's surface.

Greenhouse gases are estimated to add about one-quarter watt of energy per square foot (two and a half watts per square meter) to the earth's surface. Estimates for the forcing exerted by aerosols vary from a positive forcing of an additional half a watt to a negative forcing of four watts. The weight of the evidence is on the negative side, but just how negative is a very open question.

Aerosols are hard to measure because they are typically released on scales much smaller than those recognized by even the most robust climate model, and they are hard to approximate (what scientists call "parameterize") because we have no way to measure on a large scale how many of what type are in the air at one time and at what level of the atmosphere. Not only that, the aerosols react with one another, and their combined properties resemble their separate properties very little, if at all. Nevertheless, it is fairly clear that the overall effect of aerosols has been to damp global warming. Maybe a little, maybe a lot. But this fact does not mean that we have found a silver bullet to prevent climate change.

Black-carbon aerosols are a principal cause of respiratory disease. In China, where aerosols blown in from the Gobi desert combine with sulfates and black carbon, mortality is expected to increase by 11 percent for each doubling in the amount of sulfate pollutants. (The Chinese recently declared their weather forecasts a state secret.) And both sulfate and nitrate aerosols are very acid in reaction. When they are carried into the Adirondacks and Maine from power plants in the Midwest, or into northern Scandinavia from the Ruhr valley and industrial Britain, they carry rains acidic enough to kill lakes. Even the "cleaner" aerosols emitted by automobiles and power plants in the developed Western world lead to epidemic increase in the incidence of asthma and other inflammatory lung diseases.

The same climate models that map and predict greenhouse-gas forcing also have been used to assess aerosol forcing. Although for years the aerosol pollutants may have masked climate change, they can have a serious and unexpected effect on a whole region. As an example, seasonal rains in the Sahel savannah, south of the Sahara desert and at the north edge of the Intertropical Convergence Zone, depend on motion of the thermal equator. That equator moves north with the sun in the summer of the Northern Hemisphere, and south with the sun in the summer of the Southern Hemisphere. When the thermal equator moves north, the area beneath it experiences increased uplift and convection. Vapor is lifted to its dew point, and rain falls. Climate models suggested that if the sea-surface temperature in the Northern Hemisphere declined with respect to the same temperature south of the equator, then the rains would not move so far north as once they had, and the savannah would be left dry. The vapor would reach its dew point and rain out of the sky south of the great Sahel.

But what could cause such a decline in sea-surface temperature? In the three decades following World War II, the emission of sulfur-based aerosols increased dramatically over the industrialized regions of the north, over Europe, North America, and Japan. From about 1950 until the mid-1970s, this change in aerosols forced a modest cooling of the climate in the northern region. In response to this cooling, the models showed, sea-surface temperature would have declined. Storms would have stayed farther south. The Sahel would have baked and dried. And indeed it did.

Efforts to control air pollution in the industrial world intensified beginning in the 1970s. The aerosol load declined. The northern ocean (and air) temperatures began to rise again in the 1980s, and the Sahel drought weakened.

Aerosol pollution will never prevent greenhouse warming. Although schemes to fill the air with aerosols have been proposed, they are regarded as ineffective and possibly poisonous. When we treat the air as a dump, just as we have treated the dirt, the invisible tides of garbage do not just go away. As composter Clark Gregory once elegantly put it, "There is no such place as away."

The Winds

Who can sound the depths of the winds? Whence comes the
life-creating blast of icy air. Yesterday—so quiet and sultry—
today so wild & cool. When the wind is blowing we must expand & swell else we be blown away. Trees grow tall and with
stiffened trunk[s] let their limbs relax to be waved and tossed
at the will of the wind.

—*Charles Burchfield, summer 1914*

In 1781, the French physicist Marcellin Ducarla-Bonifas had a
brainstorm. He observed that in nature copious rain fell on the
windward side of a mountain range, while little or no rain fell on the
leeward side. The east side of the Andes, for example, was as he put
it, "like a dry sponge." He proposed—in thought, at least—to build a
wall almost two miles high (roughly ten thousand feet) near the Paris
Observatory on the left bank of the Seine in central Paris. The wall
would face east and west. He predicted that if the wind were coming
from the east, then there would be "a perpetual deluge" on the east
side of the wall, while there would be "an absolute desert" on the west
side. The air on the windward side, he reasoned, would have to rise in
order to cross the wall. In so doing, it would cool. All the water vapor
in it would reach its dew point, condense, and rain out. The air on the

other side of the wall—now bone dry—would descend, compress, and warm as it did so.

He never built his wall—like the impossibly tall mountains painted by Albert Bierstadt, it likely would have fallen over in a high wind—but he was right about two things. Wind and rain in any local area depend largely on whether the air is rising or falling and on whether it is wet or dry.

I grew up on the peninsula south of San Francisco. To the west of the peninsula was ocean. A low coast range and bayside land made up the peninsula itself. To the east was San Francisco Bay. We lived on the bayside land. To the east of us, across the bay, was the East Bay, and beyond that the Central Valley.

Every summer afternoon, like clockwork, the wind rose. The conditions might change from a tolerable day for playing in the sprinklers or visiting a pool, to sweater weather, in the course of ten minutes: winds blowing fifteen to twenty-five miles per hour out of the west-northwest. When we first moved to the Bay Area (I was five), I thought this was a temporary condition, something that might soon go away. But it never did. In fact, it has likely not gone away for as long as there has been a San Francisco peninsula. We get used to this wind with which we live. It accompanies our lives, like a note that is sounded again and again. It marks the summer with its cadence.

When I returned there to visit my father a few years ago, we went out to sit on his patio at about three in the afternoon. It was bright and sunny. The *Callistemon* tree was full of big red bottle brush flowers. A ruby-throated hummingbird was visiting them. As I walked out the door, he handed me a sweater.

"What's this for?" I asked, forgetting. I had been living in the east for twenty years.

"The wind," he said, with a resigned shrug.

Sure enough, we had not been sitting more than fifteen minutes when it started to blow.

A cold current runs south along the edge of the Pacific Ocean past San Francisco. The water temperature is only about 50 degrees Fahrenheit in midsummer. A typical offshore temperature on a summer afternoon is maybe 53 or 55 degrees. On the east side of the coast range, in the valley of the bay, the land heats up much faster, so on that same summer afternoon the temperature might be 75 or 80 degrees. Over in the East Bay, it might be pushing 90, and in the Central Valley beyond, it might reach 98 degrees.

An ocean breeze sets up. The cooler ocean air has a higher pressure at the surface than the warm air inland. The farther inland you go, the warmer it gets, and the lower the pressure. The gradient starts the flow of a cool breeze off the ocean and into the bay area.

The monsoon of South Asia is closely related to the sea breeze in the Bay Area, but on a vast scale. Rather than just sounding a note, it creates the symphonic structure by which the oldest civilizations in the world have subsisted and survived. The high Himalayas top even Ducarla-Bonifas's dream of altitude. They face north and south, rather than east and west, but they do three things: They block northern storms from reaching south into India. They add to rainfall coming from the wet warm southern ocean by lifting up the air to its dew point. And they direct the subtropical jet streams, the high-level winds that either draw up air or push it down.

In the dry winter of India and southern China, the jet streams converge. When they collide they exert downward pressure, causing the air aloft to flow down toward the ground. Just as the French physicist saw, the effect warms and dries the air, suppressing rainfall. The air flows downward and out toward the Indian Ocean, preventing the wet ocean air from riding over the continent. There is a prolonged season of hot dry weather.

As the land heats up with the oncoming summer, the pressure over the land becomes lower than the pressure over the ocean. The flow reverses, and warm wet Indian Ocean air now streams over the subcontinent and over South China. The jet stream switches from northerly to easterly. Now, its winds are divergent, lifting up air instead of pushing it down, further decreasing the air pressure at the surface and lifting the moist air. Finally, the massive Himalayas interrupt the northward-flowing air, pushing it up to the very top of the troposphere.

Ducarla-Bonifas would have been delighted. "A perpetual deluge" is exactly what you get. As much as 125 inches of rain can fall each month in the regions affected by the monsoon. That is better than four inches per day! On the other side of the Himalayas, on the Tibetan plateau and out into the Gobi desert, the wrung-out air subsides and almost no rain falls: the physicist's "absolute desert."

Benefiting from this stable, dependable source of rain, South China and the Indian subcontinent were among the first places to experience agriculture. The steadiness of this rhythm has maintained those civilizations for more than two thousand years, and when it occasionally falters, dynasties fall.

The early Mediterranean civilizations had a superficially similar climate, only here the wet season was the winter and the dry season the summer. But the winds and the rainfall were nowhere near as dependable as in South Asia. Indeed, the winds were so various and so destructive that one of the earliest epics of Western culture—Homer's *Odyssey*—was based on the not-unbelievable fiction that god-driven winds keep Odysseus from reaching home for ten years after the fall of Troy.

The most poignant moment in that story comes after Aeolus, the keeper of the winds, has tied all but the gentle west wind, Zephyros, up in a bag bound with a silver cord. Delivering the bag to Odysseus, he instructs the hero to keep all of the other winds tied up until he reaches home. Odysseus and his crew set sail. After a smooth voyage, they approach Ithaca. Homer reports that they can see the smoke from the fires burning in the stubble fields.

Odysseus lies down for a nap. His men, always curious about the big bag tied shut with a silver cord, decide that it is full of treasure that their captain means to keep for himself. While Odysseus sleeps, they open the bag. Out fly all the contrary winds, and the ship is blown right back where it started from.

In Roman Greece, just before the dawn of the Christian era, a Greek architect built an eight-sided tower in Athens to summarize the gifts and the disasters of the eight Mediterranean winds. It was topped by a weathervane—the fish-tailed god Triton holding a wand that pointed into the prevailing wind—and so it served as a kind of forecast center.

Boreas, the north wind, is represented as an old man huddled under a cloak. He blows through a conch shell. Kaikias, the north-east wind, carries a platter full of hailstones that he scatters on the ground. Apeliotes, the wet east wind, holds handfuls of grain and fruit. Another old man is Euros, the southeast wind, wrapped up well in his winter coat. Notos, the south wind, pours water out of his urn over Europe. Skiron, the north wind, brings coal and ashes. The west wind, Zephyros, is the moist spring wind that brings flowers out of the dead land. And Lips, the southwest wind, is represented by a lad propelling a boat by pushing on its stern.

These winds came (and come) with a hundred variants, and most— except zephyr—have different names today. The mistral—the north wind that flows south through Provence—is one inheritor of old Boreas. It is a wind of winter and spring that is driven by and steered between high-pressure clockwise spins in the Atlantic between northern Spain and southwestern France, and low-pressure counter-clockwise cyclones in the Mediterranean Gulf of Genoa. The wind flows—sometimes at speeds topping fifty knots for three days to a week at a time—down the valleys of the Rhone and the Durance and out to the Mediterranean. The mistral flows more or less downslope. It does not generally become warm, but it does bring weather that is clear and dry, so dry that it is often accompanied by fires. Over the ages the flora of Provence—like that of southern California—has adapted to this cycle of wet and dry, so that it benefits from the fires that come with the mistral. In Provence, all of the doors to the houses face south, and in the Christmas crèche, at least one shepherd is seen holding onto his hat, in honor of the mistral.

To the east of the mistral blows the foehn. This is a true downslope wind. The same cyclone lows that suck air down the river valleys southward in the mistral, blow up against the north-south facing Alps to the east. The wet wind off the Mediterranean drops its rain or snow on the south side of the range, then descends the north side, where, as Ducarla-Bonifas predicted, it compresses, warms, and dries. It can change the winter temperature by as much as 40 degrees Fahrenheit in a few minutes, and so is famous for melting midwinter snow. While the mistral dries the mud in the south, the foehn eats the snow to the north. Early in the twentieth century, a German manufacturer named its hair drier a *föhn*. *Föhn* is now the general word for hair drier through most of middle Europe and into Scandinavia.

The opposite wind, in every way, is the sirocco, which blows up from the Sahara and crosses the Mediterranean into southern Europe. This wind has many names and characters. It is driven directly by a low-pressure cyclone—often one that starts in the same Gulf of Genoa. The storm system sweeps into North Africa and the Sahara, where it picks up hot dry air. As the spin carries the dust over the Mediterranean, the warm air vaporizes the seawater and carries it along.

When sirocco reaches the south coast of Europe, it is hot, wet, and dirty. It brings lashing rain, often laced with red and yellow mud. The dust storms that look so poetic when they are seen in photographs taken by a NASA satellite orbiting high above are much less pleasant to those living where the wet dust falls. It can turn a whole town—trees, houses, cars, streets, cobblestones—red or yellow with sticky dust.

In North America, the wide-open topography writes the same

effects but larger. The Chinook wind comes in winter when wet air climbs the west side of the Rocky Mountains, drops its load of snow, and descends the east slope. Chinook is the foehn with a vengeance. When there is low pressure east of the mountains, the Chinook can whistle down through the canyons at more than ninety miles an hour. Like the foehn, it can change the weather in the blink of an eye. When the Chinook blew strong at the start of the 1988 Winter Olympics in Calgary, Alberta, it melted the snow on the race courses. The ski events were delayed by three days.

Unlike the foehn, the Chinook has to deal with a vast plain to its east. The cold air in place at the base of the range may be stronger than the descending wind, causing the Chinook to flow over the top of the cold air and never reach the ground. If the Chinook strengthens, it can burst through to the surface, only to be forced aloft again. On a winter day in Rapid City, South Dakota, a person could head off to work with the temperature outdoors at 32 degrees Fahrenheit, arrive at the office when the thermometer tops 100, go out for lunch with the temperature at 14 degrees, and arrive home in the evening to 95 degrees. The changes are not often that extreme, but wide winter temperature variations in the region are common.

In the spring, winds that cross the Rockies and descend on the east side form the cap that can give rise to tornadoes. In the fall, when high pressure sits over the range, winds instead might descend the west side of the mountain range, flowing over the southwestern deserts and into southern California. These so-called Santa Ana winds can have temperatures topping 104 degrees Fahrenheit, but crossing the desert is not what makes them warm. Rather, it is that steep descent and compression coming down the mountain. The winds bring hot dry conditions at a time when, toward the end of the dry season, the flora is already parched. Fires are frequent when the Santa Ana comes.

The fires are a disaster for human communities and homeowners, but they are a necessity for the chaparral landscape. There is never a more beautiful crop of wildflowers in southern California than in the spring after a major fire. Some of the native plants—called fire followers—germinate only after fire. And many of the common wildflowers—like California poppy—bloom more profusely after exposure to smoke.

When wet wind is cooled, rain or snow occurs. Nowhere does this happen with greater result than in the lee of the Great Lakes. In a way, it is the American monsoon. In Buffalo or Syracuse, New York, when lake-effect snow is falling, the depth is measured in feet, not inches. Areas of the Tug Hill Plateau in western New York, downwind from Lake Ontario, can receive more than three hundred inches of snow in a winter. That is twenty-five feet.

The people who knew the lake effect best—if they did not die as a result of it—were the pilots who flew airmail across the Allegheny Mountains, back and forth between Cleveland and New York, during the 1910s and 1920s. Their planes had open cockpits, and they were completely innocent of navigation aids, except for compass and altimeter, which were as often faulty as not. As winter approaches, the water temperatures over the lakes are higher than the temperatures over the land to leeward. When winds blow the water-laden warm air over the cooler land masses, the temperature and dew point meet. Precipitation begins to fall. When, in addition, the wet air is lifted over a mountain range—modest as the Alleghenies are—the conditions for flying deteriorate rapidly. Pilots call it "zero-zero"—zero ceiling and zero visibility. They can see nothing below them and nothing in front of them. At least thirty-four airmail pilots came to grief trying to cross the Alleghenies in such conditions. They would fly at an elevation of a hundred feet or less, trying to stay below the stratus clouds or fog. One pilot reported trying to skim along beside the insulators on the telephone poles. When the weather closed down so low that even this feat was impossible, a choice had to be made: set down wherever they were, or try to climb up out of the weather. In winter, the top of the cloud layer might be nine thousand to fourteen thousand feet up. Without any aid to show whether they were right side up or upside down, pilots would try to feel their way to the top of the layer.

In turbulence, vertigo is common. If pilots did not keep their sense of gravity, they might fly straight into the ground upside down. If they made it to the top of the stratus, they caught a break. Until they ran low on fuel, they might get to fly east or west in brilliant sunshine, with the soapsud clouds beneath them, and hope the clouds broke. If the clouds didn't break, they had to take a deep breath, say a prayer, write their will on the back of an airmail envelope, and push the stick forward.

Pilot Jack Knight reported one such descent in search of an airport in Bellefonte, Pennsylvania, which was at eighteen hundred feet smack in the middle of the Alleghenies. His altimeter took him below twenty-four hundred feet—the top of the tallest nearby peaks—and then to eighteen hundred feet, seventeen hundred, sixteen hundred, fifteen hundred. By rights, he should have been dead. He was three hundred feet lower than the airport in a place where the ridgelines were generally at two thousand feet. Finally, he saw a road and a field. He was little more than two hundred feet in the air. He followed the road to the airport.

The lake-effect snows and rains come when warmer lake waters are lifted and pass over colder land and over mountains. They are phenomena of winter and early spring, when the land is relatively cool.

Why, then, were my summer afternoon breezes in the Bay Area so often followed by thick cold fog? The land at that time of year is much warmer than the sea. The cold California current that flows south along the edge of the continent is the cause. Water out in the open Pacific is much warmer. When that sea breeze sets up on the summer afternoon, it draws in air off the ocean. The warmer air chills as it crosses the 50-degree waters on the shoreline. It reaches its dew point, and thick ground-hugging stratus clouds—otherwise known as fog—form. The fog pushes up against the coast range. If it is only five hundred feet thick, it might stay on the coast side, making people in Half Moon Bay see their breath. If it builds up to a thousand feet thick, over the hills it comes.

As a child living in the Bay Area, I was mystified by some of the things that people from the East said. (To me, the "East" began somewhere beyond Reno, Nevada.) Poems by Carl Sandburg were often read aloud in school. Being a kid of a fogbound coast, I was supposed to respond to his notion that the fog comes in "on little cat feet." Maybe *his* fog did. My fog came in like my father's thick Brer Rabbit molasses, which he poured religiously over his porridge. The fog would froth up on a hilltop, and I would wait, holding my breath. Maybe the wind would turn northerly and blow it away. More often, it started to slump down every canyon and every fold in the hills, like arthritic fingers exploring a wound. Then, the mass would spill over the summits and ooze slowly but surely downhill in my direction. You could see it coming. You would smell the wet cold whiff of it as the first fingers reached you. Time to button up the sweater or put on the down vest, in the middle of a summer afternoon.

In literature in eighth grade, I read poems by James Russell Lowell, who opined, "For what is so fair as a day in June? / Then if ever come perfect days." I knew that both he and Mr. Sandburg must live in a world very different from mine. So much depends on the water in the air, and whether and when it cools enough to come out of hiding so you can see and feel it.

Firestorm

War is the struggle of all the state apparatuses and chiefs of
staff against all men old enough and able to bear arms.

—*Simone Weil*

S imone Weil wrote this in 1938. In the totalizing state, there is no
distinction between soldier and civilian. Because all the resources of
civil society are meant to be put at the service of that state to prosecute
its wars, all civilians are really just plainclothes agents of the state. Thus,
they become legitimate targets. The generals regard it as fine to turn the
civilians' air into fire. Hitler tried this out at Guernica, but he was an
amateur compared to the Allies and to British Bomber Command. Not
that Hitler would not have returned the favor had he had the chance.

To bomb major cities, you needed four things: big airplanes, good
navigation, precise targeting, and effective bombs. At the outset of
World War II, neither the Axis nor the Allies had any of these. In
1939, in a daylight exercise, only 44 percent of British bombers found
their targets, and they were flying over friendly cities. But by 1943,
the British and Americans had everything they needed for a carpet
bombing campaign. The Avro Lancaster and the Flying Fortress were
big, reliable bombers. Newly minted radar could at least distinguish
a city at night. And the bombs were really terrific: big and explosive,

eight-thousand-pound blockbusters and four-thousand-pound cookies, whose bursting would open up buildings and blow out windows and doors so that a rain of little four-pound magnesium, phosphorus, and petroleum-jelly bombs could start fires that would spread.

Above all, brilliant tactical work had created a system of targeting that made precise, accurate bombing a reality. The No. 5 Group of Bomber Command pioneered the system. First, they would send in Blind Illuminators, bombers flying by radar who would locate the city and light it up with flares. Then two-seater de Haviland Mosquito bombers would dive low over the city, sight the designated targets, and drop red or green air-burst bombs over them. Circling the city at a high altitude, the Master Bomber would direct the waves of bombers to their targets. Often, the bombers would radiate from an illuminated target area like the spokes of a wheel—wave after wave after wave, often at intervals of only a minute or two.

It occurred to some bright soul that if the British did this with precision and good timing, and if they had the right weather, they could create a firestorm. The Germans had created a firestorm in part of London during the blitz, and the Allies had created one in Hamburg. But these were likely inadvertent. The British decided to hit the ancient city of Dresden on the night of February 13 and the early morning of February 14, 1945, with the intent of creating one.

A firestorm is aptly named because it occurs when a fire creates its own weather, and that weather—a set of violent updrafts—creates more fire. The classic firestorm before World War II occurred in and around the town of Peshtigo near Green Bay, Wisconsin, in 1871. It was the product of human stupidity coupled with bad weather luck, and so it was the mirror image of the Dresden firebombing, created by human ingenuity with "good" weather luck.

Fire was a common industrial tool for most of human history, though nowhere more so than in the upper Midwest at the end of the nineteenth century. The farmers cleared new land with fire. The loggers who were felling the millennial forests—the Peshtigo Mill put out sixty million board feet of lumber per year—often burned off the slash created by their cutting and the waste from milling. Even the railroad workers cleared the woods in their path by burning them.

A pall of smoke over the landscape was generally viewed as a sign of progress and civilization. In the summer of 1871, however, it was also viewed with trepidation. Though the spring had been wet, the summer had been dry, very dry. Some of the ground fires, intentionally started, did not go out but instead spread along and even under the ground. Winds whipped up serious fires into the crowns of trees, scorching them and threatening Peshtigo and other towns in Michigan, Wisconsin, and Illinois.

As autumn drew on, the weather cooled, and there was hope that the fire season was almost over. And besides, the fires had already killed many trees near town, leaving them mere skeletons. This, it was thought, was a cordon sanitaire that could discourage further fires. But on the evening of October 8, the weather changed. A storm crossing Nebraska brought a southerly wind into Peshtigo. A stream of cold, fast-moving air flowed over the top of the smoky lid that covered Peshtigo, punching holes in it. The inversion layer—warmer air lying over and compressing the colder air beneath it—was breached. Where the inversion was torn up by colder air, the surface air was warmer than the air aloft, and so it rose rapidly. Through these chimneys of colder air, the ground breeze rose. As it did so, it sucked in oxygen that gave new life to the isolated fires that were still smoldering all over the region.

The fires blazed up, heating the atmosphere and starting intense convective updrafts. The fires grew, moved, and began to meet and join other fires. The continuing low jet stream swept away the air as it rose, replacing it continually with a colder air that egged on the convection and increased the flames. As the fires increased in intensity, they began to control and direct the weather, forcing hot air aloft and dragging in cold air from all around.

Intense whirlwinds began. Father Pernin, Peshtigo's Roman Catholic priest, saw a canary and its cage ripped from his housekeeper's arms and carried off on the wind. In the room where he went to recover the chalice, the air was full of noisy sparks that popped with the sound of many small detonations. As he went out the door to his wagon, the wind carried away the planks of the house, the gate, the fence. As he went down the street toward the river, the wind overturned his wagon and blew it and him away.

In a firestorm, the heat is so intense that the air is full of flammable gas, waiting for a floating spark or cinder to ignite it. Even those who had run into large clearings to escape found the stumps of trees beside them turn into blazing torches, and isolated cabins suddenly burst into flames. The supposed cordon sanitaire of dead trees burned, as did whole landscapes that had been dried by the drought and the earlier fires. More than seventeen hundred people died in the Peshtigo fire. Yet that was nothing compared to Dresden. And Dresden was intentional.

The same ingredients were there. The old center of town was chiefly made of wood, long aged and ready to burn. The first wave of bombers with their blockbusters and cookies would break open and shatter the buildings, clearing passages for air and fire, just as the earlier fires had dried and opened the landscape of Peshtigo. The next waves with their balls and clusters of incendiary bombs would light little fires one after another in every corner where they rolled, just as the individual fires would smolder around Peshtigo, waiting on the wind.

Bomber Command dropped 1,471 tons of high-explosive bombs and 1,175 tons of incendiary bombs over Dresden in two well-coordinated raids, one after another. Pilots in the second raid, indeed, could not see the red and green marker bombs because of the intensity of the fires that were already burning in the city, so the Master Bomber told them to drop their loads wherever the fires seemed most intense.

A steady west wind brought cold air through the city. The heat of the fires started intense convective updrafts. The west wind kept them going. The little fires spawned by each four-pound incendiary ball joined into middling fires, and middling fires into bigger fires. Soon, the fire whirls were self-sustaining, sucking in oxygen from all around and creating intense cyclonic winds. Gale force winds spun into the center of the fires, sucking combustibles, animals, bricks, beams, and people into the maelstrom. The asphalt in the streets turned to molten black rivers. In the superheated air, people asphyxiated or died from breathing the hot gases. Structures apparently far from the fire front would suddenly burst into flames.

By dawn on Valentine's Day of 1945, the old city of Dresden was a burning ruin. Because the city was at the time a place of refuge for those fleeing from the collapsing eastern front, no one will ever know how many people died. It is thought that thirty-five thousand to forty thousand is not an unlikely estimate.

Antoine de Saint-Exupéry—who as writer, flyer, and official of Aéropostale, the first transatlantic mail carrier, had done more than anyone in the West to promote the romance of manned flight—was sickened by the air war. Although he did not live to know Dresden— he was lost flying a reconnaissance flight in 1943—he accurately predicted in 1938 what total war would become: "Night after night, [each side] launches squadrons that torpedo the enemy in his entrails, blow up his vital centers, and paralyze his production and commerce," he imagined. "Victory belongs to the side that rots last. And the two adversaries rot together." Presumably, he did not imagine the firestorm, since then instead of "rot" he might well have written "burn."

Shortly after Dresden, on March 9 of the same year, the Americans got their turn. Three hundred twenty-nine B-29s dropped 1,665 tons of incendiary bombs on Tokyo, Japan. The city was largely made of wood. The firestorm destroyed sixteen square miles and killed more than a hundred thousand people. It was the first of sixty such attacks on Japanese cities.

Flying

Dragged Aloft

Some time in the spring or the fall, on sunny warm days when the wind is light but the air is rising, about half the small spiders in the world get ready to take off. They climb to the top of a blade of grass, a cornflower, a stem of timothy, a twig of hawthorn, a fence post, a rose hip, a milkweed fruit. Once there, some will drop down on a dragline, hanging in midair. Most will stand on tiptoe at the top of their perch, their heads down and their bellies in the air. When the time is right, each begins to emit slender silk from its spinnerets. The silk can reach three feet in length or more.

Most flying or gliding animals depend upon lift exceeding drag. Spiders are lifted by the friction between their silk and the air. The rising air catches the almost weightless gossamer, stretches it out like a streamer, and tugs at the spider on its perch or its line. When the time is ripe, the spider lets go.

Not infrequently, the silk catches on a neighbor stem, and the spider travels only ten to twenty feet from home. There, however, it is poised for another try, and as long as the wind is right, it will go again. Students of the spider have once or twice tried to follow an arachnid in flight. It isn't easy. It works only when the flight aborts. The one published report suggests that the five individuals the scientists tracked went only about ten or twelve feet.

But spiders can go near or far. They are aeronauts that depend almost entirely on the whims of the wind. By splaying out or balling up, they can influence their ability to remain aloft, but they will otherwise go where the wind wants them to. Mariners in the Age of Sail frequently reported spiders landing in their sails when they were hundreds of miles from the nearest land. One air sample taken at about sixteen thousand feet—looking for fungi and bacteria—also caught a spider. When a submarine volcano lifted the island of Anak Krakatau out of the South Pacific in 1929, the first colonizers to arrive were airborne spiders.

Not all spiders travel by air. Many bridge stem to stem, throwing out a line and following it. This is overland travel, slow and expensive. You have to generate a new line for each leap, and you have to pull yourself across. While you are in the middle of the traverse, you may look tasty to a passing bat or bird, and your chance of escape is small. On the other hand, you have some control over where you are going. You will not end up on a sail or in an air sampler or in the blue Pacific water.

When they do fly—or "balloon," as is the proper term for arachnid aerial locomotion—it is for one of two opposite reasons. If conditions are good where they are living, it may get pretty crowded pretty quickly. Ballooning is a way to reduce the surplus population. (Thomas Malthus would be pleased.) Or if things are not going well where they are living, it may be the better part of valor to try someplace else.

Young or old may travel by air. In one species of the very common Linyphiidae family, more than 99 percent of spiderlings take to the air to found new colonies. (About 2 percent succeed.) When adults travel, it is often the gravid females, who lay eggs upon landing and so make an instant outpost.

However many leave, there is no shortage on arrival. One arachnologist kept count of the spiders arriving by air on one agricultural field during an entire growing season. The total amounted to about nine hundred spiders per day, and a little more than a hundred thousand per acre during the four-month season.

A spider on "tiptoe," preparing to balloon. (Courtesy of Nicky Davis)

Occasionally, even large spiders take to the air. Some scientists had suggested this, but were challenged by colleagues. The standard wisdom is that spiders heavier than one milligram seldom, if ever, balloon. Stung by the challenge, the first team of scientists went out to watch.

It was a hot January day in Namibia, and strong convection currents were rising from the surface of the land. Around noon, the scientists saw twenty fairly large females—each probably weighing at least seventy milligrams—tiptoe on the end of a branch. They emitted silk and took off, only to hang up in a nearby shrub. The next day, watching another colony in the late afternoon, they saw six comparably large females begin to tiptoe. Each put out one gossamer thread and then another. Before they took off, there were more than a hundred threads wafting upward in the rising air. Each spider had made a triangular kite of silk at least three feet wide at its far end. When they let go, all the spiders rose straight into the air. After a few seconds, they were ninety feet up and still climbing. The investigators never saw them again.

Saab in Flight

The little sixteen-seat turboprop can't wait to get off the ground. When the wind shifts a little, the port prop makes the sounds of a sawmill or of a train that quickly comes and goes. Impatient vibrations pass along the airframe, forward and back, back and forward, side to side. Sometimes they meet and propagate in a shudder right at my seat amidships. Tenth in line for departure!

The pilot again laments the weather, the sticky baggage door, the change of runways. He affects the drawl that every pilot seems to use for talking to his passengers. Or did they all learn to fly from the same Texan?

I am convinced that in this unseasonable air—a big southerly in January, sweeping up the eastern seaboard after spawning at least one tornado in Georgia—the sticky baggage door spells doom. It will shake open in flight, spoiling the perfect flow over the airframe, sending eddy waves of turbulence out of us, turning us from an airfoil into a spinning leaf.

But the little Saab does not believe this. She believes in her own smooth frame and in the wings that want only the right thrust and the right angle to get her into the air. There they will not care how big the holes in the air are, how quick the lifts, how sudden the shifts. There she will just move. She will bump, fall, jump, bank, pitch, yaw.

There will not be this annoying sticky ground to restrain her. She is made for the air. A wing cannot tolerate the ground, unless, like a falcon, it is hooded and caged, perfectly sealed from the temptations of three free dimensions.

"Number Won for Takeawf."

At last.

In Spanish, the word used for "takeoff" is *despegar*, to come unstuck.

Almost instantly, the ground is out of sight. The air is like a martini shaker, and my fellow five passengers and I are like ice cubes in it. I wish that I were happier with the situation than I am.

What a chance to observe the weather from inside it! What luck! I tell myself.

I recall that Pliny had the great good fortune to observe the eruption of Vesuvius from a nearby ship, but it was his last observation. Or as a young seismologist said more recently from his observation tower near Mount Saint Helens, "This is it. This is the big one!" And said no more.

But we survive the ascent. We rise to about ten thousand feet, where we are the meat in a sandwich between two cloud layers. The lower layer had been flat on the bottom—rain clouds usually have a flat bottom because the condensation nuclei that form raindrops or snowfall are gathering rapidly there and growing rapidly in size, all within a few feet of the lifting condensation level—but it is puffy and wispy on top. Every wisp is a different current in the air. As we fly through the wisps, we feel in our bones the truth of this assertion, since each pretty curl translates into a shake or a bump.

The Saab hums. In one of the carry-on baggage bins, something is loose. Big bumps make it tick. Each of us is affectedly sleeping, looking, reading, or otherwise pretending not to notice that the room is leaping all over the place.

I read in the morning weather report that there will be an unusual amount of mixing aloft. Sure enough, our two neat layers of cloud soon present a haze before us. Right there, the winds are mixing not only side to side but up and down. Two layers become one, and we bounce right into the mix.

I watch what appears to be snow flowing in streaks over the cowl and dissolving in the murk behind us. Condensation nuclei, indeed. I begin to watch for ice buildup on the wings. I hope the instruments are working, since otherwise no pilot can fly for long in cloud without banking and eventually spiraling out of control. I remember the baggage compartment door. I wonder about that ticking. I recall that before we boarded, I saw the pilot meditatively turning the port prop by hand, watching it move. Was there a problem that is about to be revealed? I feel my shoulders tense. My fingers in the pages of a book are wetting the paper. Shortly, a sidewise jiggle joins the bounce and shake.

The pilot reports that the headwind is so massive we will be in the air an extra half hour, but that ahead the clouds are breaking. A glimpse of ground appears: forests on the hills, farm fields with standing brown cornstalks in conservation tillage, river and oxbow meanders. Tidewater country. I have never set foot on that particular land, but already I have a story to tell about it.

It is clear and windy over Charlottesville, Virginia. The Saab bucks happily in the stiff gusts as she descends. At the last moment, as the port wheel touches down, she just doesn't want to settle the starboard side. The right wing stays just a few feet aloft. At last, she surrenders to gravity. The pilot backs the engines full, to stop the plane before it overshoots the runway. "To land," in Spanish, is *aterrizar*, to be-earth oneself.

As we deplane, I ask the attendant, a cheerful woman with a soft chin and round cheeks, if this kind of ride is normal.

"Normal enough at this time of year," she answers. "It used to make me as white-knuckled as anybody, but not anymore."

I shake my head, relieved to hear it.

She adds, "I just don't feel the need to go to an amusement park. Ever again."

The Common Crane

My wife and I like to spend part of February in the west of Spain, in Extremadura. So does the common crane. We were out for a drive one day, passing a long line of open stubble fields to our left. I noticed standing crops in one of the fields, but the stems were very fat. It was odd enough for there to be standing grain in a winter field, but it looked as though it were growing enormous torpedo onions above ground.

"Are those *birds*?" I asked.

"Can't be," she said. "There'd have to be thousands."

We pulled over and got out of the car to resolve the dispute.

The field was thick with cranes, with their slender legs, bulbous gray bodies, long black necks, and heads striped black and white and blotched red. There easily must have been a thousand of them and possibly many more. They were milling about, but they did not look restless. Now and again, a group of them would set up a clamor that seemed to be passed among the multitude until it died out somewhere near or far.

At least since the last ice age, these birds have been spending their summers in alder thickets in Scandinavia and their winters in southern Europe and sometimes even Morocco. Maybe sixty thousand cranes winter in Extremadura, arriving in November and heading north again in February. Through the winter, they eat seed, straw, rice, insects, snails, ants, and a lot of holm-oak acorns to fatten up for their journey back north. We were likely seeing their gathering prior to departure.

Cranes are among the most wonderful and versatile flyers in the world. The birds are big, weighing ten pounds or more, with a wingspan of six to seven feet. In order to take off, they have to get a good running start. They look like sprinters lunging for the finishing tape as they develop the thrust needed to get into the air. Then they flap their wings.

In all powered flying machines except for helicopters, the part that provides lift, the wings, is separate from the part that provides thrust, the engine. In the flying bird, the wings provide both lift and thrust. In fact, a bird's wings are much more like a helicopter's rotors than they are like an airplane's wings. Like the helicopter's rotor, the bird wing has a rotary motion. And like the helicopter pilot, the bird increases and decreases lift by setting its wings at different angles to the oncoming wind.

The downstroke is the power stroke in the bird. Angling its arc down and forward increases lift; angling it up and backward decreases lift. The upstroke must return at a different angle in order not to cancel the thrust that comes from the downstroke. Only insects, which are able to radically change the shape and orientation of their wings, can get additional power from the upstroke.

Birds and airplanes are much more similar in the way they turn. The Wright brothers made the first successful flyer when they learned the art of turning from birds. The trick is to generate more lift in one wing than another. The best way to do this is to change the angle at which one wing meets the oncoming air. A higher angle—that is, a higher angle of attack—creates both more lift and more drag. When one wing has more lift, it becomes the outside wing of a bank in the opposite direction. In other words, if you increase lift on the left wing, the plane (or the bird) turns right, and vice versa.

The bank will keep getting steeper as long as you keep the lift unequal. When you have the angle of bank you want, you equalize the lift on both wings. When you want to go back to straight and level flight, you apply unequal lift on the opposite side.

In an airplane, the ailerons do most of the job. (The Wrights did the same thing by actually warping the wings.) Move the yoke to the right, and the aileron on the right wing goes up while the aileron on the left wing goes down. The plane turns to the right. A bird does the same but by using a different shrug on one shoulder than another. And because the wings also provide the thrust, a bird can change lift by changing the amplitude of its wing strokes. Not only that, the bird can shift its tail, its body, and its weight to change the depth and character of a turn.

An airplane is a stiff, awkward contraption compared to the simplest bird. Still, it is much easier for a small bird to fly by flapping than it is for a large one. There is a limit to the power that animal muscle can generate. The drag that fights lift is mainly increased by the weight of the flyer, so a heavier bird must work harder to stay aloft.

For this reason, some larger migrants, like storks, flap only when the alternative is to fall to the ground. They fly an even longer north-south route than do the cranes, starting in Europe and ending in West or East Africa, a distance of more than four thousand miles. They travel almost exclusively by soaring. Looking for rising air in thermals—where differential heating of the ground makes for chimney- or ring-shaped updrafts—they circle higher and higher until the updraft dissipates. Then they glide downward at the angle that gives the most distance for height lost, until they come upon another thermal. They climb once more in the thermal and glide once more when it has gone. Storks' migration then is like a game of chutes and ladders, or corkscrews and slides. They circle up, then slide down.

The soaring flight of the storks is great for conserving energy, but it limits when and where they can fly. In the absence of thermals, they sometimes use the orographic lift from winds that flow perpendicular to mountain ranges. Usually, however, when conditions are cloudy and thermals are few, the storks are grounded. At nighttime, too, they cannot fly unless they flap. And instead of venturing out straight across the Mediterranean, they must detour around the sea's eastern shore.

Cranes are as large as storks, but perhaps because they fly only about half as far, they are willing to flap as well as soar. And in their migration, they regularly traverse the Baltic Sea, where thermals are rare. Whether they flap or soar, they keep in a pattern that takes advantage of the tiny amount of lift created by the bird in front of them.

In the inverted V formation—really shaped more like a Greek lambda—in which cranes and many other migrants fly, one bird follows another, keeping in the upwash created by its predecessor. The bound vortex that keeps each wing in flight sheds trailing vortices with an opposite spin behind them. If the following bird keeps in the right place, it can be supported on the upward leg of that vortex. It is free lift. The only bird not to get this benefit is the leader, so the lead must periodically change, or the leader will falter and the formation fall apart.

The angle and tilt of the V are not only a function of efficient use of energy. The birds also have to keep in sight of one another. The line of the formation allows a more or less constant angle between the eye of the follower and the wingtip of the predecessor. And each bird flies slightly above the one before it—even though the strongest lift is in the plane of the preceding bird's flight—because looking down allows it to see its predecessor below the horizon, making it easier to keep formation.

Colin Pennycuick once studied the flight of cranes by following them in light aircraft, making S turns and flying near his own stall speed. He watched them rise in thermals as high as six thousand feet above sea level, though usually they were much lower. On one afternoon's flight, he reported the following:

> Initially thermals were good, under a sunny sky with small cumulus clouds, and the Cranes achieved a series of good climbs in the height range 500–1300 m a.s.l. [above sea level]. Then they entered an area where the cumulus clouds had coalesced and cut off the sun from the ground ("overconvection"). Thermals were weaker here, and the Cranes progressively lost height to about 300 m, but made their way back to 1300 m soon after emerging from the overcast area. Later the cumulus clouds ceased altogether as the air became stable, and the Cranes again progressively lost height in the weak, inconsistent thermals. When we left them, they were within 150 m of the ground, and obliged to resort to flapping flight.

For any flyer larger than the size of a puppy, the greatest anxiety in flight comes when it is time to get ready to land. For small insects, the landing is really of little consequence. Insects such as flies and bees generally just put forward their legs and crash into their landing sites. A stork that did so would break its legs and never be able to get that running jump it needs to take off again.

A human pilot is much more like a stork than a bee. Landing is an unforgiving moment. You must somehow turn the plane so it is lined up with what seems to be a very thin ribbon of runway. Then you take the plane down at an angle and rate fast enough to reach the runway but slow enough not to overshoot it, while staying above the speed at which the plane would stall and fall from the sky. If there is a crosswind to boot, then you must angle the nose of the plane into the wind—a maneuver appropriately named "crabbing" because it makes you seem to scuttle at an angle toward the ground. You must

*The common crane extending its legs, increasing lift, and shedding speed
for landing. Throwing back its wings, it stalls and lands.
(Illustration by Nora H. Logan)*

fly toward the runway at that angle so the whole plane stays lined up
with the runway end. Only at the last moment can you kick out the
crab and land with the nose straight in.

At least cranes don't have to land on runways, but still they must
slow themselves down enough that they do not break their legs, and
pull off enough lift so that they do not bounce back into the air. Just
as angle of attack can be used to climb, to descend, and to turn, it
can be used to land. At the critical angle of attack, as a pilot knows,
a plane or a bird has maximum lift and maximum drag. Pass over the
threshold, and either will stall. Young cranes learn all about stalling.

Flying

Cranes learn to do this trick intentionally. It is beautiful to watch them as they settle to the ground. Their wings ride forward as if to hold a ball, while they drop their long legs and slow down. Just when they are about to land, they lift up the leading edges of their spread wings to an impossibly high angle of attack, as though they were maestros receiving a standing ovation. They stall and settle to the ground.

Stall Practice

What makes a wing fly? This is an interesting question to a student of aeronautics, but a question of even more importance to the student pilot in a Cessna Skyhawk cleared by Caldwell Tower for takeoff on runway 28 northwest bound, VFR. For only the pilot's fourth time. Ever.

Winds are at 240 degrees, eighteen knots gusting to twenty-five, the ATIS (Automatic Terminal Information Service) drones in its computer-generated, Swedish-sounding voice. (Pilots and seamen call the weather voice "Sven.") My teacher—thirty years my junior—is cheerful as he notes the crosswind on takeoff and tells me how we will crab a little to get a straight departure.

As we turn onto the actual runway, we see that the windsock is flying at an angle to the runway. As low-tech as this device might be, it is still the best way to assess wind direction at takeoff or landing.

Then my teacher says, "Your airplane," which means that I am the one who has to fly it.

"No," I respond, with a tremor in my voice.

I have yet to take this plane off the ground, and the wind today is high and gusty.

"I'll help with the crab," he adds cheerily.

I clutch the yoke with both hands.

"One hand on the throttle at all times," he counsels.

"Full power," he adds helpfully.

I push the throttle in as far as it will go. The engine makes a noise like a room full of lawn mowers all mowing at once. Takeoff is not quiet in a little plane. That is why we wear headphones and communicate with each other—as well as the tower—by radio.

"Full power," he repeats, as if to confirm what he sees and hears.

The Cessna starts to roll.

"Rolling."

We check the gauges to make sure nothing—like oil pressure—is off-kilter.

"Gauges in the green."

The airspeed indicator passes fifty knots.

"Airspeed alive."

At about fifty-five knots, I pull back on the yoke as gently as I can manage.

"Rotate."

I have asked my teacher why when a plane takes off, a pilot says, "Rotate." He explains that it is because the plane must rotate around its lateral axis, tilting the nose up, to get enough lift to leave the ground.

Easy for him to say. When a small plane takes off, it is by no means balletic. Or perhaps it is the pirouette as the ballerina, not the audience, feels it.

My teacher tells me to climb out at eighty knots. This is Vr, the speed at which we get the most climb for distance traveled over the ground. I have to remember to push on the right rudder to keep the plane from turning to the left, but what most impresses (and sometimes terrifies) me is the thought that we are now in a world where another dimension is alive.

On the ground, if I want a car to go faster, I step on the gas pedal. If I am at the top of a hill, I can add less gas and let gravity help me add speed as I go down. In the air, I can at any moment trade airspeed for altitude, or altitude for airspeed. Except on takeoff and landing, I am always at the top *and* the bottom of a hill. If I go down, I speed up. If I go up, I slow down. I need to add power to climb, and back off power when descending.

"We will cruise at three thousand feet, heading zero three zero."

When I level off at the altitude, I do what my teacher intones again and again: "Pitch, power, trim."

I pitch by pushing the yoke forward gently to achieve level flight. I watch my airspeed indicator, which climbs steadily as I transition to level flight. The airspeed is no longer being traded for altitude, so it increases. When it passes my cruise speed of 110 to 120 knots, I pull back on the throttle, reducing power to maintain that airspeed. Finally, I use a small auxiliary surface on the right elevator, moving it gently up or down relative to the horizontal stabilizer, to trim the aircraft, helping to maintain it easily in level flight.

If I want to gain speed, I can always do it in one of two ways: either by adding power or by nosing down. At a comfortable altitude of three thousand feet, with the russet and red autumn woodlands giving way to farm fields, some plowed, some a yellowing green, this fact seems much more believable than it does on takeoff or on landing.

As if to prove the point, my teacher pulls the power back to idle.

There is a deafening silence as the motor's threshing din sinks to a sort of feeble ticking.

"Now, we're a glider," he says, with the usual happy lilt in his voice.

I have been told what to do. I can recite it, like an incantation. A Cessna has no trouble gliding to a landing. I must first establish the angle of glide that will give me the most options. I recognize this angle by the airspeed that accompanies it, about sixty-eight knots. If I hold this speed, I will get about a nine-to-one glide ratio. For every thousand feet we descend, we will travel nine thousand feet over the ground.

Then, I am to pick a landing site and set a course for it. Then, if it were a real emergency power loss, I could try to restart the engine. If I have plenty of altitude, there is plenty of time. Or so I am told. But in the moment when the power is taken away, I feel like Scrooge on his windowsill, as the Ghost of Christmas Past asks him to step out into the air.

"But I am a mortal and liable to fall!"

"Bear but a touch of my hand there [on Scrooge's heart]," the shade replies, "and you will be upheld."

It is practically as great an act of faith to trust a wing, for in both cases we are upheld by the invisible. Indeed, a technical definition of faith is "the evidence of things unseen."

As the descent begins, however, we *do* glide. The quiet of the idle engine becomes a comfort, not a terror. The unseen indeed upholds us, through the medium of this long flattish thing called a wing. It does not matter so much whether a wing has that odd keeled shape that most wings have, with a hump on top and a bit of hollow beneath. This shape—the wing's camber—improves performance and discourages stalling, but it is not necessary. If it were necessary, every aerobatic pilot who flew inverted would fall straight to the ground.

The important thing is that the wing be finite, flattish, and that it be propelled through the air. A barn door makes a wing, a poor one, but a wing indeed, as does a piece of plywood, a sheet of paper, a bit of tin foil. All these things have the right stuff—a shape that lets the streamline of the air run smoothly over it. Lift and drag are properties of all objects when they meet the moving air. If lift is greater than drag, then the object will fly. A man or woman does not have anything like this shape. Drag will always win over lift for a squat and lumpy human. So we must put on wings to fly.

For any given wing, however, the ratio of lift to drag depends only on the angle at which it meets the rushing air. A business card, for example, can do a descent pretty much like the one that I was doing in the Cessna. Take such a card in your hands. Hold the short ends between the first and second fingers of each hand. Launch gently forward. The card will travel a bit, then acquire a backspin and make a steady descent to landing. If you have launched it with topspin, it may plunge to the ground, or it may insist on flying in the opposite direction from which you launched it.

What is happening? The card experiences lift because the air on the top side is traveling faster than the air on the bottom side. As mathematician Daniel Bernoulli discovered, whenever the velocity in a fluid increases, the pressure decreases. The relatively high velocity of the air over the top of the card lends it a lower pressure on the top than on the bottom, so the card is sustained in the air. Because it has no propulsion beyond the initial push of your hand, it descends, though were a wind to rise, it might sustain itself for longer.

But why the spin? If the Cessna's wings spun in the manner of this business card, I would experience not pleasure, but terror, followed by blacking out and certain death. Nonetheless, it is an invisible spin that keeps my Cessna too in the air.

Nature wants air to flow smoothly off the back end—that is, the trailing edge—of a wing. Though the air is flowing fast in stream-lines over and under the wing, at that trailing edge the air is absolutely still. If you were a very careful insect, you could walk along the trailing edge and not even feel a breeze. A German named Wilhelm Kutta first observed this in 1902, and so the phenomenon is called the Kutta condition.

In every takeoff, however, the Kutta condition is not given but won. As the plane begins to roll, the airflow curls under the moving wing, but the wing is still not ready to fly. The vortex created by the flowing air does not envelope the wing. Instead, it spins back counterclockwise off the trailing edge, growing in strength. At last, as the Kutta condition is achieved, the air off the trailing edge becomes still, no more vorticity is generated, and the starting vortex spins until

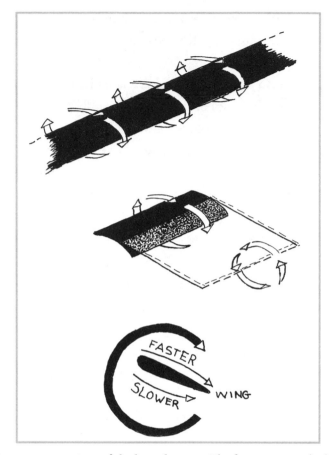

Three representations of the bound vortex. The first is on an idealized infinite wing that never takes off or lands. The second shows how in takeoff, a starting vortex is left behind as the bound vortex forms. The bound vortex speeds the air over the top of the wing and slows it over the bottom.
(Illustration by Nora H. Logan)

it dissipates, left behind in the wake of the departing plane. This is when it is safe to rotate. This is when the Cessna will not, like the business card, begin to turn somersaults.

The starting vortex has now established an equal and opposite vortex that surrounds the wing. The vortex is bound to the wing as long as it flies, so it is called the bound vortex. The effect of this circulating air is to accelerate the flow across the top of the wing—where the direction of the vortex flow adds to the normal airflow—and to retard the flow on the bottom of the wing—where the vortex flow resists the normal airflow. This is the spin that keeps every plane in the air. It is a comfort to me as we glide to feel that the smooth airflow over the Cessna's wing is enfolded and governed by a circulation that moves with us, ensuring lift and reducing drag.

In a lesson, however, we seldom enjoy anything for long. My teacher instructs me to climb to three thousand feet again. I put on full throttle, ease back on the yoke, apply right rudder, and climb. At our altitude, I practice pitch, power, trim. And there we are. Nothing to it.

My teacher is looking below us. He tells me to turn to a heading that will lead us through the patchwork of farm fields, not over the sleeping dogs of mountains. I imagine he is being thoughtful, since the turbulence is greater over the hills. But he has something else in mind.

"Now, first," he says with a cheerfulness that fills me with suspicion, "we will practice power-off stalls."

I shoot him a nervous glance. I can feel sweat forming between my left hand and the yoke.

"They're really fun," he adds, which leads me to believe that they are really scary. "But we need plenty of room to lose altitude."

Sweat starts to form on my right palm, where it grips the throttle.

The idea is to pretend we are on final approach to land, only we are giving ourselves plenty of altitude to work with. I am to reduce power to the approach setting, about 1,500 rpm, lower the flaps, and establish the approach speed, about sixty-five knots. As I reach my approach speed, I am to pull back on the yoke, raising the nose.

Remember that the lift-to-drag ratio is influenced only by the angle that the wing makes to the air. In fact, the greater the angle, the greater the lift . . . up to a certain point. I remember that this point is called—ominously—the critical angle of attack. Pass this angle, and the airplane stalls.

I don't like the idea.

"Keep pulling back," says my teacher.

I do.

The stall warning horn sounds, a high reedy whine. The plane wallows and doesn't want to do what my hands and feet are telling it to do. For a long time, however, nothing else happens. Then all of a sudden, the nose drops and the whole machine backs up through the sky, as though someone had grabbed it by the tail, yanking back and down. This is a pretty accurate description of the sensation. Beyond the critical angle of attack, a region of adverse pressure develops on the top of the wing. There, the flow starts to back up toward the front of the wing. Since the streamlines are rushing from front to back, they can still overcome this back pressure, except at the region right against the wing's skin, where the combination of friction and adverse pressure actually turns the airflow so it goes back to front.

The bound vortex gets a big bulge in it. The air behind the backup bulges out. The smooth flow separates from the back of the wing, creating a region of turbulent eddies. A region of downward pressure forms just behind the leading edge, pushing down on the wing near its center of lift. At the same time, the forward pressure on the rear of the wing decreases, so it no longer balances the backward-pushing force from the front of the wing. There is a net force backward—in the same direction as the streamlines—and drag begins to win.

You can see what happens if you take the same business card and launch it from your hands. Only this time, give it a forward spin. Instead of descending in an orderly fashion, it falls and backs up.

When you sit at the controls of a Cessna, the natural reaction is to pull back on the yoke to keep it from falling out of the sky. After all, if I tripped while running, I would lean back to catch my balance. When my horse stumbles on the trail, I pull on the reins to help her get her feet again. But in the air we do not have feet on the ground. We have traded them for wings. We are guests of the invisible.

"No!" says my teacher, a little less cheerfully than normal, in response to my reaction. "That will only make a second stall."

What I must do instead when the bottom seems to fall out of the sky is let the yoke go forward, or even push it forward, until the circulation is reestablished and the wing has lift again. Put on full power. Establish a positive rate of climb. Gradually retract the flaps.

Whew!

We practice it three times. By the third time, I am not feeling that this is fun, at all. But I have a little faith that the wings will sustain us. All I must do is reestablish them in their right attitude to the air.

Next, alas, come power-on stalls. Again, I am told how much fun they are, but my teacher adds a thoughtful reflection: "Some people find them a little frightening, because there's so much noise and you just can't see over the nose."

This exercise simulates a stall during takeoff, at full throttle, as you climb up. I remember a news report from the 1960s, when I was a kid, about a cargo jet that stalled on takeoff from the San Francisco airport and crashed in flames. I remember seeing the smoke rising over the bay.

We set up at three thousand feet, reduced power to 1,500 rpm, then increased to full throttle and pitched up to climb, adding the right rudder. To make this stall happen you have to pitch up to over a twenty-degree angle above horizontal, even a little more on a Cessna since it strongly resists stalling. You really can't see over the front of the plane. You feel that were you not harnessed to the seat, you would slide backward out of the tail of the airplane. The engine is laboring like a freight engine pulling two hundred cars over the Tehachapi Pass in California.

The stall horn sounds. It really is a reed that is inserted in what is usually a low-velocity, high-pressure area on the leading edge of the wing. When the plane is about to stall, it becomes a high-velocity, low-pressure area and sucks air out the hole through the reed, making a loud whine.

I keep pulling back on the yoke. The horn keeps sounding. I see only a slice of sky out the window. The engine rumbles and complains. It still won't stall. Finally it does. The nose drops, the whole plane slides back, a wing dips, and I nearly panic. My teacher reminds me to let the yoke go forward while he applies rudder to level the wings. If he did not, we might start into a spin.

Three times, we practice this. The third time, I almost do get the plane into a spin because I try to use the ailerons, not the rudder, to keep the wings level. The ailerons are useless in a stall. When we finally turn for home, it is a relief to practice just straight and level flight.

"You don't have to do spin practice for a private pilot's license," says my instructor. "But if you want, we can do it anyway."

I look at him in horror.

"It's really fun," he adds cheerfully.

I ask if he will please take the controls.

"Okay," he says. "My airplane."

I look out the window. The autumn country passes below us: yellow, red, russet, brown, the silver reflections of late sun off a pond. I have a lot to learn. In the air I play the role of a winged creature, and I respond to whatever happens as that creature would respond. The imagination must be directed into the part, not distracted by the roar of the engine or the sickening backward slide. And I must remember the role. It is a kind of active contemplation. Beryl Markham, who was a bush pilot in Africa during the 1930s, remarked, "[Flying depends] not only on your ability to steer your course or to keep your altitude, but upon the things that live in your mind while you swing suspended between the earth and the silent sky."

Active, responsive, not reactive. These are the qualities of a good pilot. You must give up assumptions and live alert to the slightest nuance that comes into the five senses, responding not as your supposed self, but as your wings. It doesn't sound like a bad way to live: without complaint, fantasy, or demands, but in conversation with the moment.

Wilbur and Orville Wright went to Kitty Hawk, North Carolina, in 1901 with gliders made according to all the best theories of flight at the time. They didn't get off the ground once. On the train back to Dayton, Ohio, Wilbur sighed, "Nobody will fly for a thousand years." That winter they threw out the theories. They built a small wind tunnel and started making little wings: square wings, oblong wings, wings shaped like pocket knives, wings shaped like lozenges, wings shaped like mustaches, flat wings, square-edge wings, round-edge wings, curved wings, double wings, triple wings. They tested more than two hundred in all.

The next summer and fall in Kitty Hawk, they made a thousand successful glider flights. The following year, they added an engine, and in the face of a cold December wind, they took off and flew.

The Bat, the Bee,
the Bar-Headed Goose

When I was about three, my parents bought me my first kite. My father and I assembled it. I was so excited. To this day, I remember that it was then I first learned the difference between a square knot and a granny. We walked out into the desert. He attached the kite to the string. He told me that to get the kite into the air he would hold the kite while I ran with the string. I looked at the end of the string, and realized I would be running away from the kite. I started to cry. My father asked what was wrong. Until that moment I had been convinced that I would ride on the kite. Perhaps this was understandable because we lived on an air force base where regularly my friends' fathers rose into the air on roaring wings. But I suppose riding a kite is actually a common dream.

For two billion years, all the creatures on earth breathed by diffusion. Their breath came into them across their cell walls, and their excretions went back out the same way. When some of the purple sulfur bacteria became mitochondria inside other cells, they supercharged the bigger cells, making it possible for them to process oxygen and food into energy much more quickly. As multicellular creatures evolved, it became necessary to bring oxygen to each cell. Tracheoles, lungs, and air sacs developed, all means for delivering air to the blood so the blood could carry it to the individual cells and give them the oxygen to make their fuel.

Eventually, creatures stood up, grew tall bodies, walked and ran, and spent years or even centuries alive in the wind. But only two classes of them—the insects and the birds—learned as a group to fly. That they do so is testimony to the advantages of flying: You can dodge predators more easily. You have first pick of the food the air brings. If you can get high, you can cover great distances while spending little energy.

But first you must get into the air. Few mammals can fly unaided. The mammal lung (next to the fish's gill) is the breathing apparatus least well adapted to flight. It just can't supply oxygen to the blood at the rate needed for powered flight. The flying squirrel doesn't worry about its lungs because it climbs the tree, then leaps. It is a diminutive hang glider. The main thing for the squirrel is to maintain airspeed and keep the wings extended so the miraculous bound vortex of flight persists.

Humans who try to imitate the flying squirrel are not so lucky. Any creature smaller than a puppy can survive a fall from thirty feet without serious harm. Base jumpers weigh a lot more than a puppy and jump from several thousand feet in what are officially called wingsuits, also known as squirrel suits. The suits contain cloth membranes in the angle between the arms and the body and in the angle between the two legs. The size of the base jumper makes the glide a thrill, with tremendous airspeeds and a sense of completely untethered flight. No wingsuit jumper, however, has ever landed. Instead, the jumpers deploy parachutes to slow and land. Even so, many miscalculate lift or distance from a cliff face, or currents in the air, and end up crashing, with almost zero chance of survival. What is easy for a flying squirrel, and even okay for an errant gray squirrel falling from a branch, is nearly impossible for a human.

Alone among the mammals, bats have mastered powered flight. A bat can travel 250 miles a night in its foraging runs, though it lights and goes frequently. This is very likely one reason why there are so many bats: there is no shortage of insect prey in the air, plenty for both bats and birds. By flying instead of climbing, fruit- and nectar-eating bats have a good chance of getting to their food before their competitors. One in five mammals is a bat. Only humans (and possibly rats) are as widespread across the face of the earth.

Because lungs are so inefficient, the bat economizes. Everything in a bat is squeezed in for flight. The lungs and heart are huge, the guts tiny. Every wing beat corresponds to a breath, so the same muscles can work both operations. The concentration of red blood cells—and therefore hemoglobin—in bats is higher than in any other mammal, allowing its blood to carry more oxygen per unit volume. The largest bat weighs only about three pounds, a tenth the size of the largest bird. Still, a bat in flight increases its oxygen consumption by 30 percent, and its metabolic rate quadruples. Each flight is short and acrobatic. After it lands, the bat needs about thirty seconds of heavy breathing to take in enough oxygen to make up for the deficit incurred in flight.

The wings of birds are renewed by molting. The bat's wings are there for life. They amount to flaps of skin not much more substantial than the ripstop nylon wings between a base jumper's arms and body. But the bat's wings are modified hands, not arms. Where a base jumper's control over the wing is only extension or retraction, the bat has fingertip control over the wing, in extension, angle, and camber. It can even make small adjustments to the skin on the leading edge—essentially the flaps—that increase camber, decrease stall speed, and help make bat flight the strange looping, stooping thing it is. You will never mistake a bird's flight for a bat's flight. I often feel that dusk has come only when that odd erratic pattern appears in the air above my roof. In fact, I used to imagine that bats carried the thread that stitched day onto night, making evening happen and keeping the round of days.

The honeybee has no lungs at all, but it is a far better flier than a bat. Gram for gram, in fact, the honeybee is the strongest creature in the world. Beekeepers since time immemorial have known that it is a poor idea to stand in front of the entrance to a hive. Bees have a habit of flying straight at top speed, from wherever they have been, to and through the hive entry. They make a beeline, giving rise to the phrase that means to do something without any hesitation, delay, or detour. If you are blocking their way, you might simply get a bee in the back. It doesn't often harm the bees or you, but why get in their way?

Breath is what makes these feats possible. An insect doesn't have either lungs or gills. Rather it has an intricate network of open passages called tracheoles that penetrate its exoskeleton and travel directly to each and every muscle cell that needs oxygen to make it work. The smallest diameter for a tracheole is equal to the diameter needed by an oxygen molecule to travel freely. This direct delivery system is ten times more efficient than the best bloodstream, and it means that an insect going from rest to strenuous activity can increase its metabolic rate two-hundred-fold, while the best a bird or a bat can do is increase its rate by about twenty- to thirty-fold.

At rest, an insect takes in oxygen simply by diffusion along the channels of the tracheoles. As it begins to move, the rate of diffusion increases. The faster the oxygen is used, the faster it is replaced by fresh oxygen flowing in. For a small insect, like a fly, that is all that is ever needed.

Mosquitoes, black flies, gnats, flies, no-see-ums, dragonflies, dam- selflies, wasps, hornets, beetles, ants—all belong to orders of the class Insecta—and the names of the orders refer to the character of the insects' wings. Diptera (the flies) have two wings; Hymenoptera (the bees and wasps), gossamer wings; Coleoptera (the beetles and wee- vils), sheathed wings. Students of the Insecta have flown about in airplanes with nets, catching bugs in flight. They estimate that in the summer temperate zone, there are from one to two million insects flying at any given time over one square kilometer (about one-third square mile) of land. There are perhaps twenty-two trillion pounds of insects alive all over the globe.

The best fliers in the world are in the class Insecta. They can hover, fly backward and sideways, carry huge loads through the air, and land and take off upside down. It must then have seemed like sour grapes when French scientists in the 1930s "proved" that honeybees could not fly. Because humans had recently learned to fly in machines with fixed wings, the scientists decided to fix bees' wings for the purpose of their calculations. Their stiff mathematical bees could not generate enough lift to get off the ground. The scientists would have done better asking a beekeeper who has taken one in the back whether a bee can fly.

Insects are the champions of flapping flight. The faster the flapping, the greater the lift. The greatest flappers are the best hoverers because in hovering, only the wings' motion—not their passage through space—is generating lift.

No other animal can flap like an insect does. Rates of up to one thousand hertz, that is, one thousand beats per second, have been recorded for insects. Not even a hummingbird comes close. A honeybee in flight generates three times the muscle power of the hummingbird, and thirty times that of the strongest human. It can fly five miles from the hive, pick up a load of nectar equal to its own weight, and then make a beeline back again.

Like many of the strongest fliers, a bee prepares for flight by warming up. The bee flexes the muscles that raise *and* lower its wings at the same time, rather than in succession. This creates no motion, but lots of heat. The higher temperature increases the rate at which oxygen can be off-loaded in the muscles, and so improves the efficiency of the delivery system.

There are two drawbacks to this wonderful arrangement of breath. The first is that if you are too big, it won't work. *Saturday Night Live's*

Killer Bees would have killed themselves before they could get their first sentence out. Tracheoles work only when the rate of diffusion can reach all the muscles without delay. The second is that insects are very vulnerable to pathogens and poisons. Anything that is in the air goes straight into the muscles. This is why pesticides can be as effective as they are. The insect has no filter to exclude them, and can't put on a mask or hold its breath. The whole bug breathes all the time.

Insects were born to fly, but bats and birds were not. Bats likely began as something more like flying squirrels. They learned to fly from the trees down. Birds are relatives of theropod dinosaurs. They learned to fly from the ground up. But birds solved the problem of oxygen supply far better than bats. Indeed, bird flight tests the upper edges of the air.

At the top of its arc from the Indian marshes to the Tibetan plateau, the bar-headed goose reaches heights where few animals have ever gone. Early climbers on Mount Everest were startled to see birds flying easily over the summit of the mountain the men were struggling to ascend. They were watching bar-headed geese, who were not lost or straining, but sailing on the jet stream at the very top of the troposphere to reach their breeding grounds on the Tibetan plateau. The humans were using supplementary oxygen; the geese were just breathing the air.

The bar-headed goose has been recorded at altitudes of over thirty-three thousand feet. This is the altitude where your pilot remarks that the outside temperature is 40 degrees below zero, where the great fast-flowing rivers of the jet streams set weather systems spinning. The air here contains only one-fifth the oxygen as the air near sea level, where the goose winters in lowland India wetlands and marshes. Yet in the space of a few hours, the bird can fly from the wetlands to the top of the high peaks and then out onto the world's largest high plateau.

There are lower passes through the mountains, but the goose does not take them. It may even preferentially go higher, both to catch a tailwind and to increase the delivery of oxygen to its lungs. It seems strange to humans, who cannot breathe at all at such altitudes, that going higher—where there is less oxygen—could result in greater volumes of oxygen reaching the lungs.

The lungs of the bar-headed goose are not like those in humans. In all birds, the functions of breathing air in and out, and of transferring the oxygen from the air to the blood, are separate. In human lungs, the bellows of breath is itself what draws the air over the spongy alveolar tissue where the gas is drawn into the blood. In birds, a separate network of air sacs located all over the body (and sometimes even in the bones of the wings) inhales and exhales the air. The chamber where the blood meets the air does not expand and contract. Instead, it is fed with a constant stream of air from the sacs. Both as it breathes in and as it breathes out, a bird flushes fresh air over the bronchial tissues. As a result, birds use 90 percent of the oxygen they take in, while mammals use only a little more than half.

Nevertheless, the goose should be faced with a serious contradiction. It has to expend tremendous energy to get to an altitude that contains very little oxygen. Sure, the tremendous effort of flapping may keep its wings from icing up, but how will the bird get enough oxygen to fuel this effort where the gas is less and less available? The obvious solution is to breathe more and faster, that is, to hyperventilate.

Doubtless you have tried this yourself on occasion, when driven by exhaustion or fear, or at high altitudes. Pretty soon you feel wonky, you are getting pins and needles in your fingers and toes, your head hurts like hell, and you think you are going to throw up. In humans and other mammals, heavy breathing reduces the amount of carbon dioxide in the blood, which changes the blood's acidity and leads to a shrinking of arteries that carry blood to the brain. Less blood to the brain results in poor judgment and impairment in the operation of the body.

For some reason, this constriction does not happen in the bar-headed goose, or in other birds that fly high. On the contrary, at higher altitudes the bird may get even more blood to the brain as it breathes harder and harder. Meanwhile, the colder temperatures encourage oxygen to be loaded more efficiently onto hemoglobin for transport through the body to the skeletal musculature. A number of species share these abilities. Even the common pigeon can fly happily at twenty thousand feet, an altitude at which a rat will immediately pass out. But even among the birds few can reach higher. The bar-headed goose has an additional advantage in its bloodstream.

In all living things, the constituents of proteins, the amino acids, undergo constant mutations. Many of these changes have no effect at all on how the creature looks or behaves. Some are harmful, and result in death. A few prove useful, and gradually become a part of the creature's way of life. Over the history of its begetting, four substitutions have occurred in the amino acids of the hemoglobin in the bar-headed goose. Two of these have had no effect on the goose, for good or ill. Two of them have made the hemoglobin relax.

There are two states to hemoglobin: tense and relaxed. In the relaxed state, the forces that keep molecules apart are reduced. The two amino-acid substitutions in the bar-headed goose changed the shape of the molecule in its blood, so that it is more often in the relaxed state. This increases the rate at which enzymes can work in the hemoglobin, and dramatically increases the rate at which the bird can get and move oxygen.

The bar-headed goose draws a line, as it were, at the very top of the habitable air. It did not acquire this ability in order to outcompete other geese—for none other are involved in this migration—or in order to win differential reproductive success. It did so when the first geese with the mutation realized they could just keep climbing. Perhaps the first one that sailed over the Himalayas and reached the high Tibetan plateau thought, What have we got here?

Adventure leads all creatures on. I was recently in the high Mojave Desert in a tiny town that consists of nothing but an old railway hotel, a general store, a collection of trailers, and the Union Pacific railroad tracks. There was a cactus garden in front of the hotel, and in it a memorial that reads as follows: "Ken Trongo. 1939–2006. 'Let's see where this road goes.'" When I looked up from the memorial—which consists of a steering wheel planted on a stake—I saw nothing but an apparently featureless desert, but it was apparently not featureless to Mr. Trongo.

The Lee Wave

On March 5, 1966, around two o'clock in the afternoon, a Boeing 707 operated by BOAC took off in clear air from Tokyo. It was bound for Hong Kong, with 124 people aboard. The pilot, Bernard Dobson, wanted to give his passengers a close-up view of Mount Fuji, which for once was unobscured by clouds, so he amended his flight plan to allow him to fly under visual flight rules near the mountain. He climbed to about seventeen thousand feet, then began a slow descent to allow the best-possible view.

At the time, a weather station at the mountain's base was registering winds of sixty to seventy knots out of the west-northwest. Dobson descended toward Fuji's crest on its east side, leeward of where the prevailing winds passed over the summit.

Observers on the ground noted a plume of white vapor emerge from the right side of the aircraft. The tail fin failed and fell onto the left horizontal stabilizer, detaching it. Both engines appeared to separate from the plane, and the outer third of the right wing sheared off. The forward fuselage failed. The plane went into a flat spin and fell until it hit the ground near the base of the mountain. Everyone aboard was killed.

Flight 911 had hit the powerful turbulence of a lee wave. When strong winds cross the top of a mountain or a mountain range, they often spill over the lee side in waves of turbulent air. If the air on the windward side is stable—that is, it has no buoyancy of its own but must be forced to rise—the strong wind pushes it up and over the mountain. On the other side, however, it wants to sink right back to its equilibrium level. The speed of the sinking causes the air to overshoot its mark downward, so it then must rise again to reach its equilibrium level. A gravity wave with crests and troughs can form and extend thirty miles or more to the lee side of the summit, as the air seeks its equilibrium.

In many cases, the air will rise and sink at a rate of a few hundred feet per minute, and the result is merely a rough ride. When the wind is strong and the air is very stable, however, the air might rise and fall at a rate approaching two thousand feet per minute over a distance of just a few miles, and tremendous turbulence can result. In the first few waves of the lee at or near the mountain crest, overturning horizontal vortices—called rotors—can form. These are like tornadoes lying on their sides.

If there is any moisture in the air, characteristic clouds form. A lenticular cloud—called a "lennie" by the glider pilots who ride the rising air on top of it—is shaped like a lens or a flying saucer. What gives a lennie away is that although the wind is strong, the cloud never moves from its position on the lee side of the mountaintop.

The lennie forms when the updraft side of the lee wave lowers the air to its dew point, causing the water to condense and form a cloud. A few miles away, where the wave descends again, the air is pushed down and warms to a temperature above its dew point, the condensation ceases, and the cloud ends. As long as the lee wave remains in place, the lennie marks where it rises and falls. As the rotor dissipates, the cloud does not move. It simply disappears.

Where the rotor occurs, it is often made visible by other cloud forms that actually take the shape of rough-edged barrels. Called roll clouds, they are red flags to any pilot to stay clear.

A spectacular lenticular cloud in the Sierra Wave. (Courtesy of National Oceanic and Atmospheric Administration)

Half an hour before the passage of Flight 911, lennies and roll clouds had been observed in the vicinity of its flight path, but none were present when Captain Dobson entered the area. The air was very stable. (That is why the day was so clear.) The wind was very high. But the unseen turbulence tore the plane apart.

One of the most notable areas for lee waves in the world is the east side of the Sierra Nevada crest in eastern California. There, prevailing westerlies in stable air often produce lee waves with spectacular lennies and roll clouds. The waves can have huge amplitudes, and lengths of twenty miles or longer. During the early 1950s the U.S. Navy ran the Sierra Wave Project there, to better understand the phenomenon of the lee wave and to teach pilots how to cope with (or avoid) it.

Larry Edgar, one of the project's glider pilots, survived an encounter with a rotor that tore his Pratt-Read glider apart. He was rising up over the edge of a lennie when the cloud seemed to swell up in his path. He was flung left in his seat, then to the right. As he slammed into the right side of the glider, a tremendous positive acceleration squashed him down in his seat. He remained conscious but could not see. He heard a loud explosion as his glider rolled violently to the left, and he was flung upward by a negative acceleration that banged his head into the top of the glider's canopy.

"There was a lot of noise and I felt like I was taking a tremendous beating," he remembered. "I was too stunned to make any attempt to bail out. . . . Just as suddenly as all this violence started, it became quiet except for the sound of wind whistling by. I felt I was falling free of all wreckage except something holding my feet."

He had been ripped right out of his glider. As his parachute opened, he felt the rotor draw him eastward then back westward toward the mountains. While he was descending on the chute, he watched the remains of the glider float past him. It was traveling skyward in the roll cloud.

The Wind Riders

Walt's Point stands at an elevation of nine thousand feet on the shear eastern scarp of the Sierra Nevada, a little more than five thousand feet above Owens Dry Lake. To be frank, it less stands than it leans. It is a wide dirt pullout from a steep switchback road that climbs naked grade after naked grade out of Owens Valley and up to Horseshoe Meadow at around ten thousand feet. You could park half-a-dozen cars in the pull-out, no more, and the dusty surface leans into the void at about a 10 percent grade.

The stone on the rising slope behind is broken into big taupe blocks with sparkles of quartz in them, granite that has been heavily eroded by water and chiefly by wind. The plants are sparse wind-beaten pinyon pine and blue-green artemisia. A jagged black lichen grows on the face of the more protected angles of the rock. Only when you look with a 10× loupe can you see a little purple and green in it.

When you stand here, you feel like you should lean into the slope or hold onto something to keep from blowing away. To the east you look straight out to Owens Valley and its dry lake, framed far off by a brown range of mountains without any visible vegetation. In the flats of the dry lake run ribbons and rough quadrangles of shallow alkaline blue water—the little water left in the lake—separated by blond and white lozenges of earth, with intrusions of the orange and rose-pink blooms of salt-loving bacteria.

The only sounds here on a June morning are the wind, my feet walking on the gravel, and the buzz of flies. The flies seem to be glad of company in this desolation, hung like a flake of dead skin on the edge of the world. There are only two signs of human occupation. One is a boulder laid down near the edge. Inset in it is a bronze plaque that reads, "Walt's Point / In Memory of Walter G. Millet, Sept 6, 1906–Nov 2, 1965." (You suspect that he somehow died of being here.) The other is a knot of long aluminum streamers, colored red and green, tied to dead stems of juniper atop the hill behind. These were placed by hang gliders, to tell them which way and how strong the wind is blowing.

It is my own fault that I am here. It was from this launch pad in 1991 that Kari Castle set the woman's distance record for a hang glider, more than 210 miles from Walt's Point along the Sierra crest to Austin, Nevada. The record stood for more than a decade, and when it was broken, she went right out and broke it again. She lives in nearby Bishop. I asked to interview her here. I felt that no one could have a more intimate knowledge of the air than an experienced hang glider.

She said, "Sure, I'll meet you there."

Even more than an ordinary glider pilot, a hang glider while flying lives in the full presence of the free air. There is no fuselage around her, no cabin heat, no supplemental air, no ailerons to govern banks, no elevator or rudders to shape the ups and downs. She must be alert to her flight as it passes, responding with her body to the motions of the wind and the air. She glides out looking for rising thermals, then leans into tight circles to climb up in the one she finds.

I was eager to meet Castle, despite the site.

Well, where was she? I could see down at least three long barren switchbacks toward the valley, and there was not a car on it. After about five minutes, I saw a light-colored, somewhat shiny speck creeping up along the lowest switchback. Fifteen minutes later, Castle appeared at Walt's Point on her bicycle, having taken an early-morning ride thirteen miles long and about one mile up to meet me.

She asked for a moment to catch her breath, but for all I could see, she had never lost it. I appreciated the companionship, even if for the moment it was silent. We were sitting in the dirt. She was looking out to the southeast at a spine of rock and sparse pine that rose up about a hundred yards away, the only thing that blocked the view of the valley from any vantage point.

Castle had first tried hang gliding on a whim back in 1981 in Canada. She thought she had to do it once just to say she had, like bungee jumping or skydiving. They set her up in a hang glider and stood her at the edge of a two-hundred-foot drop.

"Fly," they said.

"Nooo!" she answered.

She spent most of the day taking a running start, then pulling in on the bar, piling in, and crashing into the slope before she went off the cliff. Finally, in desperation, she just let the wing fly. "I didn't do anything," she recalled. "It just flew. And I thought, 'Oh, this is easy!'"

The routine is simple and intuitive. You are suspended at the center of gravity below the wing, in a moving sling often padded with a bag to keep you warm at altitude. You hold onto a bar in front of you. To speed up you pull the bar toward you; to slow down you push it away. To turn you shift your weight in the direction of the turn.

After one flight, she was hooked. She has remained so, despite being twice tumbled by unexpected, invisible cliffs of falling air.

Walt's Point is a site known for big air. It faces east, so the morning sun strikes it and illuminates the bare valley floor below it. On hot summer mornings, the heating of the ground overcomes the prevailing westerly winds, and broad strong thermals rise all up and down the Sierra crest. The updrafts are among the most powerful anywhere.

They can send you up at a rate of two thousand feet per minute. "That makes you feel really small," she remembered. "I think eight hundred feet per minute is plenty."

A thermal typically rises until the air condenses in a cloud, so the altitude of the cloud base is often the top of the thermal. In the summer in Owens Valley, the cloud base can be above twenty thousand feet. A hang glider is not supposed to pass eighteen thousand feet— above that is jet territory—but one day Castle and her boyfriend got into a huge thermal off White Mountain. She heard him call on the radio, "Hey, we're punching through twenty-four thousand feet, and Kari is right below me." Because her altimeter at the time was a watch-dial contraption that circled once for every ten thousand feet, she had thought she was at fourteen thousand feet. "I guess the fact that White Mountain is fourteen thousand feet tall and was ten thousand feet below me ought to have given me a clue," she remembered.

If you fly in an airliner, the interior cabin pressure is set at about eight thousand feet. Should it rise to the pressure equivalent of fourteen thousand feet, the oxygen masks will deploy. (The supplemental oxygen is meant to last only for the minutes it takes the pilot to descend to an altitude where you can breathe without it.) Castle had already been above ten thousand feet higher than the limit for better than a quarter of an hour. The summit of Mount Everest is only about five thousand feet higher.

In the 1990s, when the gliders were what she ungently described as "crap," you needed a site as high and big as Walt's Point to get a good ride. Now you can get a long flight if you are released at two thousand feet from behind an ultralight in Texas, or riding the slope updraft along the Pacific headlands at Fort Funston in San Francisco, so Walt's Point is not as important as it was. But it was from here that she set her world record distance in 1991, and the people who still come here to fly do it for the chance to ride along the summits

Kari Castle rising in a thermal after she launched from Walt's Point. The launch site is the triangular area in the road. You can find it by looking straight down from the left wing's tip. (Courtesy of Kari Castle)

of the fourteen-thousand-foot Sierra Nevada and the White Mountains, among the granite peaks, the scree falls, the chutes, the snowy couloirs, the wedge-shaped peaks of Olancha, Langley, and Whitney.

To launch from Walt's Point, you have to do something that will seem absolutely crazy unless you understand the air. You have to run off the edge heading straight for the spine of rock and pine not a hundred yards away, the one Castle was staring at when she first arrived at our interview.

"People don't believe me," she said with a sigh. "They think, Why am I heading right for those rocks and trees when I could go out into the open air right over here?"

The reason is the thermals. The spine of rock is heated on both sides by the morning sun, and the updrafts are almost always strong all around it because the morning breeze rises right up the edge of the rock. You launch right at it—Castle calls it "the house thermal"—turn right, and up you go. Right away. The people who instead launch out over the valley and turn left struggle looking for an updraft to carry them up to fourteen thousand feet or higher.

Once you are up, however, you can play the same game over and over, searching for the rock spines that appear all along the crest of the range, circling up in the thermal each one gives you, then gliding along the top of the range, gently descending, until you must look for another thermal. On her distance ride on July 22, 1991, she went almost two hundred miles north along the crest but had to stop to pee. "You spoiled a two-hundred-mile ride to pee!" her friends said with disgust. The next day, under similar conditions and wearing diapers, she spent eight and a half hours in the air and went 210 miles.

The air on the east side of the Sierra Nevada is not only big, it can be dangerous. When the wind is strong out of the west and conditions are stable, terrible rotors develop. These are death traps to airplanes, never mind hang gliders. "I know airline pilots who won't fly planes here in the summer," laughed Castle, "and I'm out there flying a frigging handkerchief!"

Once, she and a friend were sitting in a hot springs in Mono Lake. They watched three dust devils form on the nearby desert. One went straight up and traveled in a straight line over the ground. The second started on the same line but soon veered off at a sharp angle. The third went straight up into the air, then made a dogleg turn in midair and seemed to spin parallel to the ground. She has taken this as a reminder that no one ever securely knows what the air is going to do, even down to events taking place just fifty feet apart. Every thermal goes up, and at some point it spills over and descends again. If you hit that spill point, watch out. If there were three pilots out where the dust devils were, one would get a nice lift, one an unexpected detour, and one would be spit out of the air.

On a clear day in Owens Valley—a great day for flying—Castle was in a competition, doing well and feeling fine. She had just launched and ridden up to about sixteen thousand feet. She thought she would tuck in her arms, gain a little speed, and get aerobatic. The air was smooth. In an instant, she found herself on her back looking up at the sky, her glider inverted below her. She hit the crossbar, and the structure crumpled like a beer can. She and the glider started to spin and fall. She had hit the spill point of the thermal.

Every hang glider carries a reserve—a parachute to use in case of disaster—and she managed to throw hers. She crashed down on rock under the parachute canopy at about twelve thousand feet, very unhappy but still alive.

More than a decade later, in a world championship in Austria, Castle had her second tumble. This time the conditions were terrible. The local pilots said that they would never fly in them, but what were they going to do, call off a world championship? The wind was coming strong over a mountain crest, not unlike the prevailing westerlies that create the Sierra wave. The conditions were perfect for rotors to form in the lee of the mountains—rolling, roiling air masses with impossible turbulence.

Castle was up on the race course, heading for a turn point. There was a lovely spine of rock—just like the house thermal at Walt's Point—where she was sure she would find a good thermal. She did. She rose up to nearly cloud base and started her turn. "I was going around right," she remembered, "and all of a sudden, something caught me and spit me out and I wasn't going right. I was going left." Okay, she thought, if I'm going to go that way, that's not so bad. Suddenly she found her glider pointing straight down. Recalling that on her previous tumble almost fifteen years before, she had lost control because she let go of the bar, she made sure to hang on to it. "If I just hang on," she remembered thinking, "I can get it back."

The next thing she remembered was her feet touching the sailcloth of her wing. She was still holding the bar all right, but she was upside down. She and the glider turned over five or six times. "I was like a flea in a washing machine with my hang glider, getting banged and bashed," she recalled. "I was pissed!" She couldn't see the ground or the sky. She was just tumbling.

Finally, she found herself lying on top of the sail again, the blue sky above her, and her glider bent around her like a taco shell, with all kind of sharp bits sticking out. She thought that if she did not throw her reserve chute just right, it would get tangled in the wreckage, and that would be the end. She managed to get it out and open, and she descended still stuck in her taco and trying to steer her chute toward a slope where she could actually land.

What she experienced was almost certainly a rotor, the kind that destroyed BOAC Flight 911 near Mount Fuji in 1966, the kind that ripped Larry Edgar's glider out from under him in Owens Valley during the Sierra Wave Project (see page 203).

Through the hour and a half that we talked on the dirty edge of Walt's Point, I had forgotten where we were. When I looked out again at that spine of rock and pine, I could feel the life in it, the rising air. It was no small thing to be willing to join that life, to let your own be governed by it. To fly this way is like an open query. You ask, and the sky answers. You embrace the incalculable.

Castle was not flying that day, but she was glad that I had a date that afternoon to watch her friends the Sangers over on the other side of the valley, flying from a place called McGee's. That slope is only a thousand feet or so above the valley floor, and it faces west. The mountain breeze rises up along the edge of it, giving lift, and it gets its best thermals in the afternoon, when the westering sun hits full on the eastern edge of the valley. Because it is generally cooling at that time of day, the updrafts are less gnarly and the turbulence less strong. The west wind had stayed down all day, so there might be good flying at McGee's.

My wife and I rode up to McGee's in four-wheel-drive Toyotas, the road little more than a mining track. Wayne and Paula Sanger were there, along with their friend Adrian from South Africa. The couple were going to paraglide—a meditative version of soaring that is more or less like riding a swing set that rises high into the air—while Adrian had his hang glider.

The view from McGee's was homey compared to Walt's Point. Though we looked straight across at the Sierras, the valley at our feet was green with irrigated fields and fencerows. Still, a little dust devil raced by just in front of Adrian's hang glider as he was setting up. "It's pretty active today," Wayne said. "One of those things can turn a glider right over."

As the air is cooling, you have to work for your thermals. Often, a lull in the steady wind means that a thermal is rising. You launch into the lull. You can also look for bugs and swifts. Swifts feeding high in the air are often chasing insects lifted in a thermal. You launch into the bugs.

Adrian stepped into a padded suit that made him look like a cross between the Michelin man and the body of a dragonfly. He hooked up to one post of the glider a variometer that would tell him visually and audibly his airspeed and his rate of climb or descent. A radio went on the other crossbar. Then he hooked himself to the glider and stood, the wing on his shoulders. Wayne steadied one wingtip.

"The breeze is coming up," Wayne said. "We better get out of here." A steady breeze at this time of day, when the valley stays warmer than the peaks, is likely to descend rather than ascend, killing off thermals.

Adrian launched in a lull, running down the slope and gliding out into the open air. He turned left, he turned right.

"He's looking for a thermal," said Wayne, "but he hasn't found one yet."

Wayne and Paula hooked themselves into their paragliders. The quilted chutes lay on the ground. With practiced grace, they grasped the cords that attach them to the chutes. They lifted the cords quickly up and out, as though they were making a gesture of acclamation: closed hands to arms widespread. The chutes spun up into the air and caught the breeze. Both Wayne and Paula left the ground.

"This is the best part," Paula called, "when you leave the ground and you are suspended." She does as she says.

Distracted by their launch, I had lost sight of Adrian. I looked down expecting to find him still struggling through the valley, but he was not there. I looked up and around. There he was, his glider now tiny, circling tightly in a thermal. He must have been up to six or eight thousand feet already. He rode over the mountain ridge and was lost to sight.

My wife and I drove the four-wheelers back down the track to meet the flyers in the valley. When we got there, Wayne and Paula had already landed.

"It looks like Adrian got the last low thermal of the day," said Wayne. We were still looking for but not finding him.

At around 7:15 in the evening, as the sun was touching the Sierra crest, Adrian glided down into the field beside which we had left his car, having spent most of the last hour and a half above ten thousand feet.

Kari Castle has a recurring dream. In it, she flies like a bird. "I just step off and hover," she said. "When I want to, I just put down a foot and touch down. Then I puff up, get high, tuck in. Just like a bird."

On the coast of California in San Francisco is a bluff where the cool air coming over the ocean meets the warm air of the land. The convergence of the two air masses dependably lifts the air. The steep headlands up which the onshore breeze blows add to the lift. It is not big air, but it is very steady and dependable. This is where Kari's dream has come closest to coming true.

"The air there is so smooth," she said, "that you can put one foot down on a rock, then launch right off again. You can play like that. You could never do that here."

The Sangers too have enjoyed the steady lift at Fort Funston. Wayne was there at a friend's house, had a great day of flying, and got up the next morning ready to go again.

"I'll go with you," said his friend, "but I don't think I'll fly today."

Wayne realized that his friend was bored with the air. It was too steady, too nice. He was restless. Evidently, a great part of the pleasure of flying is not knowing what turn the air will take.

What Now?

Habit and compulsion are drivers in our lives. We have done something a certain way before, and so we do it again. If we do it often enough, we may feel that we *must* do it this way, or bad things may happen. Mainly, this is a good thing. It would be a shame if while driving, every time we wanted to take a right turn we had to consciously remember to turn on the signal. Better we should have it as a habit that happens without a thought. But the older we get, the more habits weigh. We have to have that glass of wine when we get home. We have to have our milk and cookies. We have to get our parking spot in front of the office. The dog has to do all his business every time we walk him. Our children have to answer our calls. Or something is wrong. Someone doesn't love us. We must complain.

A person wears so many grooves during a long life that eventually the deep-worn grooves begin to dig a grave. It is hard to have a new experience, or recognize and value one when it comes.

Here, it may be lucky to be a pilot, because the thing a pilot learns and relearns is that you do not know what will happen next. As my teacher once told me, "It's not like if you have an engine problem, you can pull over and fix it at the next cloud." There are checklists to follow in case something unforeseen happens, but the first and most important act is for you to recognize and respond not to what you expect or what you want, but to what actually occurs.

A corporate plane picks up a passenger in Palma de Mallorca. The instructions are to take the man to Barcelona. Fifteen minutes into the flight the attendant comes into the cockpit. She says, The guy is very nervous and sweating profusely. She is uncomfortable. She reports that he has gone to the bathroom but has yet to come out again. On this plane, the bathroom connects to the luggage compartment.

Air traffic control in Palma calls to say that their passenger is waiting for them at the Palma airport, and getting very impatient. Where the heck are they?

The German captain and his copilot look at one another. If their passenger is still in Palma, who is this guy? They assume the worst. They begin a very gradual turn and descent, slowly equalizing the pressure inside and outside the cabin, just in case the passenger is carrying a bomb that detonates with a pressure cue. Suddenly, the baggage compartment smoke sensor sounds off. There is explosive decompression. Every screen is red, and every bell is ringing. The ailerons won't work to turn the plane. Wreckage falls behind the plane. There is fuel leaking from the left wing. The captain surveys his instruments.

"Well," he says, "we are breathing and we have one engine. Can we fly the airplane?"

The plane is a shuddering shithouse. Because the ailerons are not operational, he can't make a normal bank to put the plane on the heading he wants. But he thinks that if he can slow down enough, pull up the nose, and drop the tail until he is almost at stall speed, then he can use the tail rudder to roll the airplane in the direction he wants it to go. Okay? As some European pilots say in English, asking for the concurrence of the crew, "Happy that?"—short for "Are you happy with that?"

Half an hour later, against all odds, the pilots are on the ground in

Palma again. To be more precise, the pilots are sitting in a simulator looking at a graphic of the Palma airport, for this entire near disaster has been a problem set by their teacher in simulator training.

Most commercial pilots now earn their certification and recertification (every six months) in simulators. These are nothing like the old television screens of the 1960s, or even of the most elaborate setup for your computer flight simulator. A simulator now is housed along with three or four of its brethren in an enormous barn. Each simulator is about the size of a hotel room, only it is fully enclosed, independent, and set on six stilts. The full crew flies the mock plane.

You have to take a safety briefing before you are even allowed on a simulator. To enter it, you cross a ramp and pass through a doorway. At the back of the room is a bay where the trainer sits in front of a computer that is capable of generating everything from engine failure to icing on the tail, to a terrorist bombing. Beyond the trainer is the full actual cockpit interior of the plane in question.

When you sit down at the controls, the trainer pushes a button. The ramp pulls back, and the simulator rises into the air. You are ready to go. A graphic of your home airport is what you see out the window before you.

The trainer tells you where you are going and gives you a flight plan, but in training you never have a nice day. Maybe the weather is awful on takeoff. You can barely see the runway. You are flying by instruments from the word "go." It is very cold outside, likely to cause icing.

You roll down the runway, you reach decision speed, you are committed to go, and suddenly you have an engine fire. There are lots of red screens, flashing lights, sirens blaring. Your heart is thumping. But you are committed. You have to fly. You rotate, get the gear up, and climb.

The engine is on fire and still running. Can you put the fire out? Will you shut the engine down? The crew thinks through the problem. The trainer has the option of causing a fire that takes one bottle to extinguish, two bottles to extinguish, or one that won't go out at all. In this case, the crew get the fire out, but they have to shut the engine down.

The engine fire has damaged one of the hydraulic systems, and its fluid leaks out, giving them another set of red warning signs. In all this commotion, you have forgotten about the icing. The anti-ice was on for the engines from the moment they rolled, but you can't turn on the wing anti-ice until you have airspeed over the wings. With your focus on the fire, you didn't turn it on.

The trainer's temptation is to point out the mistake, but his duty is to keep mum.

You turn the plane to set up for an emergency instrument landing, but it is slow to respond. You keep having to add power, when you should be taking power off for your descent. You set your landing speed, but it is in the yellow warning range. What is going on? you ask yourself and your crew.

Someone says, "We must be heavy or something."

"Oh, ice!"

You turn on the anti-icing for the wing, just in time.

You call for "gear down." The copilot complies and checks to see that it has happened.

You call for "flaps in" to reconfigure them for landing, but the copilot is distracted by the icing problem.

Now you are getting a red message for excess airspeed. How can that be? The copilot looks out the window. The flaps have not retracted. Of course not. The hydraulics on that side are damaged.

Here you are, in horrible weather with icing conditions, an engine fire, and a hydraulic system failure. And now you are going to make an emergency approach on one engine with the flaps out because the flaps are stuck.

Happy that?

You bring the plane down safely. But this is just the day's first exercise in mayhem.

The trainer is happy with his students because they figured it out in time, and they did it by working together. To the trainer, the situational awareness that makes for a good pilot is not the result of steely nerves or autocratic control, but of clear communication and a wide-angle view of the surrounding world. "A good pilot," the trainer said, "is a Renaissance person. He's alert to the smallest change in any of his senses, and he responds by asking what is *that* about?"

The right stuff for a pilot is not godlike independence. Rather, it is presence. It is the ability to respond to noise and trouble by querying your senses, the instruments, and your companions. To fly a plane through trouble is a creative act.

Behind most accidents is a failure of communication, caused by distraction, exhaustion, nervousness, fear, or even a bad mood. When Eastern Airlines Flight 401, a Lockheed L-1011, went down at the Miami airport in 1972, it was because the crew let a little problem distract them. The nose gear apparently wouldn't go down. They were on final approach at two thousand feet.

The copilot asked the pilot, "Do you want me to fly?"

The pilot didn't answer. He was busy working on the gear problem. The copilot decided to help him. No one was flying the airplane. The pilot may have thought that the copilot was, but he had not given him control or responded to his asking for it.

It was night. A horn sounded. The copilot looked up and saw that the altimeter read fifty feet. Instead of adding power and gently pulling back on the yoke, he asked, "What's going on here?" It is the last thing he ever said.

As a worst-case scenario, they might indeed have landed the plane without the nose gear. True, it would have settled on its nose, and passengers would have had to be lifted to the ground, but it would have been a cosmetic problem at most.

Autocratic captains are the worst. Instead of learning, asking, adapting, they assert, sometimes with fatal results. The best captains are almost always the ones who ask for input. Captain Richard Siano began his career as copilot on TWA Lockheed Constellations, those four-propeller three-tail behemoths at the end of the prop era. He had to fly them on short hops through the Alleghenies, the very worst weather for flying in the United States. Instead of flying over the weather, the short-hopping Connies flew right through it. The young Siano took advantage of this to learn everything that his captains and his flight engineers could teach him about flying weather.

Siano ended his career as a senior captain flying 747s on international flights, but his favorite airplane was the Boeing 727. "You could fly it at Mach .86," he remembered with pleasure, "but on landing, you could bring it down to eighty knots." This amazing versatility was owed to its four sets of flaps and slats, two on the leading edge and two on the trailing edge of each wing. He recalled setting down the stretch version of the 727 on twenty-one hundred feet of runway at LaGuardia Airport in New York City, which had notoriously short runways. That was less than a third of the runway's length. "And I wasn't even trying!"

However, the 727 had a peculiarity. The engines powered down easily, but if you suddenly gave them full power—pushed the throttle up to takeoff power—they could take up to seven seconds to respond. (This may have been because the engines were based on those of the Pegasus missile, which did not have to worry about speeding up or slowing down. It just went where it went and blew up.)

A captain training a new copilot on a 727 coming into Salt Lake City in 1965 either didn't know or had forgotten this. He set his student on a high-sink descent—the Salt Lake City airport is ringed by tall mountains. When the copilot, who perhaps remembered the 727's tendency, tried to increase thrust, the pilot pulled it off again. When he realized his mistake, he applied full takeoff power, but the engines were too slow to respond. Forty-three people were killed in the crash landing.

At the end of the twentieth and beginning of the twenty-first century, passenger jets changed as much annually as they used to change in a decade. On board, redundant computers consult each other on every detail of the flight plan. They can perform all routine tasks, including navigation, climb out, descent, and landing. While I was flying in a corporate jet simulator with a teacher, we got to talking and by the time we stopped, our jet had landed itself at our destination, my home airport in Caldwell, New Jersey.

The need for what pilots call "hand flying"—that is, flying the plane manually—is dwindling, but lack of those necessary skills is the biggest flaw in the wonderfully efficient systems. If you can't fly a plane manually, what do you do when you *must*?

What happened to a Bombardier turboprop flying into Buffalo, New York, in bad weather on February 12, 2009, illustrates this. The weather was lousy all right—low visibility, wind, snow, and icing—but 109 other flights had flown safely in and out of Buffalo on that same date. When the Bombardier got a stall warning on approach, the copilot mistakenly thought it was a signal that the wings were icing. (In fact, the wings were fine; the tail was icing.) She pulled in the flaps to let her speed up, but in the confusion of the moment she forgot to add power at the same time. The pilot did not remind her. Not only that, but when the computer tried to help by automatically adding power, the pilot took the power off again. The plane was lost.

The computers do not always help, especially if they disagree. One teacher likes to set his students problems of this kind, because they are likely to find them in modern airplanes. The pitot tubes are speedometers calibrated by the air that rushes into them as the plane flies forward. If a pitot tube is clogged—it doesn't matter if it is clogged by a bug or by ice—it will not read the proper speed. In fact, it will claim that the plane is going much more slowly than it actually is.

There are two pitot tubes in an airplane, each tied to a different computer system. If one of the tubes goes bad, the information in the corresponding computer will be worthless. When the teacher freezes up one of the tubes, his students usually get it that they must disregard the data from the frozen tube and depend on the information from the one that is working. But the computers don't reason so clearly. They are upset that the two systems disagree, and in response, they shut down the autopilot and the flight director. All the helpful tools that make flying easy are gone, and as usual, the weather is awful. The problem is compounded by the fact that when the computers think the airplane is going too slowly, they may change the sensitivity of the controls, so it becomes very easy to overcontrol the airplane, possibly sending it into a spin.

The crew confers. They realize that although they are ignoring the bad data from the clogged pitot tube, its computer is not. They pull the circuit breaker on the computer with the bad information. As it dies, the other computer is happy to have no contradictory information. It turns the autopilot and the flight director back on.

Knowing where the circuit breakers are is becoming a part of the pilot's response kit. On an early demonstration flight of the Airbus A320, the plane was supposed to make a low pass over an airport, then climb again. The computer evidently insisted that the plane was going to land, and it did: right in the forest at the runway's end. It is said that all Airbus pilots know where the circuit breakers are, because if a computer malfunctions they must disable it in order to get manual control of the plane.

Often, though, it is just a matter of saying where you are and asking for help. One evening in Vietnam, as he was flying his A-4 Skyhawk back to Chu Lai, Dave Oguss felt really good. There was a big thunderhead out in front of him, gilded by the setting sun. He had plenty of fuel. He shot straight up in a vertical climb beside the cloud, rolled the airplane, and suddenly did not know which end was up. Fortunately, the A-4 was a two-seater. He told his weapons officer, "Hey, I've got vertigo." The other pilot talked him back to straight and level flight.

Telling

The Wilderness of Pheromones

The world is awash in perfumes. Some are specific to the creature that emits and receives them. Some can be eavesdropped by others. Some are intentionally faked by predators to attract their prey. All depend on the physical movement of chemicals or groups of chemicals through the air from sender to receiver. This exchange of signals—what in mammals like us would be called sniffing, but in others involves the flick of a tongue, the rustle of an antenna, or the rubbing together of heads—is by far the most common form of communication among the living. It orients. We chase and follow it. It can lead us instantly not only through space but through time. As Vincent Dethier pointed out in his wonderful lecture entitled "Sniff, Flick and Pulse," this ability is predicated not on a single fixed response but on a varying response to intermittent signals.

Sniffing itself creates this mutability because it gathers the air in discrete samples, with each inhale and exhale. Humans get repeated but distinct takes on the strength of an odor, and so can better recognize and follow (or flee from) it. Insects do it differently, since they sniff with their antennae, but to better vary the incoming signal they flick their antennae at it. On the sending end, female moths make sure they will be found by males by intermittently releasing the sex pheromone in pulses.

There are more interactions mediated by pheromones in the animal kingdom than by any other kind of signal. And it is not only animals. Chemical communication embraces all the kingdoms of life. Bacteria use pheromones. So do all ants, most insects, snakes, salamanders, foxes, mice, voles, bats, elephants, and moths. In fact, elephants and moths use some of the same chemicals to attract the opposite sex. (Whether moths are attracted to elephants, or vice versa, is not known.) Strangest of all, perhaps, plants emit pheromones, and sometimes they give off pheromones that imitate those of insects, in order to attract the predators that prey on those insects.

Though many creatures equally use sound or sight to guide them, an advantage of pheromones is that they are cheap to produce. A boll weevil, for example, uses about 0.2 percent of its daily energy to generate the pheromone used to attract its mate. The cricket uses about half its energy to creak.

To be a part of nature means to be born, and to be born means to start searching: searching for food, for a mate (or mates), for friends, for enemies, for a place to live, for the way home. The world for every creature—of whatever size or scale or length of life—consists of these common needs. And for most of the living world, pheromones point the way to fulfill them all.

Female moths emit a pheromone that attracts the opposite sex. Male moths come with pheromones derived from the poisons of the plants on which they feed. Females typically choose a male with a good dose of these pheromones, since they will use the poisons to protect their eggs.

In many mammals, the male emits a pheromone that will cause females to go into heat. And a female in heat will emit chemicals that attract the male to her. Writer François Rabelais concocted the tale, in chapter 22 of his book *Gargantua and Pantagruel*, that the hero's teacher Panurge got his revenge on a lady who had spurned him in the following way: on Corpus Christi Day, as she was following the procession to church, clad in her finest red satin dress, Panurge surreptitiously sprinkled on her a poultice made from the appropriate organ of a bitch in heat. "He had barely finished," reports the writer, "when all the dogs hanging around the church came running at the lady, drawn by the smell of that which he had sprinkled on her. Little ones and big ones, fat ones and thin ones, they all came, penises at the ready, sniffing and snuffing and pissing all over her." According to the author, she was pursued home by 600,014 dogs.

Exaggerated perhaps, but not far off the mark. In fact, the situation in nature is even more creative. Sometimes a female mouse will accept a male who has signaled to her, but if she senses other male pheromones in the area, she might prevent pregnancy while she receives as many other males as possible.

Recent experiments suggest that pheromone cues can even influence human sexual behavior. Women who have a concoction of another woman's underarm essence painted on their lips will begin to have their periods in synchrony with the other woman. Women who live in the same house or work in the same office are also said to develop this synchrony.

Once a female has laid her eggs, she might emit a particular pheromone to mark the spot. Certain female lacewings use this cue to dump their own eggs into sites cleared and marked by another female. Apple maggot fly mothers, on the other hand, mark a parasitized fruit so that neither she nor another fly will mistakenly lay too many eggs in too limited a larval food source.

Sex is one need in the world, and food is an equally powerful one. Many creatures mark the trail to where food can be found so that their friends can find it too. The pheromone might first cause the creatures to come together in large number—as do bark beetles on pine trees or tent caterpillars on cherries. Trail pheromones then mark the ways to the best food. Ants often use pheromones to mark trails to food. As more individuals follow a trail, the trail gets stronger and lasts longer. The assumption is that a good food source has been found, so the trail increases in intensity until the food runs out. Most ant species work this way. Army ants—who are completely blind—orient, gather, and go on their raids entirely by means of pheromones.

Other animals mark their territory by means of pheromone points, and some, such as badgers, mark each other. The signal can mean "mine" or "keep out," but most often it is the starting point of negotiation. So long as a marker is acknowledged and respected, cooperation as well as competition can emerge.

When enemies appear, creatures of all sizes emit scented alarms All species of ants do. So do lacewings, aphids, deer, voles, and mice. If you recall how danger makes you sweat, you might be ready to believe that, at least vestigially, humans do too.

The response to an alarm may be to drop from a food source and flee, or in social insects, it may be to mobilize soldiers to defend the colony. In a few cases, almost unaccountably, the response to an alarm pheromone is to throw the nest into disarray, along the lines of the mock adage "When in danger or in doubt, run in circles, scream and shout."

The Japanese honeybee is among the most skillful defenders. Japan is home to a species of giant hornet that loves fresh bee. When a hornet first finds a hive, it might pick off a flying bee or two and hurry home to eat it. (A single bee is no match for a single hornet, which can kill about forty bees per minute when it concentrates.) After a visit or two to this source of fresh food, the hornet marks the hive with a pheromone. Other giant hornets get the point: "Here is a good restaurant." They begin to appear at the hive. At first, they pick off the bees one by one, but when three or more hornets are gathered at the same time, they switch strategy. They attack the whole colony. At forty bees per minute, a team of thirty giant hornets can kill a hive of twenty thousand honeybees in just a couple hours. Later, they might inhabit the hive for a time, gradually bringing the larvae and pupae back to feed their own young.

But the Japanese honeybee smells the hornet the moment it marks the nest. A hundred workers rush to the hive entrance and stand in a circle outside. They shake their rumps at the hornet, perhaps inviting the creature many times their own size to devour one or two of them instead of continuing to mark the hive. At the same time, they release their own signal that attracts workers to the hive entry. They then duck inside the hive entrance, where a thousand more of their fellow workers are already waiting. These bees are spoiling for a fight. They have in fact heated up from their usual body temperature of about 95 degrees Fahrenheit to over 110 degrees.

When the hornet enters, it is immediately surrounded by rank after rank of bees. They form a buzzing ball many bees thick. The ball quickly heats up to a temperature of 117 degrees Fahrenheit, just hot enough to cook a hornet but not quite hot enough to cook a bee.

Alarm pheromones can also mobilize friends of other species. More than two thousand kinds of butterfly larvae are protected by ants in return for receiving food from them. In all cases, if their protégés emit alarms, the ants catch the scent and rush to their defense. Some ants even protect gardens of fungi. If they sense the odor of a creature they know to harm the fungi, they will carry the offender away. This might not work well against a bird or an anteater, but most smaller predators are well advised to flee.

Pheromone cues are even used to plan the building of houses. Certain termites make burrows that are more than ninety feet in diameter. Each is filled with passages, and each passage is supported by laboriously constructed pillars. The location and the strength of the pillars are indicated by pheromones emitted by the insects as they work.

For better or for worse, not all the senders or receivers of such chemical signals are honest. A certain parasitoid fly senses the sex pheromone of the male spined soldier bug. It zeroes in on the bug and lays its eggs in the hapless individual. Four times as many male as female soldier bugs are parasitized in this way. For this reason, a number of male soldier bugs have learned to keep silent. They might not advertise their prowess or attractiveness to the females, but they wait near one who does. In the end, the silent bug gets the girl, while the flashy one becomes a long slow supper for a larval fly.

Detecting the scents of others is a way of life to many creatures. There are ticks that settle on the spots marked by antelopes, knowing that other antelopes are bound to touch the same spot. Hornets smell the sex hormones of masses of fruit flies, and fly in for a feast. The blind snake follows the scent trail of the blind army ants, and devours their brood. The robber bee enters the nest of the stingless bee and emits such a quantity of that bee's alarm pheromone that the defenders give up and rush about aimlessly, dying one by one as they are eaten.

Sometimes, the approach is gentler. A beetle makes for itself the recognition pheromone of a certain termite. The beetle is welcomed into the termite's nest as though it were another termite, and it is fed by the termite workers.

Among the greatest deceivers are the orchids. Of the roughly thirty thousand species of orchids now known, about one-third get pollinated by pretending to be what they are not. Some use visual cues, but many emit faux pheromones. One synthesizes and emits the sex pheromone of certain bees. The bees mate with one flower, then with another, all the while carrying the pollen. Another orchid is even more devious. It has black blotches near the throat of the flower that more or less resemble feeding aphids. But to make sure of itself, it also makes and produces very precisely the alarm pheromone of the aphids. Syrphid flies that feed on the aphids appear and are fooled just long enough to get a dose of pollen, which they carry on to the next pretender.

Not only is there communication that stretches back and forth from bacteria to humans, but also there is copious communion among all the kingdoms of life. Supposedly senseless plants tell parasite wasps and predator beetles where to find their prey. When armyworms attack the leaves of corn, the entire plant—not just the injured leaves—sends into the air a signal that means "I am being attacked by armyworms. Please come and get them." The signal is strong enough to be perceived from far off, is unambiguous in meaning, and is emitted when the pest is present and the predator on the prowl.

It takes corn an hour or two to muster its tale and send it off on the wind. Cotton plants store the message in glandular hairs, releasing it as soon as the pests begin to chew. Lima beans respond to spider mites by inviting predatory mites. The cassava plant tells a related predatory mite about its problem with mealybugs. There are no isolate individuals. Anywhere.

Mother and Child Communion

Everybody comes out of a womb, but nobody remembers it. What happens directly afterward for every human being, however, is a school of love. First, it is dark, you float, you are supported on every side, and your food and oxygen are supplied through the umbilical cord. In a normal pregnancy, you want for nothing. Occasionally, a smooth pressure from the outside—ascending, descending, circling—outlines the part of your body that is closest to the world.

When you emerge, the situation shifts unfathomably. From dark to light, from damp to dry. There is noise; you are squeezed. The midwife pats your butt to get you breathing, cuts the cord, and lays you near your mother's breast. From that moment on, you are a creature of the air.

You are also hungry, something you have never been before. How do you find food? Well, if they are not crazy, they have laid you right next to the source of all goodness. But how do you find the breast and learn how it works? Likely, all you see are contrasts of light and dark.

Yet very few babies have any trouble at all. The reason is in the air. During pregnancy, a mother begins to make five volatile compounds in the glands that surround her nipples and in those in her armpits. She never made these smells when she was not pregnant, and she will stop making them after she stops breast-feeding. The newborn baby is very sensitive to these exact compounds. Stefano Vaglio and his colleagues, who discovered the compounds in the study they performed in 2006, have a wonderful way of putting it: the odors, they write, "are an Ariadne's thread that permits the infant after birth to find its mother." Ariadne, you will remember, is the young lady whose carefully laid thread Theseus was able to follow to escape the labyrinth and its Minotaur.

Within an hour of birth, the baby will turn to the mother's breast even if it is pitch dark. Within six days, the baby will choose its mother's own breast odor over that of any other woman, lactating or not. Within two weeks, the baby will recognize its own mother from the smell of her armpits alone, without any further clues and without fail. This is perhaps not too surprising, since in the first hours after birth millions of synapses are formed in the brain as the infant responds for the first time to the stimuli that become part of its world. The odor of the mother—and particularly of her breasts and armpits—is among the first traces written on the brain. Likely, it comes with a flood of endorphins, so the baby learns on the very first trial.

The mother learns a similar trick. If you present her with two T-shirts, one worn by her own infant and one worn by a stranger, in four out of five cases the mother will sniff once and immediately recognize her baby's shirt. She is not guessing. As she hands back to the enterprising scientist the garment she has chosen, she says things like, For sure, or Of course, or No question. She can continue to do this for the whole childhood.

The beginning of the bond between mother and child is a few smells that pass back and forth between them. There is an argument about whether to call these odors pheromones, but that is not important to us. The important thing is that key knowledge is passed invisibly through the air, and it has importance only for the two of them.

You may say that nature has simply supplied an obvious need. The baby must find the mother's breast if it is to live, so nature has put an unmistakable sign on it. And it must find the mother, so nature has made the mother's more penetrating body odor also an attractant for the child. Pure chemistry. Nothing to it.

But this is to miss the action. The baby is placed on the mother's chest. It turns to her nipple. She holds and guides it. She enfolds the baby in her arms, thereby doubling and trebling the dose of underarm odor. (God help us if the mother has washed or been washed too clean, for then the baby will be at a loss.) It feeds happily, God willing. It then rests upon her chest, and she continues to enfold it.

Outside the womb the baby finds a world where one is still fed, still supported, still cradled. There is beginning to form before its still-only-partly-discerning eyes the figure of another who provides gladly and sometimes even with delight these benefits.

The babe has not sold or bartered for these things. It makes no exchange to receive them. It has not bargained, wheedled, or cajoled. All these actions might come later, and alas, a woman who has too many doubts may well spend her time wondering if she is motherly enough or happy enough or indeed happy at all. Nonetheless, mainly it is all, rather, simply given, and the more the baby takes, the more there is to receive. And the more the baby takes, the more the mother experiences the baby as giving her its life and its acceptance.

This free exchange is a type and pattern of love. It is not based on scarcity, rationing, sales, or craving. There is indeed need involved, but real love happens only when it is joined to need. (Robert Frost got it exactly right in "Two Tramps in Mud Time": there he wrote that "Only where love and need are one" can anything be done "For Heaven and the future's sakes.") Real love is a mystery, in the technical sense of the word, because we cannot account for it and we do not exactly know why it should be. But we *live* in the mystery. For all every mother and child will forever after regard each other as a problem—perhaps the biggest and most troublesome problem on God's green earth—we live in the mystery.

And if, afterward, we fall away from this? If we fall to haggling, withholding, diverting, idolizing, bargaining, overwhelming, insisting, ignoring, or neglecting, whose fault is it?

Allure

But when from a long-distant past, nothing subsists, after the people are dead, after the things are broken and scattered, still, alone, more fragile, but with more vitality, more unsubstantial, more persistent, more faithful, the smell and taste of things remain poised a long time, like souls, ready to remind us, waiting and hoping for their moment, among the ruins of all the rest; and bear unfalteringly, in the tiny and almost impalpable drop of their essence, the vast structure of recollection.

—Marcel Proust, Swann's Way

Perhaps the greatest book of memory in the Western world—Marcel Proust's thirty-two-hundred-page *Remembrance of Things Past*—begins with the smell and taste of a cookie dipped in linden flower tea. This experience, asserts the author, puts him back into his childhood suddenly and completely, with all the emotions it evoked, as though he had gone back to that time. This is one of the most famous opening gambits in all literature. It is also a fact.

Smell holds a unique place among the senses. At once concrete and ethereal, pungent and invisible, and always a mixture of all that the air brings in that moment, an odor has a signature that infuses emotion into remembrance. It also gives all the nuance to taste. The taste buds sense only sweet, sour, salty, or bitter. All the details are provided by the nose. The word "recollection" is perhaps best for what happens, since around the odor gather at first a few and then more and more associations, until a time and place, with their meaning, are present once more.

The odor draws us. Literally, it is alluring: *ad* + *leurre*, meaning to draw toward, as a falcon flies toward the lure. A group of scientists recently studied the memories associated with campfires, popcorn, and newly mown grass. The participants were presented with visual, aural, and olfactory cues for each of the three and asked to report the memories they elicited. Almost to a person, the subjects reported that the memories evoked by the smells were not more detailed, but rather more vivid, present, and emotionally alive than those brought forth by the sight or sound of the same stimuli.

Most people would describe the smells of campfires, popcorn, and grass as pleasant, but it isn't only sweet smells that allure. Sometimes, the contrary is the case. One man cried whenever he smelled a certain flower, since masses of them had been placed in front of his father's picture at a memorial service. I, on the other hand, am powerfully drawn to the scent of urine and damp stone.

Once, I had to visit a late Gothic basilica in Saint-Maximin-la-Sainte-Baume, a town of about fifteen thousand souls in the Vaucluse in Provence. I was told that Mary Magdalene had come to this town, fleeing persecution in the Holy Land, and had lived as a hermit in a cave in the mountains above the town. (Of course, like so many saints, on her death she was said to have been carried aloft from her cave by angels, leaving a sweet smell in her wake.) The church was dedicated to her and to the town's patron saint, and its crypt was said to contain Mary's remains. The Black Death had interrupted the building campaign, and the basilica had never been finished.

I drove an hour to find the place. The church was closed. A passerby pointed me to the house where the sacristan lived, suggesting he might open the church for me. The man was reluctant to come out of his house, but when I said I wanted to see Magdalene's relics, he grudgingly agreed to let me into the church. Perhaps he regarded it as a religious duty.

When we entered it, the church smelled musty, not quite clean and probably leaking from half-a-dozen holes in the roof. But this was nothing compared to the crypt. We descended stairs that led through an arched vault of fluted limestone beneath the high altar. With every step, the stench of urine increased. I asked the sacristan what was happening. "Yes," he said, "it stinks. That is one of the reasons we close the church. People use the crypt for a *pissoir*!"

He turned on a dim light at the bottom of the stairs. I could barely distinguish a kind of rough frieze of statuary and three or four stone caskets. An hour out of my way for this! I thought. I turned to go back up the stairs. As I was climbing them I noticed some kind of graffiti scratched in the stone wall. There was an upside-down U with two straight scratches running top to bottom inside it. Then, I noticed another similar one, this time with three vertical scratches.

I started to explore the walls in dimmer and dimmer light, as we retreated farther from the bare bulb beside the tombs. There were not just two or three, or even twenty or thirty of these signs. There were two or three hundred, maybe more. Wherever a person could reach, the inverted U and its scratches had been carved.

The sacristan noticed my exploration. "Yes," he said, with the same weary voice. "Some of the women when they marry here sneak in and make these marks."

Why would they do that? I asked.

"That arch mark," he replied, "is the cave above town where Mary Magdalene lived. That is why our town is called 'la-Sainte-Baume,' the Holy Cave. The scratch marks are the number of children the young women want to have."

I no longer was eager to leave the place, much to the sacristan's disgust. I went from cave to cave counting the number of children each woman planned to have. Later, I learned that one of Magdalene's local miracles had been to bring safely to childbirth a pagan queen who had been given up for dead. So the young women were in a sense making a talisman for safe delivery.

But they were also scrawling their hopes on this *pissoir* wall, and committing these wishes to the care of a supposed spirit of benevolence and help. The Gothic stone masons who had started to build this place before the plague took them could certainly have made more skillful carving, but I believe they would have praised and shared the women's impulse. Indeed, some of the most interesting marks on Gothic stone are the masons' marks likewise simply scratched into the surface, usually to tell where a stone went but sometimes with still-undeciphered meaning.

I have never forgotten that sight or that smell. Now, when I sniff the right combination of stone and piss, I am carried back to that crypt and its hopeful caves. The odor brings the scene to life and spreads it before me, much as a smell itself is first whiffed and then confirmed. One reason why odors might be such powerful mnemonics is indeed that they are formed by a singular concatenation of scents. It is not only the piss, but the damp stone, the moss, the dust on the floor, perhaps the sacristan's odor and my own. All these together make a signature that can be evoked but never repeated, unless by the same place and participants.

Someone supposedly asked Ralph Waldo Emerson why he had never traveled. He is said to have replied, "I have traveled much in Concord," the town of his birth, life, and death. When we are led by olfactory memory, we travel back through our lives, whether these lives have been lived in a single place or all over the world.

My earliest memory is cued by the odor of pine. I was only three months old. The odor evokes a scene that has broad black masses to its left, a kind of low goalpost in front, and green high above and all around. I am told that this corresponds to a place where my parents stopped after crossing Berthold Pass on our way to California. My milk bottle had evidently exploded from the pressure change at altitude, so I might have been startled into such an early memory. None of the details of place and time come from me, only the sensation, which I can still see perfectly before my eyes, but I am known to haunt Christmas tree lots.

Sometimes, an odor is fixed to a person. My grandmother wore Guerlain perfume—lots of it. When she arrived for a visit, we smelled her before we saw her. To bury our heads in her clothes was to be buried in her scent. We would rush to open her suitcase, which smelled even more strongly of the perfumes she carried. We would open the bag that contained her Indian jewelry and pore over the turquoise, silver, squash blossom pendants. We would unzip the bag that contained her strange compacts, shallow coin-shaped silver boxes that would pop open with the push of a button, showing a mirror, a powder puff, and a scented powder or an unguent. Finally, we would come upon the six pack of frozen pecan pies that she had brought as a gift from a place called Van De Kamp's, which seemed to us beyond the ends of the earth. Her scent and her bag were heavenly to us.

Though many odors allure me, I am aware that the word "allure" is meant to be used for sexual attraction. So much of a modern woman's life is devoted to wearing that which will allure. This includes an array of perfumes. It is interesting to me that the very same woman who shaves her armpits so as not to smell musky then puts on an artificial musk to replace what she removed. The wise inform me that in many cases that is exactly what she does, since that artificial musk is a compound that is very close in chemistry to what her underarms and their resident bacteria would have emitted anyway.

The number of attractants and other communicative chemicals in the universe of animals and plants is small and their chemistry often shared. One of the ingredients in recent perfumes is identical to the alarm pheromone emitted by giant hornets in Japan. When they sense this chemical in the air, the hornets make a beeline for the spot to defend their confrere. If you happen to be wearing that perfume, there is a chance that you will be skewered by at least one giant hornet.

Researchers would dearly love to find the sex hormone that will unfailingly attract the opposite sex among humans. In middle Europe, girls used to think it best to carry a slice of apple under their armpits and then to feed it to the swain of their dreams. His devotion was supposed to be ensured. Likewise, an enterprising young man might carry a handkerchief under his own armpits while exercising. That evening, at the dance, he would gallantly wipe the perspiration from the brow of his partner, using the same handkerchief, and she would become obedient to his will.

I had a somewhat different idea. As a young and very inexperienced freshman in college, I was in love with two things: the library and every girl who walked by. (I had gone to a high school where females were scarce, and now I was in the middle of New York City.) There was a wonderful girl whom I realized actually liked me. Given how slow and dense I was about such things, she had probably done everything to get my attention, including feeding me the scented apple.

I wanted to show her that I too liked her. One evening, while our friends were playing poker in the common room, I invited her to go for a walk. I had a plan, though perhaps not the one she hoped I had. You see, I knew how to go through the subterranean tunnels of the university and reach the library stacks after it was closed. Down we went to the basement. We made turn after turn in the tunnels, and I found the door that led into the library basement. The odor of books rushed through it. I for one was intoxicated. She, I believe, was rather amused and charmed, but not excited. That night we were caught by campus security, who also appeared to think it charming, though they sternly warned us against any repetition of the event.

I have not seen or heard from her in forty years, but I still often visit that library. When I do, the smell of the books reminds me of her, and I wish her well. Apparently, books can also make a pheromone.

The Atmosphere of the Beloved

When Napoléon was coming back from a campaign, he is supposed to have sent a note to Josephine. "I will be home tomorrow night. Please do not bathe." On the other hand, upon Josephine's death in 1814, the workmen dismantling her boudoir found the walls so infused with musk—the deep pungent scent taken from the glands of the musk deer—that they felt quite sick.

We are trained almost from birth to respond first to visual and aural cues. Shake the colored rattle in front of the baby. How pretty, how colorful, and what a racket it makes! But it is made of plastic and so has only a very slight acrid smell. When we are a little older, we are propped in front of a television or read books full of large bright pictures. When we are older still, we graduate to images that more and more contain at least suggestive pictures of persons of the opposite sex. We respond to the shapes and curves of their bodies, to the thickness and turn of their lips, to the look in their eyes, to the way they are standing.

And this is not just an artifact of a culture addicted to imagery. Long before photo offset and long long before the Internet, Immanuel Kant put smell in its place. If any of the senses could be dispensed with, he thought, smell would be the one. As many odors were distasteful as were good, and the pleasures that the sense of smell could lead to were annoyingly brief. It is no surprise that Kant never married and that he thought sex a sordid transformation of love into appetite.

He is surely right about that. Intimacy is about scent. Is this mix of rubbing, sniffing, licking, leaning, twining that we experience with the beloved a mark of wisdom or of folly? Wisdom, you might think, because *sagax*, the Latin for "wisdom," also means a person with a keen sense of smell, and the *sapientiae*—that is, the wise—are those who have and know flavor. No, folly, you might object, remembering all the crazy things you have done in the name of love, and those nights when you walked up and down an evil-smelling avenue in the heat of summer, beneath the window of the one you wished to touch and hold, not sure if you dared call her or if you did, whether or not she would let you near her at all.

But then you call. Then she says come on up. Then you end up in each other's arms, maybe after a big fight or maybe after a meal. You might leave the light on, but usually you will turn it off. There is something to the intimacy of lovers that wants to dispense not with smell but with sight. And if it is a hot summer night, and you are young and without air-conditioning, you will soon be in a steam room of your own making.

As nearly hairless as we may be, the human has more skin secretions than any other higher primate. The average person has about six square feet of skin, but the most prolific producers of scent are the cheeks, the upper lip, the hair, the forehead, the armpits, the nipples, and the genitals. I do not think it is coincidence that these are the places on the beloved's body that the lover most frequents.

In 1886, a Frenchman by the name of Augustin Galopin wrote a book called *Le parfum de la femme, et la sens olfactif dans l'amour*, or *The Scent of a Woman, and the Sense of Smell in Love*. He had no doubt of the role that odor played in throwing up a bridge between the visible and invisible. "Odor is the precursor of love," he wrote, "and air is its messenger." The lovers interpenetrate one another through one after another emanation that seems as solid as stone yet is completely invisible. "The two lovers explore one another in the chiaroscuro of their souls," he asserted, "and lovingly taste their great good fortune. They alone understand the link between the bestial nature of human beings and the spirit of God."

I would add, however, that as lovers live together, they not only continue to share these perfumes. They build together a mutual scent that each carries about, whether or not they are together. It is a scent compounded not only of their skin secretions but of the mud on his boots, the henna in her hair and eyebrows, the garlic hanging from the hook, the insides of shoes, half-dry towels, toothpastes, and window cleaner, the dust held in the corn broom's strands, the old pair of paint-stained jeans, always overripe bananas that the fruit flies crowd around in angular flight, the cedar chest leaking infinitely slowly its balsam, olive oil soap and herbal essence shampoo and sharp-smelling Chinese liniment, the half-filled compost bucket waiting to go out, the glue that holds the books together, mosquito repellant, sunscreen, firewood, the ash in the fireplace . . .

Galopin noticed that in the days when people still had trades they tended to marry within them. This fact he thought not a consequence of social immobility, but rather of the fact that, for example, a lady of Marseilles loved a man who, like her, smelled of garlic and onion, or a collier loved a woman who loved the smell of coal.

As I am sitting in the library on a warm afternoon, a young woman in a crisp shirt and skirt snippily asks me to move my notebook away from an outlet. She wants to plug in her laptop. I am briefly annoyed at her tone, but then a light acrid floral perfume reaches me across the table. Instead, I am charmed that this mistress of the prim has a scent. But when I go back to my reading, I find that I have been smelling the back of my hand. It is warm and pungent and peculiar. It is a way of touching base, of going home.

I remember one great pleasure of making a commitment to the beloved. It was when I began to call her by one of the few names that everybody uses for their own beloved. Though the names quickly become routine, at the start they are redolent of a new way of regarding this other person: Honey, Sweetie, Dear. The first two describe an odor or flavor, and the third means precious, costly. The trio is not incongruous, since through most of human history the most prized scents were very expensive. Gold, frankincense, and myrrh were the three dearest things in ancient Egypt and were the sort of gift you would give a king, so the three kings were giving Christ the most precious things they could find, two of which were scents.

Royalty could overdo it in sweetness. To receive Mark Antony, Cleopatra had herself rouged with henna, penciled with kohl, and rubbed with an olive oil scented with flowers, jasmine, gum, and resin. She sailed toward him burning the most precious Egyptian incense, *kyphi*, a concoction of cinnamon, acacia, juniper, peppermint, cassia, fragrant roots, flowers, resin, and myrrh, mixed in a blend of wine and honey. Her sails were soaked in rose water. Plutarch comments that the winds themselves were seduced and lovesick for the queen.

For most lovers, a little perfume is plenty, or even too much. It simply adds to the whole bouquet. As often as not, it is metaphor. Robert Herrick, the unmarried seventeenth-century English poet who composed song after song to beloved women, was particularly in love with their smell. He often wrote poems to one Julia, whose sweat he described as oil of blossoms, lilies, and spikenard. To one Anthea, he wrote the full truth of the matter under the heading "Love Perfumes All Parts."

If I kiss Anthea's breast
There I smell the Phoenix nest [i.e., cinnamon]
If I her lip, the most sincere
Altar of incense, I smell there

Hands, and thighs, and legs, are all
Richly aromatical
Goddess Isis can't transfer
Musks and Ambers more from her;
Nor can Juno sweeter be,
When she lies with Jove, than she.

And all those aromatic perfumes, even when really worn, are simply anthologies of attractants. To the perfumer, a scent has three notes, as Michael Stoddart points out in *The Scented Ape*. The top note is the floral hint that is first perceptible. The middle note is a resin that warms the scent. The bass note makes it last. All three either are or smell like sex attractants: The top note, scent of flowers, brings bees. The middle note has the steroid smell of attractants across the whole animal kingdom. The bass note is a real musk or an imitation one, a long-lasting perfume that by itself smells vaguely of piss or feces, like the sign left by foxes in the woods, a note that you can both smell and taste as you walk by, even if you have a cold.

Whether or not she has daubed on scent, the beloved is always perfumed to us. Even in old age, as one gallant put it, she smells of dried rose petals. What an older man smells like, I do not know, but I hope like well-seasoned firewood.

All of this to Kant, of course, is nothing but base appetite. It leads us away from moral responsibility. But I would say that without love, morals have no ground. As a mother is to a baby, so are the lover and beloved to one another. They are chances to learn love.

Zooming In

I went walking with a friend on a new trail in my favorite woods. It runs up past what was once a racetrack. Along the way it bumps right into a family cemetery. There is one solid obelisk in the group, but the rest are slender gravestones the shape of slices of toast. Some have broken their backs. Some lean against walls or stumps. A few lean together into a tepee shape, like a stack of rifles in a Civil War camp. The start of the letters on a first name may be crisp, but by the time you get to the last letter, there is scarcely a shadow on the stone to suggest the curve of an "e" or the pretzel of an "s." Black cherry and white ash have grown in around them. Grapevines hang from the trees.

It is a musty, shady, and disheveled place. Over in one corner are roughly piled the beautiful, rusting, filigree remains of the cast-iron fence that once surrounded the plot. The whole scene makes me think of the word "decomposed."

As I often do in this used, used land, I wonder who these people were and where they lived. It must have been nearby, but now there is only woodland and I have yet to find a cellar hole. At least, however, I can tell you where their fields were. President Franklin D. Roosevelt, when he was contemplating moving starving farmers off the land in Appalachia, experimented here first, in the New York uplands. The Civilian Conservation Corps was here, making plantations with its seedling white spruce and red and scotch pines. When these families were moved off the land to take city jobs in Albany, Cohoes, Watervliet, Schenectady, and New York, their fields were sewn up as woodland with line after line of pine.

We walk through a grove of red pine. It is as ugly as most mature pine plantations are. The bottom twenty to thirty feet of each tree is full of whorls of dead branches, like so many fish skeletons, shaded out by the canopy above. The understory is messy and confused. A few dead pines, however, look livelier than the living ones. They show hundreds of fat, flexed, flat-white tongues, sticking out in our direction and all around and up and down the trunks. Maybe only one in eight or nine of the pines has this odd decoration, but when they have them, they have no shortage of them.

On closer inspection, we find that each of these tongues is the fruiting body of a fungus, emerging from the hole made by a pine bark beetle in its attack on the tree. The fungus is *Cryptosporus volvatus*, a very strange polypore first described by the New York State botanist Charles Horton Peck, whose office was not more than thirty miles from here. My friend and walking companion was Peck's successor, so he is particularly happy to find this uncommon mushroom.

He picks one and folds back its veil. "Look under there," he said. "It looks like a puffball, but really it is a polypore." He shows me the covered cavity full of tiny holes, in each of which reside thousands upon thousands of spores. These spores, like those of most fungi, travel by air, but the fungus also spreads by hitching a ride on bark beetles. The beetles bore through the fruiting body, feeding on the fungus, and carry off bits of the mycelium when they fly to infest another pine. When they arrive, they deposit their load of fungus as they bore into the tree.

I was interested in the fungus, but more interested in the fruits because they marked the holes by which hundreds of beetles had attacked each tree. It was a graphic example of the ways of the pine

The scolytid beetle that attacks red pine may carry and spread the polypore basidiomycete Cryptosporus volvatus. *The holes in the bark are exit holes dug by the beetles, some made larger by woodpeckers. (Photograph by William Bryant Logan)*

bark beetles. Unlike most insects, in order to stay alive they must not only weaken but also kill their hosts.

There are over six thousand species of bark beetles in the world, and they have been with us a long time. In Baltic amber from the Oligocene, twenty-five to thirty million years old, are found perfect specimens of bark beetles that are almost identical to those found today. Jewelers love to sell amber pendants and earrings that have bona fide bugs floating in the warm yellow brown of the jewel. How did the beetles get into the amber? That is the story.

Pines respond to insect attack by mobilizing defensive chemicals carried to the site by copious gummy resin. The healthier the pine, the stronger the dose and the greater the pressure with which the resin arrives. Sometimes, the first bark beetle to drill into a potential host tree is squirted right back out of its new hole and onto the ground by the pressure of the terpene-filled sap. If it cannot inhabit the tree, it cannot mate, it cannot lay eggs, and its larvae cannot mature, feeding on the pine wood. If that were all, the bark beetle should have been history after two or three seasons, not survived for thirty million years.

The entombed beetle is a representative of the struggle that still goes on today. The first beetle to penetrate might indeed resist drowning or being crystallized in the gooey resin. Students have watched a mountain pine beetle swimming through the exuding sap, trying to scoop it out of the hole, surfacing for air occasionally by pressing its abdomen out of the fray and lifting a wing, below which is an unclogged spiracle through which it can breathe. If it succeeds in making a place for itself, the fight has just begun. More resin will be mobilized, more terpenes emitted. To win, the beetle must overwhelm the pine's defenses, and to do that it needs help.

Many species enlist the help of the fungi they carry, either on their carapaces or in special chambers in their heads. The fungi help defeat plant defenses. They cause the tree to work very hard to prevent the fungi from penetrating far into the interior. A lot of the energy that might have gone to fighting beetles must be used instead to fight the fungus.

In the meantime, the lone beetle calls its friends. With its first meal, it makes feces and an odor. The odor is composed of some chemicals internally generated by the beetle and of one chemical made by modifying the pine's own defensive terpenes. Both feces and pheromones exit via the hindgut, and the pheromone plume floats off downwind.

Within a day, there might be eight hundred more beetles, attracted by the odor, ready to try their luck with this tree. Each one that succeeds emits the same pheromone, increasing the strength of the signal and attracting still more beetles. For each beetle, the tree must spend more and more energy to defend itself.

Not only the beetle's friends receive the signal. So do other bark beetles. Some might be attracted, but for others the pheromone of their own species blocks that of their competitors. Predators also get the message. Within a day of a sustained attack on a pine in California, there were a hundred new insect species living on the tree, many of them feeding on or laying their eggs in the bark beetles. In one forest study, the researchers trapped six hundred thousand bark beetles along with eighty-six thousand predators.

Still, when the number of bark beetles reaches about forty per square yard, the tree is doomed. It cannot make enough resin to squirt out or entomb that many bugs. It runs out of reserve energy and begins to decline. This is what the beetles, individually and as a group, require. With the nasty terpenes and resins in decline, they can safely mate, lay eggs, and leave their larvae to feed and make galleries in the dying tree.

At this point, there must be a stop to the arrival of new beetles. If there is not, they will overcrowd the tree, and everyone will die instead of live to procreate. But because the pheromone that attracts them is partly made out of compounds from the tree itself, as the tree stops making the terpenes, the pheromone weakens and stops acting as a signal. New beetles cease to arrive.

This is a real contest. In many situations, the tree is as likely to win as the beetle. Although a few of the red pines by the cemetery were dead and sprouting little white tongues, most were still alive, with maybe a single or a couple of empty and abortive beetle holes.

But epidemics occur. The largest ones in living memory have destroyed, over the last few decades, more than thirty billion conifers in the Canadian and American West. Climate change is to blame for part of this disaster. A smaller number of beetles lost to winterkill owing to warmer winter weather increases their population. Equally damaging has been Smoky the Bear. The misguided policy to prevent natural forest fires has led to a buildup of overmature, declining trees, which leads to beetle population explosions.

The virulence of the beetle attack is the product of the number of beetles and the resistance of the trees. Pine and other conifer forests

As of 2011, more than 30 billion conifers had been killed by mass beetle attack. (Courtesy of the U.S. Forest Service)

have evolved to pass regularly through fire. (Some cones won't even open unless they are burned.) If fires are forestalled—whether to maintain property values, preserve timber harvests, or make parks look more perfectly manicured—the forest builds dense knots of older trees. When resistance of the trees is weak—because they are old, crowded, wounded, or in decline—each beetle attack in such trees is more likely to succeed. Each successful invasion generates an order of magnitude more beetles, which find nearby still more weakened trees to colonize. Finally, the number of beetles is so great that they can begin to attack even the healthiest pine. Instead of one landing and trying its luck, one hundred might do so. When they gain a foothold, several thousand might follow within a day.

Aphids in the Invisible World

Most aphids are fat, soft, and slow. There is the occasional social aphid species whose sterile soldiers respond efficiently to an alarm by skewering the intruder on a pair of horns, but in general an alarmed aphid has good reason to fear for its succulent life.

When attacked by a predator, an aphid secretes drops from its cornicles, a pair of tailpipes that extend from its back. The drops are very sticky, and in some cases will glue shut the predator's mouth. Whether or not the glue holds, however, the drop also releases volatile hydrocarbons that reach neighbor aphids, alerting them to the disaster. In response to the alarm pheromone, the aphids jump or drop from their feeding sites or scuttle away, leaving the predator with at least a long chase to find a second tasty aphid.

The chemical is sensed by other predators too—by ladybird larvae, for example—which might hurry to the place in the hope of alarming and gobbling the fleeing aphids. But the pheromone might also attract allies.

Many aphids are attended by ants, that farm them. The ant approaches an aphid, rubbing the insect with its antennae. The aphid releases a drop of sweet honeydew, which the ant captures and carries back to its nest. Ants rest on the branches near where the aphids are feeding, waiting to milk them and, as it turns out, primed to protect them. After aphids release their alarm pheromone, the ants rush to the scene and attack the intruder, removing it summarily from the pasture of their flock. Instead of fleeing, the aphids simply waggle their tail ends, as if to say, "Nyaah, nyaah, nyaah, Come and get me, sucker!"

How do we know that the ants are responding to the invisible signal and not just to the sight of the enemy? L. R. Nault and his colleagues performed an ingenious experiment. First, they established relations between an ant species known to tend aphids and a group of aphid species by putting them together. Uniformly, the ants rubbed their antennae on the aphids. If they got honeydew in return, they set up shop as aphid flock guards. If the aphid species did not give honeydew, the ants instead seized the aphids themselves and carried them to their nests, after which the aphids were never seen again.

Having established thriving flocks with ant shepherds, the experimenters took forceps and carefully squeezed the cornicles of selected aphids. The juice came out, and the alarm pheromone wafted through the air. The ants were instantly aroused, turned toward the source of the odor, and rushed the forceps, antennae waving and mouthparts gnashing.

Just to be sure, the researchers distilled the essence of the pheromone and attached varying concentrations to bits of paper, which they waved behind the backs of the ants. At too low a concentration, nothing happened, but at a minimum amount, the ants swung around fast and made for the paper. They reared up on their hindlegs, reached out with their forelegs, and tried to bite the paper.

Thus, although predators or parasites might well be attracted by an alarm pheromone to an aphid colony, they attack it at their peril. To gain safe entry, some create fake documents. The larvae of certain lacewings, for example, dote on fresh mealybug. This woolly aphid, however, is usually surrounded by ant protectors. The lacewing larvae tear pieces of the white waxy covering from their aphid prey and glue it to their own bodies. When the ants approach, they smell aphid, and let the lacewings pass. Aphid carnage results.

This world of invisible communication guides visible beings. Some ladybird larvae even find their way to a flock of yummy aphids by following the pheromone trail laid down by their guardian wood ants. The ants have placed the trail to make sure they can find their way from their own nest to the flock, and back again. The larvae are uninterested in the ant nest, but love to feed on the flock. For reasons still unknown, although the wood ants will ferociously attack adult ladybirds, they let the larvae pass.

The Bolas Spider

I n *New Seeds of Contemplation*, Thomas Merton writes that people are discontented because they are selfish. They do not understand the complete unselfishness of God in creating the world and all that is in it. They grasp for themselves, and so fall away, when rather they ought to imitate God by giving freely.

"Pleroma" is the Greek word for the fullness of God's power. The word suggests that he made and makes absolutely everything that could and can possibly be made, with every permutation, combination, and improbable adaptation. The idea of natural selection is one description of the means by which the pleroma is fulfilled in creatures. The bolas spider is a fine example.

This tribe of three genera of spiders is in the family of the orb weavers. The orb weaver, like our garden spiders, usually weaves large, circular, netted webs that in the mornings are dripping with dew. But the bolas spider is not any good at it. Instead of weaving a wide, netted web, the female sleeps by day on a leaf. At night, she drops down on a line from beneath her leaf, and at the end of that line she fashions a clear sticky ball. (At this point, the word "bolas" might begin to ring a bell. It is the name of a cord with heavy weights at the end, a tool used by the gauchos of the pampas to trip up cattle. In fact, it is a tool of great antiquity in the Americas, having been used by pre-Columbian peoples to trip up llamas and guanacos. The spider is aptly named.) The spider waits on her leaf, her end-weighted line held in her two front legs. When a moth flies near, she winds up and throws. If she is lucky, she hits the moth.

Orb weavers in general are bad at catching moths. The slender web threads might catch a wingtip, but the wing simply sheds a few of its exterior scales onto the web, and the tasty end of the moth flies away. The sticky ball, however, has mass and staying power. It penetrates through the layer of scales to the integument of the wing. The moth is caught and quickly wrapped up for later consumption.

Bolas spiders are such good pitchers that a student of one species named it *Mastophora dizzydeani*, for the baseball pitcher Dizzy Dean, whose deceptive curve ball was his most feared weapon. He also is said to have thrown a bean ball. But if you were a moth, why would you ever get anywhere near *M. dizzydeani* or any of her relatives?

That is where the deception comes in. It turns out that this entire tribe of spiders is expert at manufacturing and releasing the sex pheromones of their moth prey. This is no easy task, since sex attractants are a quite species-specific concatenation of varied ingredients, often made through different enzymatic pathways and mixed in different proportions. Expose a moth to only half the dose of sex pheromone, and she will shrug her shoulders and move on. Expose her to the wrong mix of two ingredients, and she will likewise turn away. The bola spiders get it right: they make, mix, and vary the pheromone contents to bring their prey to the plate so they can bean them. The music of adaptation—how a creature fits perfectly into a world it did not make—is what delights the scientists of life. Who would have thought up a bolas spider?

Calling

What Is Sound?

When at night a watch cricket stops chirping in a Japanese house, the whole family wakes up to find out who has come in. The living—even when sleeping—query the air to learn that others are there, to learn where, to learn how, to learn why. Whether we are archaeans, aphids, or people, the senses are the means by which we come into communion with a world of change. Our human eyes shake, shimmy, shudder, and vibrate constantly at frequencies of up to a hundred hertz, so that even a still object is not still to our eyes. We sample a sight all over at all times. Scientist who have laboriously managed to cancel or compensate for this eye movement in experiments—erasing the variation in the signal—find that the subjects cannot see what is in front of them.

Exactly. Orientation—a sense of place, time, rhythm—is what holds us to the world and in it. Indeed, Humberto Maturana and Francisco Varela—two biologists from Chile—believe that it is only the constant mutual perception of the world's creatures by its creatures that makes the world be at all.

Sound holds a unique place among these queries that make our world around us. It is the archetype of pulsing, intermittent signals, because there is really nothing to it but variation. Sound is the product of vibrations that propagate through the air. (Unlike light, they will not propagate in a vacuum.) Sound is a pressure wave that radiates from its source, in pulses of alternating compressed and rarefied air. Apparatuses in living beings have developed to receive these waves, often by setting up a corresponding vibration that is transferred to a trembling fluid and thence translated through nerves. The variations in sound are nothing but regular variations in the pressure of the air.

Smell can be complex, but it is instantaneous. It mainly affects us by its mixture and its strength. Sight and touch appear to map and hold a world of identifiable others, the things we can call by name. Moreover, they provide narrative. They occur continuously and trace a moving world. Sound is likewise narrative—it has loudness, rhythm, qualities of richness, thinness, buzziness, deepness, purity, shrillness, scratchiness, all of which we summarize as timbre, pitch, volume, and tone—but although it points us at things, we do not mistake it for the thing. It is pure signal.

Sound has an astonishingly complex syntax. We speak of musical phrases, and musicologists speak too of sentences, of period, of ternary bits (not binary). This is an understatement, and even the syntax of a "Good MOR-*ning*" can put us in a good or foul mood, according to how it is inflected, how the syllables rise and fall, and the quality and speed of the voice that has spoken it. Even the hum of the air conditioner has a pulse that we respond to as a varying signal with a hundred meanings.

Sound has syntax, but its semantics—its level of meaning—is forever floating, present but untouchable and unseeable. It is like proportion in geometry. We know that we love how this building or painting looks, but we cannot exactly describe why. The why is hidden in the proportions. Likewise, humans around the world will agree on which musical tones are consonants—that is, what tones sound harmonious or "good" together. Strangely enough, this consonance corresponds to regular, repeating vibrations that are related to one another by ratios of whole numbers. Nonetheless, one culture will admire those "good" tones, while another will value every little dissonance as a mark of beauty, the way the mole on a woman's shoulder or the wrinkled skin of her toes makes her seem surpassingly beautiful.

The world of sound is the most mysterious of all the sensual worlds. When we listen to music, we—including those of us who cannot even grasp the rudiments of trigonometry or calculus—are transported into that mathematical realm of rates of change, of rise and fall, of many and few, of addition and multiplication and order of magnitude.

It is sad then that we now seem to be destroying our sonic life. Climate change is only one of the horrors that a civilization of rampant consumption has foisted on the world through the air. Every day I must travel through New York City and around the region looking at trees to earn a living. Every day I have the radio on to three different stations in a futile effort to learn what the traffic is like so I don't spend the whole day stuck on the road. As I flip the channels, I become more and more struck by the unvarying rhythms on the radio. This situation has got worse even over the fifteen years I have been doing this, and much more since the days when I used to travel cross-country.

You can easily do this experiment. Turn on FM radio. Start scanning channels. Count how many times you hear a heavy pounding beat. You will hear it on rock stations, on Latin stations, on black music stations, at sports events, even behind the news headlines on talk radio. It pounds out of the commercials and even on the country stations. You will find a little more modulation of beat and tone should you hit a jazz station, or a classical station, but especially during the day you are likely to get rocking jazz and horn-accented overtures. The Christian stations often sucker you in with a nice soft hymn, only to ask you for a donation the next minute. The only dependable place to hear an absence of the driving beat is in commercials that are trying to sell you some life-saving drug by telling you the story of a poor soul who was dying but was saved. Usually, such commercials prefer strummed-guitar folk music.

Federico García Lorca sensed and wrote about this beat long ago, in his *Poet in New York*, a book of poems responding to his sojourn in New York City and rural Vermont at the beginning of the Great Depression. The visit was shocking to a man who had grown up in southern Spain, where people still took four-hour lunch breaks, and where the highlight of the day was seeing your friends, not the big meeting with the client.

When I lived in García Lorca's Granada during 1976, I was struck in exactly the opposite way. Here was a place where people still valued rest, play, friendship, contemplation, to an extent that frankly shocked me. I remember one party in the Albaicin that lasted five days. It traveled from place to place, and we who belonged to it would simply pick up its trace and find it, coming and going as we pleased.

In García Lorca's 1929 New York—and much more in our own!— no one wanted to rest for even a moment. Anyone who tried, he suggested, was likely to be swept up, whipped into action, or put into a coffin and pushed out of the way. The rhythm of life in New York he described as "a single furious gesture of advance."

Try listening to our business radio stations, and this is exactly what you will hear. Though there is no backbeat playing behind the talk, it is indicated in the mantra. Almost every interviewee—whether a banker, a broker, a trader, or an economist—will say more than once the phrase "going forward." Going forward, we expect the price to rise by x percent. We hope that going forward, the trend will continue. Well, there was too much uncontrolled risk taking, but going forward . . .

I am not saying that money is the cause of this, but a relentless commercial culture most certainly abets it. Rest and contemplation are suspect; only continuous striving is permitted. Otherwise, there is the specter of failure. The ubiquitous big backbeat is this culture's signature. While it may enrich us in goods and services, going forward, it impoverishes our sonic life with an emotional pollution that makes it hard to hear and love any tempo that is not a solid *bum bum bum*. Fast or slow, back or front, but always *bum bum bum*.

Canids and many other creatures have better noses than we do. Birds see the ultraviolet tracks of voles. But we have among the finest ears in the animal kingdom. They ought not to atrophy. Our sonic life today is less lively than the ordinary conversation of parrots, the howling of wolves, or the clicking of bats and of the blind.

Parrot Duets

I knew a parrot in Venice many years ago. He was a Colombian exile. All day long he sat in a window overlooking a canal. When the fit took him, he would shout with his loudest call, "*Viva el partido liberal!*" No wonder he—or rather his master with him—had had to flee Colombia. With a bird trained like that, it would be hard to keep your feelings a secret.

This parrot did not know what he was saying, though he said it with gusto. But the African gray parrot Alex—trained by his mistress, psychologist Irene Pepperberg for thirty years—almost certainly did understand what he was saying, at least in a limited way. He could recognize a door key of a type he had never seen before and correctly call it a key. He created a new word for apple, "banerry," possibly believing it to be a cross between two fruits whose names he knew, the banana and the cherry.

Very impressive as this is, it betrays a strange and unwarranted anthropomorphism. Why should we teach a parrot to talk human, as though that were the only way in which a pair of beings could communicate intelligently? Why not listen to what parrots say among themselves? Indeed, the great student of the Central American yellow-naped Amazon parrot, Timothy Wright, has observed that his subjects have not only syntactical languages but also dialects. If a parrot moves from one place to another, he or she must sometimes learn a new dialect of yellow-naped Amazon.

But what are the requirements for such a language, or for any language? Three things: syntax, phonology, and semantics. Syntax is the ordering of sonic elements or repeated phrases in a way that has structure but that can be infinitely varied by elimination, super-addition, repetition, or substitution. Phonology is the production of certain ranges of sound with certain inflections, allowing for the recognition of syntactic elements as well as of emotional tone such as interrogation and exclamation. Semantics is the reason behind the other two. Why do it? What do we achieve by exchanging these patterns of sound through the transparent medium of the air between us? That is the hardest part to grasp.

Yellow-naped Amazon parrots live in dry forests, where they feed on seeds, everything from acorns to mangos. They make a mess when they eat, scattering the fruit everywhere to get to the tasty seeds, which they rip open with their hooked beak. These large parrots sleep by the hundreds in communal roosts that typically do not change from year to year, for decades or longer. But they live in pairs; they mate for life. The pair hunts together during the day, either alone or with a small group of pairs, although a great acorn-laden oak can gather quite a crowd of them. The couple nests in cavities of trees or palms, returning to the same nest every year. The two feed their young together, and when the young are fledged, they fly them back and forth to the roosting site so that the young birds can learn their way.

These parrots have a language that is also antiphonal song. The two members of the couple sing repeated duets, every morning and evening, at least. The male and female of the pair make their unique contribution to this music. There is a syntax common to the whole species for this communication, but there are many dialects, with varying phonology and phrasing.

Wright has extensively studied what he calls the northern dialect.

Here is how it goes. The duet begins with a pair of contact calls. Typically the female calls first and is answered by the male, whose call often begins just as the female's is ending. Thereafter, female and male notes are produced antiphonally, again with male following the female. The calls are specific to their sex. The opening contact call—a wawa—is the only note common to both sexes. Once the opening has been made, however, the two modulate to their sex-specific words. The female has a scree that begins with an upsweeping warble and ends with a noise. The male scree differs, and the male will also repeat the wawa within the duet, while the female will not. The male also has a distinctive word, "yoohoo." The transliteration "yoohoo" is a good representation of what happens, since there is little change in pitch, with two harmonic phrases.

As the talk or the song (or is it both?) goes on, the amount of noise in the screes tends to be shortened and its internal warbles lengthened. Likewise, the male's "yoohoos" tend to get longer and more melismatic in the "yoo." Elements can be repeated or eliminated, and can recur many times in a session with different patterns of warble and noise. A couple will typically run through seven or more of these duet sentences in a single event, which Wright calls a session.

There is unquestionably a syntax involved here—a structure that facilitates the communication by creating a set of expectations. And the variations in delivery and in the character of notes allow for infinite variations in the tone and extent of what is communicated. But what exactly is communicated?

This is not an easy question to answer, even in human communication, whose elements we better understand—hopefully. In the heyday of generative grammar, linguists like Jerrold Katz and Jerry Fodor sought the "semantic atoms" that they believed must underlie human syntax and phonology. In other words, they wanted to know how words come to mean. But they were unable to find the supposed atoms.

Noam Chomsky's famous sentence is a case in point. "Colorless green ideas sleep furiously," he wrote, is a sentence that is grammatical but meaningless. We in the poetic end of the linguistics department begged to differ. "Furious sleep" is enormously suggestive. Meaning seems to exceed and surpass any limits we try to place on it, because it is always and everywhere enacted in the instance of communication. It takes place, and the meaning emerges through the context.

What is true for human semantics is even more so for brute beasts, even the yellow-naped Amazons. When we see what appears to be fulsome communication among the animals, we tend to find a univocal explanation for it. Wright frankly says that he cannot say what these duets mean, but he lists the main possibilities: "maintenance of the pair-bond, joint defense of territory, and simultaneous acoustic advertisement and mate guarding." I suspect that the parrots are involved not just in one of these meanings, but in all of them in shifting proportions from moment to moment, just as humans are.

Here is an example. I recently went out to dinner with my wife and two friends. Originally, it was to be a dinner among one friend, my wife, and myself. Normally, my friend and I would meet alone for our dinners or we would meet with our wives, as two couples, but his wife was out of town. So we decided to dine together, the three of us at a local restaurant. When we arrived, a common friend was just coming in the door. He was alone, since his wife too was out of town. We invited him to join us, and we were four. Three guys and my wife. What a situation for mate guarding, particularly as my two male friends are uncommonly handsome, witty, and intelligent.

My wife immediately displayed what I regarded as acoustic advertising by mentioning a number of episodes relating to a previous boyfriend, and I was stimulated to mate guarding by recalling to her a number of episodes about which we agreed deep in our hearts. She spoke for me in raising an issue about fairness to political opponents, thus helping to maintain the pair-bond. My friends joined in eloquent acts of display, both noting the rightness of their indeed quite righteous opinions on an important issue of the day. Because of my daily contact with people whom they regard as political opponents (and total idiots), I jumped to the defense of these opponents, suggesting that they were not idiots but had many provocations to believe as they did. This was certainly acoustic advertisement on all of our parts. My wife did her best to side with me on an issue we have discussed repeatedly, exhibiting wonderful joint defense of territory.

In short, it was an interesting evening, and a good time was had by all. I put my credit card on the table at a certain point, to indicate that I had been up since five in the morning and was ready to retire to my roost. But that is certainly not all that the dinner was about. In each exchange, there was a wish to be in communion, to create a common and perhaps new understanding, to come out of the conceptual shells in which we live and experience life in a fresh way. At very few moments did we get there, but that is what conversation is about. It is many things at once, not just one meaning for one event.

Late in the dinner, the fourth friend started a story about his childhood and about how it had caused him to reject a very lucrative job because the job was dishonest. Sure, there was display involved in this, but sure too he was opening himself to expose something that had actually happened to him. These are the moments in a conversation that tend to stay with you and to influence reflection.

I am not trying to say that the yellow-naped Amazon is a reflective bird, or just like a human, but there is much more to all forms of communication than we are accustomed to think. The duets between parrot pairs may take place as a kind of contest with other nearby pairs. Perhaps indeed they are warning off the others, or asserting their right to their territory, or both. But the pairs also sing these duets when no other birds are near. Sometimes, I bet, they are simply singing, "You're with me, and I'm with you. Yoohoo, yoohoo, yoohoo."

The Answered Question

Bats ask and the universe answers. More than seven hundred species of bats continually send out their queries, at a rate of a couple-hundred calls per second. The echoes that the world sends back to them orient them in space and time, tell them what is out there, and guide them to their meals.

When sound reflects back to us from something in the world, it will sound as reverberation if the interval between the emission and the reflection is less than one-hundredth of a second. Reverberation makes the sound seem fuller, louder, more resonant. If the interval is longer, the ear will hear the source and the reflection as two different sounds, as an echo.

Bats depend on the lag and precisely measure the echo. A human can hear frequencies as high as twenty thousand vibrations per second (or hertz). A bat can hear frequencies six times higher, up to 120,000 hertz. The sounds it makes at these high frequencies reflect off an object as small as a moth, with no loss of signal strength. The time it takes for the signal to come back, and the rate at which that time interval changes, allow the bat to home in on the moth, even in the darkest night.

Lazzaro Spallanzani had first realized this in 1773. Noticing that bats seemed able to fly through dense foliage in the dark without crashing, he observed blind bats and saw that they too never collided with the world around them. Spallanzani was a Roman Catholic priest and wide-ranging scientist who also contended against the idea of spontaneous generation and for the idea that decay was caused by invisible microbes traveling through the air. Louis Pasteur would later confirm the Italian's ideas about microbes, but the priest's notion about bats was ridiculed by the famous naturalist Georges Cuvier as more in tune with faith than with sober science.

It wasn't until 1938 that Donald Griffin and Robert Galambos proved that Spallanzani had been right about bats too. They placed bats in a small room filled with slender, almost invisible wires running floor to ceiling. When the bats had shades over their eyes, they never hit a wire. When their ears were plugged or their mouths were taped shut, they crashed continually until they gave up trying to fly.

To establish that bats really were calling into the void, they used a tool made by Galambos's mentor, emeritus physics professor George Washington Pierce. It was a device that looked like a cross between an ice box and a Victrola. It translated the inaudible high-frequency calls of the bats into sounds that humans could hear. When they simply agitated bats in a cage, the two young scientists heard a buzzing from the machine recording the bats' response. When they released the bats to fly through the room full of wires, there was a cacophony of static from the machine. The evidence was telling, but it went so against the notion that humans as the crown of creation must be in every way superior to mere beasts, that one older scientist at the first meeting where Griffin and Galambos presented their findings grabbed Galambos by the lapels, to try to shake him back to his senses.

As it turns out, however, most bats know this trick that Griffin and Galambos first elucidated, and as a result the bats are the most widespread of all the orders of mammals. The bats send out high-frequency calls, and by the echoes they can sense the presence and exact location of what is around them. They know the position of stationary objects in space, their range and their position both vertically and horizontally. They can track a moving object, home in on it, and pounce.

For a bat, the world of fast aural vibration is more revealing than the human world of sight. Using a narrow-band, constant-frequency call for detecting objects at a distance, a bat can pick out a tiny insect by the aural glinting of its wings. If the insect's wings beat sixty times per second, the bat is likely to record six of those beats as an exciting decibel surge. As it closes in on the insect, the bat switches to a broadband, frequency-modulated (FM) signal. This sweeping acoustical barrage blankets the insect, giving the bat a spectral image of the texture, speed, and direction of its prey. Just before the bat reaches its victim, there is a constant buzz of soundings that guide the animal over the final centimeters to its goal.

Bats locate not only flying insects this way. Some bats fish for aquatic insects or even minnows. Their aural senses key on the echoes from tiny ripples in the water. Nectar-feeding bats are attracted to the wonderful, sound-focusing, cup-shaped leaves that have evolved in their favorite food sources to ensure that the bats will be guided to them so they can be pollinated. The cup shape focuses and perfectly reflects the incoming pulse of sound.

Insects, of course, would rather not be eaten, and their tympanum ears are especially sensitive to ultrasound calls. When the calls are of comparatively low frequency, the moth can theorize that the bat is still far off and seek to fly away. If the signal is high frequency, the moth might instead take sudden evasive action, figuring that otherwise it is about to meet an untimely end. Some tiger moths even put out their own ultrasound pulses, perhaps to jam the bat's sonar.

For a part of nature, then, the world of hearing is more powerful than the world of sight or smell. The strange thing is that not only bats and a few birds echolocate. We humans can do it too. To some extent, we all do. A carpenter knocks on sheetrock to find the studs. An arborist sounds a tree with a rubber hammer and listens to the response, to locate a hollow. A doctor listens for the tone that might indicate disease as he palpates the chest and the abdomen. A stranger knocking at a door theorizes about what is on the other side by hearing the sound of the echo inside. A person tells the distance from a thunderstorm by counting the seconds between a lightning flash and the rumble of thunder.

A few blind people, however, echolocate so well that they can hike, mountain bike, and play basketball, querying the world with clicks and getting their cues from its response. The click—usually made with the tongue against the palate—is of much lower frequency than the bat's inaudible high-frequency call. The bat wants to distinguish an insect a little more than an inch in length. Typically a person does not need such fine discrimination.

It is interesting to see this skill in action. These blind people might circle an object, clicking continually as they do so and turning their head first this way, then that way. Presumably, they are unconsciously determining the different times it takes for the echo to reach each ear as the ears themselves shift position. After a few ranging and clicking moments, they will identify what is before them.

Lore Thaler and colleagues at the University of Western Ontario studied two blind people with this skill—one who had been blind for most of his life and another who had lost his sight as a teenager. Both men were far more skillful at distinguishing what was before them by clicking echolocation than were two sighted control subjects who were blindfolded for the experiment. By closely observing brain activity in all the subjects, the researchers were able to learn that the echolocators were using the visual-processing part of the brain to make the aural distinctions of echolocation. They had, in short, invested a tremendous amount of gray matter—usually reserved for eyesight—in this new way of perceiving.

The skill evidently can be learned. One of the blind subjects in the experiment had in fact taught the skill to the other blind subject, and others have experimented with sighted people kept blindfolded for a week. As the temporarily blind became accustomed to their new state and as they were trained to listen and click, by the end of the week they had already advanced to a quick game of blind one on one.

Nothing in It but What Goes through It

One of the most beautiful buildings in Europe is the modest stone abbey of Sénanque, set in a small narrow valley in the Luberon mountains in the south of France. They have dressed up the environs with long rows of lavender in recent years, so the church seems to be cloaked in odorous pin stripes, but that isn't what I'm talking about. Sénanque is not so beautiful for its setting or for anything it contains. Sénanque is beautiful rather for what it does not contain. Like the human heart, it is an empty chamber. There is nothing in it that does not go through it. Sénanque was built for song. Indeed, you might say that the church is a musical instrument in which the choristers are the plucked strings or the vibrating reeds.

Music as we perceive it is based on the harmonic series. When you pluck a string or sing a note, along with the primary note come undertones, or harmonics, of the other vibrations related to it. The harmonics are related to the primary note by whole-number ratios that create what musicians call octaves, fifths, thirds. The resonance of all these tones sounding together when a note is played gives richness to the sound of the instrument. This is as true for the abbey of Sénanque as it is for the finest violin.

It is no accident that the building acts as an instrument. That is how it was planned. The designers had faith that harmony of proportion to the eye would bring harmony of sound to the ear. They were right. The builders of the twelfth century had few tools to help them set a building straight. They had a compass and a rule to do layout on paper. They had a knotted cord and a measuring stick—denominated in the length of palm, hand, and elbow—to help them lay out the structure on the ground or in the air. As a result, they depended far less on precise measure than we do, and far more on proportion. They could not get a line exact in length, but they could place it in relationship to other lines.

The most elegant proportion, the builders experienced, was also the simplest one. Just as consonance in music is perceived by vibrations that exist in simple, whole-number relations to one another, so in visual proportion they decided that harmony would come from simple, nested relationships of length, breadth, and height.

The simplest relationship, they thought, was an analogy with three terms.

$$A:B::B:C$$
$$2:4::4:8::8:16$$

Just to see the succession of numbers is settling and pleasant. But there is an even simpler and more elegant way to refine this relationship. It is an analogy that relates the three different quantities, but using only two terms.

$$A:B::B:(A+B)$$

One quantity is to a second quantity, as that second quantity is to the sum of the first and second quantities. This proportion acquired many names over the centuries—golden section, golden mean, golden ratio, divine proportion, the ratio of Phidias—but the Cistercian builders likely only knew it as the ratio of extreme and mean.

Is this relationship simpler or more complex than the three-term analogy? It is more complex because it makes an additional relationship inside one of the terms. But it is simpler because it uses only two, not three, different terms to establish the relationship. In short, it is *both* simpler and more complex. It nests complexity within simplicity.

Here is a canon of beauty. The ABC three-term proportion is apt at representing growth or decay. It multiplies or it divides. It is like a cell in this regard, growing more or less by replication in series. The golden section, on the other hand, implies its origin in every step of growth. There is an internal link that ties the terms together not only according to their relative size but also according to their origin.

One great achievement of Sénanque and the other pure Cistercian abbeys is that they use both forms of the analogy. The designers based the nave and sanctuary on two golden-section rectangles, and the transept on two ABC-analogy squares. The elevations of front and sides were likewise based on angles derived by linking the vertices of golden section rectangles. They embodied in their architecture their conviction that the origin, source, and eternity of the living came into relationship to what grows, decays, and passes.

Every day, eight times a day, the monks of Sénanque enacted the assertion by singing it in this very space. Bernard of Clairvaux, the Cistercian founder, knew that human desire and love must pass through the flesh to come to God. "Through the beauty of the sensible," he wrote, "the soul rises to the true beauty."

The great Gothic cathedrals now look pretty spare, but at one time they were brightly painted. Not so Sénanque. It was always unpolished and unpainted native stone. There were no statues, no gargoyles, not even any fluting in the columns. There were no tapestries or hangings. The windows were simple and small. At the crossing, where one might at least have expected four capitals at the four corners, there are instead four concave hemispheres in the stone.

There was only proportion and stone. In part, the founders may have wished to avoid distraction, but more important, every bit of Sénanque focuses its sound. The low unornamented dome of the crossing—itself raised on a golden section proportion—receives the music and reflects it back, spreading it evenly through the space. The concave capitals of the nave do the same, focusing sound, just as the cupped-shaped leaves of the fruit bat's food plants send back strong signals that the plant is waiting.

All the proportions of the building created a space that is acoustically alive. The rectilinear stone walls triangulate reflected sound, multiplying its strength. The whole building reverberates deeply, particularly in the frequencies at which Gregorian chants were sung. The reverberation not only makes the sound full but also brings out the harmonics, so although Europe was still a century or more away from polyphony, the singing had a rich, polyphonic resonance.

In this and the other Cistercian abbeys, it was impossible to preach a sermon. The acoustics were so resonant that the first word would come back at you a dozen times while the second was in the air. Even a whisper would resonate through the halls. The abbeys had to have a separate hall in which the abbot preached, and where the monks made their plans for work.

The Cistercians admitted only ten tones to their singing of the psalms. There was no organ or any other instrument in their churches. (A great Cistercian, Aelred of Rievaulx, spoke of an organ as "the terrible snorting of a bellows, more like a clap of thunder than the sweetness of a voice.") They sang the purest Gregorian plain chant that they could muster.

Recently, a slender young woman with straight black hair and in a short black coat visited Sénanque. As she walked near the crossing, she began to sing. She sang intervals reminiscent of Thomas Aquinas's melody "Adoro te devote." She was alone and she did not even stand still, yet the resonance of the space—the open physical proportion reflecting sound from the top and sides of the church into the crossing—made her single voice into a group of voices and made a solo sound like a choir.

Imagine what it would be like to be a choir of monks singing the psalms at Matins, Lauds, Prime, Terce, Sext, None, Vespers, and Compline. I am sure that, like everything on this earth, on some days the songs sounded very old and tired, but on others the music taught them as very few other things on our planet might teach: that the harmony of one sense responds to the harmony of another. The proportions we see in Sénanque translate directly into the songs we hear. Sight and sound share this canon of beauty: an irresolvable and inexplicable order that gives back more than it takes.

Enchanted

Songs, prayers, incantations, poems—all open a channel that we hope will make the thing they sing about be so. There is something to the enactment of words with their rhythms that lends them power. The word "enchanted," in its origin, means "brought into being by song."

A song requires two things: breath and a listener. Nothing can be said without exhaling. Try it. It is very frustrating. The air leaks out of you as you try to vocalize. You must release your breath to say, to chant, to shout, to sing. And for there to be a word, an invocation, a call, a song, there must be a listener, a creature with a vibratory apparatus attuned to receiving and encoding what you have just spoken into space or yodeled across a canyon half a mile wide. Of course, you can listen to yourself, but then you simply play both roles. The point is that these acts suppose or create a community and thus a world.

In Genesis, God speaks the whole universe into being. "Let there be," he proclaims, and in that moment what he says is so. John will later characterize the Creation and maintenance of the world as the work of the Word. The Kabbalists will ever after seek the original words by which all things were made. Aquinas will conceive that in God each word is instantly enacted in the universe at large. But human naming also has power. (In the Abrahamic traditions, at least, humans are said to be made in the image of God, that is, to be in some ways like Him.)

The most powerful singer of antiquity, however, had no Judeo-Christian roots. Said to have been the son of Apollo and Calliope, Orpheus was a mortal, but he played the lyre and sang so sweetly that the beasts left off devouring one another and lay down together to listen. Mountains softened and leaned toward him. Trees uprooted themselves and gathered at his side. When he went to hell to recover his lost wife, Eurydice, Sisyphus stopped pushing his stone and sat down on it to listen; the eagle stopped eating the entrails of Prometheus to lend an ear; Charon quit poling his ferry and sat down in the stern. When Orpheus sang of his sorrow and his loss, the Furies cried for the first and only time, and Hades and Persephone gave him back his bride.

Not for long, it is true, but among mortals the songs of Orpheus have had the highest prestige for almost thirty centuries. Indeed, some Christians tried to claim dignity for Christ by calling him the Divine Orpheus. When in the sixteenth century Marsilio Ficino translated what he thought to be Orpheus's original songs, the Florentine philosopher took up his lute and sought to make of himself a second Orpheus.

Ficino was an intimate of the powerful Medici family, for whom he had translated both Plato and hermetic texts including the *Asclepias* of Hermes Trismegistus and the Hymns of Orpheus. He set out to heal by means of song. Following texts that he regarded as ancient—predating Moses and Plato—he conceived that the universe was constructed on three levels: the formless intellectual realm of the Invisible Creator; the middle world of the stars and their angels; and the lower world of matter, species, form.

There was no pejorative attached to matter, but he believed that matter depended for its sustenance and renewal on the two levels above it. In particular, the *spiritus mundi*—a very light and hot air said to descend from each star and each of the seven spheres of our system—was what gave each material species its form and kept it in being. The Orphic Hymns, as translated by Ficino, were invocations to the lords of *spiritus* and to their attributes. There were hymns to night, to heaven, to the stars, to the moon, to Jupiter and Juno, Neptune and Pluto, Jove as the Thunderer, Jove as the maker of lightning, Proserpine, Mercury, Apollo, Bacchus, Tethys, Semele . . .

In his work as a healer, Ficino chose the appropriate song and played it on his lyre while he sang to his patient. Often, there would be a prescribed incense to accompany the song. The words and tune together were not meant to compel the gods to help. Rather, they were meant to open the hearts and minds of the listeners to the high realm, so the *spiritus* could flow from the heavens and heal them. In this, Ficino believed, he was only following his master Orpheus, whose words he used, by taking his listeners out of the world of daily thought and into a world of higher act, a world of enchantment.

Ficino was polite compared to his contemporary Giordano Bruno. In his *Incantations of Circe*, Bruno created a detailed set of incantations in which his heroine Circe cited the qualities, the names, the important places, and the titular animals belonging to each of the deities, in order to enlist their aid against unjust and beastly men. Again, this is not so much a forcing of the gods to act as it is the creation of a palace of words and images into which the gods may come to meet and help us. In Bruno's work, Circe indeed turns men into animals—as she did to the crew of Odysseus—but for Bruno, her just purpose was to reveal in evil men their real beastly natures. Although the words are set in the mouth of Circe, Bruno clearly agrees with her. Indeed, he wrote the book in part to vindicate her magic.

The incantations do not read like poetry so much as they do like immense shopping lists, but try to read the original Latin out loud. I think that Bruno created a poetry of lists. For Venus, he began with the birds and animals he regarded as sacred to her:

Oro te, prome tuas columbas, turtures, pavones, ficedulas, galgulos, passeres, pelecanes, harpas, pifices, olores, cygnos, palumbos, sturnos, chenalopices, & non nominatas aves tuas. Lepores, hinnulos, equas, formicas, fringillas, caeteraque specierum istarum animantia. Phocam, ruticillam, sagum, vitulum & vndicola tibi natantia

What an astonishing pile of life! It is like one of those paintings heaped with foods of all kinds. It fills the mouth with words. He goes on to praise her qualities:

Venus alma, formosa, pulcherrima, amica, benevola, gratiosa, dulcis, amena, candida, siderea, dionea, olens, iocosa, aphrogenia, foecunda, ignita, conciliatrix maxima, susceptrix optima, amorum domina, harmoniarum ministra, musicalium dictatrix, blanditiarum praeposita, saltationum moderatrix, ornamentorum effectrix, vniuersorum compago, rerum vinculum

Frances Yates pointed out how much Bruno relied on the similar lists made by Cornelius Agrippa in his *De Occulta Philosophia*, but as like as they are in the piling on of words, there is a great difference. Agrippa's Venus exists to be fecund. After a line or two of praise, he quickly gets to the point: she is the source of children, the beginner of parents, the principle that gave rise to the great diversity of life and the variety of animals. She is, in short, a highly placed functionary.

But Bruno's Venus is "nurturing, shapely, surpassingly beautiful, friendly, benevolent, gracious, sweet, willing, pure, starbright, heavenly, daughter of Diona, odorous, playful, fecund, beneficent, quiet, delicious, ingenious, fiery, best of conciliators, mother of luck, mistress of love, minister of harmony, singer of music, . . . governess of dance, maker of adornments, the universal matchmaker, the binder of all things." This Venus is not a functionary, but a living being, and Bruno's massive homage is itself a love poem. Indeed, this is perhaps the sexiest incantation ever written, beginning with a long list of adjectives that perfume her with every loveliness, and continuing with a dancing set of two-word Latin phrases that praise her powers.

The Renaissance Neoplatonists—Ficino, Bruno, Agrippa, Pico, Dee, and others—had a whole philosophy to back their magic. Their books were collected by princes, and their systems of talismans and of magic memory learned by the wealthy. Ficino treated Medicis, not millers. But in fact, they were all wrong about the *spiritus mundi*. They conceived it to be some particularly fine kind of air. It just *had* to have substance. (For centuries afterward, following Ficino and company, early scientists would fruitlessly pursue the elusive ether.) They could not grasp that this power of incantation comes not from some fine material that it conjures but from a relationship that it invokes.

Fortunately, the conviction that the enacted word can change the world was not limited to any class or culture. It is as widespread among humans as is echolocation among bats. Millions who reflected little on its origin made daily use of it.

The folklorist Alexander Carmichael traveled the highlands and the Scottish isles at the turn of the twentieth century, collecting prayers from a largely illiterate people. Many were formal incantations, meant to accompany the day's work: lighting the fire, caring for the animals, helping a ewe to give birth, feeding the family, starting the fire, rising in the morning, going to bed at night. Each song called on the powers of heaven to accompany the acts and to help bring them to a happy conclusion.

It was no trivial matter to start a fire on a treeless windswept island during an Atlantic gale. Once a wife had her fire going, she did not want it to go out ever or at all. (Well, those who celebrated Beltane let it go out once a year, so they could relight it with the new fire, brought from the community hearth.) On every evening, but that one, she would divide the embers in the circular hearth at the center of the home into three equal sections, leaving a small complete circle in the center. She would lay down peat between each of the sections, one in the name of the God of Life, one in the name of the God of Peace, one in the name of the God of Grace. She would cover the whole preparation with a light layer of ash, which would keep the fire smoldering until morning. When she was finished, she would recite an incantation.

Carmichael recorded three different incantatory prayers for this process, which in Scottish was called smooring. One of them went like this:

The sacred Three
To save,
To shield,
To surround
The hearth,
The house,
The household,
This eve,
This night,
Oh! this eve,
This night,
And every night,
Each single night.
Amen.

Another of the smooring chants calls on an angel to watch over the fireplace:

An angel white
In charge of the hearth

Til bright day comes
To the embers.

The chants were not a substitute for careful work, nor a guarantee of it. They were rather, like Ficino's songs or Bruno's brimful lists, a use of the product of breath to bring heaven and earth into harmony.

It is easy to believe that this use of language is long gone now, an artifact of the days before science and matches and pilot lights, an example of superstition, but it is not necessarily so. Incantation is woven into our daily lives so closely that we do not even notice it. I am not talking about the perversions of song occasioned by advertisers. I am talking about "good-bye" and "hello," about "good night" and "good morning," about phrases like "sleep tight / don't let the bedbugs bite" and "see you later, alligator / after 'while, crocodile." Each of these expresses faith and calls for its fulfillment. By a formula said out loud, it enacts communion and calls on it to continue. As automatic as it may be, it is one of those small daily acts of love.

My paternal grandmother was from Texas. She had an accent that seemed to slow her speech to half the speed of ordinary mortals. When she came to visit us, she always came into my room to say good night. "Good night, lamb pie!" she would say from the doorway. It seemed to take her about a minute to get out those four simple words. Guuuuuuuuud naaaaight, lammmmmmmmb paiaiaiaiai. After Gammy's good nights, I could usually fall right asleep, and although I might well still have nightmares, I did not lose sleep from the fear that they would come.

Sonata Form and Chaos

*If all musical sounds were to be forever silenced—orchestras, bands,
human voices, birds & insects—and I were allowed to retain one
sound to cheer me, I would ask that the wind might play in the tree-
tops. The wind! Motion is life. All is dead that stands still.*

—*Charles Burchfield, summer 1914*

Music stops thought. It comes into us through the air, but it
takes us out of ourselves.

Sometimes, I have trouble sleeping after about three in the morning. I wake up and start thinking, worrying, troubling, doubting . . .
A friend told me that I should think of having sex. That worked once
or twice. It shut off the worry. But what works best, I find, are piano
sonatas. I have been listening to so many of them that now they
come to me unbidden. When I wake, I hear the flow and cadence
of Haydn's Piano Sonata No. 4 in G major, or Mozart's No. 14 in
C Minor, or Beethoven's No. 1 in F minor. Sometimes, I mix them
or switch one for the other. They stop me from thinking, and I sleep
again. I realize that Haydn, Mozart, and Beethoven might not have
been entirely gratified to hear that a postmodern geezer was using
their great music as a sleep aid. Oh well, I remember the music during
the day as well. It comes to me along with last Sunday's hymns.

The Beethoven sometimes puts me back into a large room with a marble-lintel fireplace, a piano that was never played, a sofa covered with sewn-in effigies of leaves and bugs, a few easy chairs with bright striped upholstery, the big fireplace flanked by two hurricane lamps that never once were used, and the very deep-piled white carpet with its light pileus of dog hair. My tall, slender, long-necked mother would be there too. She moved like a great blue heron, stepping deliberately. Her head did something between a dart and a jerk when she shifted it. It seemed that it was a little too large for her slim neck. Not that she was not beautiful, but in my experience she was very often uncomfortable. I felt that she did not quite fit into her own skin, and that she was aware of this unfortunate situation. When she sat down on the edge of the lawn to weed the flower beds, she seemed to fold up into herself.

She was an expert in duty and in worry. The two together drove her nuts. She typically had to anesthetize them at evening with a couple martinis and a glass of wine. From an early age, I learned to make a good martini. I knew the vermouth, the olive or the onion, and the little stir she liked. As she and I grew older, the recipe changed. When I came home from college one year, I noticed there was no vermouth. She told me she didn't use it anymore. Nor olive nor onion. Just vodka. And she was buying the store brand. She didn't drink much more than she had, but it was evident that the fun had gone out of even that.

The one pleasure she allowed herself was music. I remember sitting in that living room with her again and again listening to Verdi or Berlioz, but particularly to Beethoven. When the first two thunderclaps of the Eroica sounded, her eyes were shining, and by the end of the eighth bar, she was in tears. Perhaps in part because of its effect on my mother, I was instantly drawn to Beethoven.

I liked a lot of other music too. I carried my transistor radio on my belt while I was mowing the lawn. Since I used a push mower, I could hear the music. I loved the driving rhythm of "giddyup, giddyup 4-0-9" in the Beach Boys' song, especially when it was followed by a slow and soulful harmonic ballad like "Surfer Girl." In Beethoven, I seemed to get these different pleasures all rolled into a single, uninterrupted piece of music. What is more, all the different tempos, timbres, rhythms, instruments, inversions, deletions, rises, and falls were somehow inscrutably related.

When I left home a couple years later, I had in my possession a great gift from my parents: the complete Beethoven symphonies in a boxed set. I can still see the cover in my mind's eye, Herbert von Karajan and the Berlin Philharmonic. There was a picture of the conductor looking as romantically disheveled as a German could manage. I listened to those records until the box had broken at two corners and the cover picture was peeling off.

Certainly, the music reminded me of home, but also as I came to know some of it by heart, I found that I could inhabit it. On the one-hundredth hearing, I was no less moved by how surely it seemed to process through such doubtful turns and through such sudden dynamics, through twists of melodic weaving, then breaking into staccato phrases, then reweaving with a whole different range of instruments or in a different key or register.

Suddenly, I stopped. For two decades afterward, I completely lost touch with classical music. Don't ask me why. It probably had something to do with leaving home and mating. I came back gradually, backing into it through the radio. As I drove around town, the relentless beat of the sound on every station made me frantic. I was reduced to listening to the classical station, where at least the drumbeat of progress would occasionally give way to a slow dance.

I think it was a Haydn piano sonata that caught me again. I was stuck in traffic and getting ready to explode when it came on. It was so clean and clear. The theme was simple. It did not strain to evoke some mood or storm. It passed from high to low, got broken into parts, turned upside down, run into a repetitive string, then passed back and forth and up and down. It settled for a moment in a lovely cadence. Then something else began—slower, more meditative, in another key, but somehow related. Finally, it came back to the opening theme and ended with a flourish. When it was over, I noticed that I was once again driving at the speed limit, and that I could not remember where all the traffic had gone.

I was hooked once more. I have since particularly come to love the sonata allegro form, not in preference to all the other parts of a sonata or a symphony or a concerto, but as their archetype. In this supple, dependable but ever so changeable form is summarized what has always delighted me in classical music.

Sonata form is like the great weather systems. It enacts what is at once predictable and unknowable. Like an extratropical cyclone as it sweeps over North America, a movement in sonata form plays the border between order and disorder. It rehearses repetition, modulation, sudden change, intense falling, speeding and slowing, the vast pleasure of taunting partial repetition and the momentary contentment of restatement.

In the music as in the weather, the opening theme is simple and universal. An eddy begins to form, and its fronts to differentiate. A string of notes—sometimes as few as three—makes a melodic statement. The first high cirrus floats in, presaging the lowering of the clouds and the arrival of stratus and rain.

It seems that the possibilities are endless, but they are actually constrained by the prevailing westerly winds and by the boundary along which the fronts meet. Likewise, the music seems free but is constrained within universal bounds. All over the world the same pentatonic scale made by the overtones that are created when a string is plucked or a bugle blown makes music to the human ear. Some cultures prefer some keys, some another. Some use more of the overtones, some fewer. (The first overtone is an octave, and because men and women typically sound an octave apart, it is tempting to think of music beginning with the singing of octaves and then one by one bringing in the fifths and thirds and other overtones.) Some prefer more dissonance in a tune, some less. But all recognize the overtone series, and all know the difference between consonance and dissonance.

The opening theme calls out one from the twelve possible keys, by using the notes that comprise it. Sometimes, the theme will leave out the main tonic note or interpolate a stranger, but if it does so, it is the more excitingly to bring in the satisfying home note a little bit later.

Early writers about the sonata form counseled composers not to seek some perfect, evocative melody for their theme. Rather, they wrote, begin with a simple theme, something memorable so people will know when it comes back, but malleable so you can work upon it all the changes that will make the real beauty of the piece.

The development of a cyclone depends on the evolving relationship between a circle and triad. The eddy spins counterclockwise, carrying the fronts. But the cold, warm, and occluded fronts evolve not only because of the eddies but also because of the character of what arrives from outside. Together, they create the unique sequence of disturbances that constitute this particular storm. Likewise, the sonata depends on the fertile marriage of a rounded form and a trio of ideas. The theme sets out a home key, tours through the development into at least two or three other, related keys, and finally returns everything to the home key. Within this circle, however, there are three parts to the theme: first, the exposition that lays out the theme and home key, then transitions into a related key, creating tension; second, a development that reworks the theme and introduces new material in the new keys; and third, a restatement of the new material and the original theme in the original, tonic key.

Like a great storm, a fine movement in sonata form makes the pattern, but with a spin that you feel has never happened before and will never happen again. A theme can appear in a rising tone only to be answered by the same notes falling. It can be expanded by repetition, or be broken into separate phrases and recombined. The same musical motif can be taken up by different instruments at the same time in different registers, with different tones, and at different speeds, so that counterpoint is created. A theme can be inverted or two themes joined. One can be elided and another expanded or augmented. Two themes can be embedded in the same phrase. All the while the movement is pursuing its journey from the tonic key to the key of the fifth, to other keys, and then back again, as the wind blows the storm from west to east, turning its cyclone in a counterclockwise gyre.

How to describe this pleasure? It is intellectual, emotional, visceral, mathematical, syntactical. Like the songs of Ficino or the incantations of Bruno, it lifts us from a world that can be confined by assumptions and explanations into one where only experience brings meaning, and where meaning is constituted not by one phrase or thought but by the whole act of making and hearing.

The Aeolian Harp

The air can play the harp. When a steady wind blows over taut strings—or even over telephone lines or ship's cable—it can vibrate the strings side to side. Lord Rayleigh—the same person who gave the first convincing explanation of why some of the sky is blue—was the first to understand the phenomenon. He understood that the steady wind, when it meets the blunt edge of the string, swirls around both sides. Behind the string, there arises what is wonderfully called a "vortex street." Because the first man to study it was Theodore von Kármán, it is properly called Kármán's vortex street. It is a street that bends alternatively to one side and then the other behind the obstacle around which it passes. This alternate motion will make a slender and moveable obstacle vibrate as the vortex shifts from side to side.

Hence, the wind harp. Ralph Waldo Emerson, who was so delighted by the Aeolian harp that he kept one in his study window, wrote, "It trembles to the cosmic breath / as it heareth, so it saith / Obeying meek the Primal Cause / It is the tongue of mundane laws." For about a century, the Aeolian harp was popular in the cultured homes of northern Europe. Some who had read Tobias Smollett's *Adventures of Ferdinand Count Fathom* may have lamented the count's reprehensible lack of a moral sense, but been impressed by the success with which he seduced the beautiful young Celinda through the use of the ravishing melodies of the Aeolian harp. Such harps were a popular gift to the beloved from her swain.

How ravishing were the melodies? Some who have the harps today can hardly get them to play, but this is usually because they need a strong and steady breeze. Often it is better to have them a bit aloft as the air along the ground is frequently full of turbulent eddies. When they do play, however, the sound is haunting, both because you do not know when it will start or stop and because as it continues it plays all the overtones of the string. Remember that the universal language of music is drawn from the overtone series, and that a vibrating string, if it goes long enough, will vibrate in all its different sections, producing all the tones possible on its length. The first three overtones—octave, third, and fifth—create the major scale. Beyond them lie tones that sound sometimes haunting, sometimes sad, sometimes screeching and dissonant. If the wind is steady, you are likely to hear them all.

This sound was not really music, but it was the condition of vibration and ear that made music possible. The harp's innocence and naturalness likely helped it to seduce, as well as the chance that the maiden would put it in her bedroom window upstairs, thus having a nightly reminder of your devotion (and your possible wish to join her there). But it was not as an instrument of seduction that the Aeolian harp was best known. It was adopted by poets from James Thomson to Samuel Taylor Coleridge and William Wordsworth, to Emerson, as an emblem of something they longed for but could not quite grasp. To the poets, the Aeolian harp was about the reception of a truth inaccessible to science. It was quite literally about inspiration, since it was the breath of the wind that made it play, just as in a wind the spirit had descended on the Apostles at Pentecost and allowed them to speak truths that everyone from every place could understand.

The Aeolian harp waits patiently for the right wind, and sounds according to what that wind dictates. It is perfectly receptive. Emerson recorded with delight a question from his young son about the

Aeolian harp that he had in his study: "Waldo asks if the strings of the harp open when he touches them."

To be open to what nature brings was what the Romantic poets most wanted. Coleridge wrote that perhaps all beings received their thoughts and feelings in this way and so sounded as the harp. Shelley thought that all men were played upon by a constant stream of internal and external impressions, and that it was the work of the poet to make harmony of the inner melody they receive. In his "Ode to the West Wind," however, he forgot himself, asking the wind to make of him its lyre, just as it made the forest moan.

Breathing

The Tarpon's Breath

I was about sixteen years old. I stood a few feet back from the edge of a sheer cliff. There was a rope attached to two big tree stumps that snaked its way to the edge and then fell into the abyss. Beside me, an older man had just stepped into a figure-eight sling, hooked a bright blue rope through the carabiner on the sling, slung the free end of the rope over his shoulder, and jumped off the cliff. I watched him spring quickly down the face, first to one side, then the other, taking the force as he came into the cliff by flexing his knees. They call this rappelling.

I almost fainted when he jumped. First, because it looked like suicide. Second, because I was next in line. They hooked me up in just the same way and showed me how to hold the rope and how to angle my body. They advised me to take it easy. Soon I would get used to it. I tried to sit on the edge and slide off, as though I were entering a swimming pool. No, they said, you'll never manage it that way. I stood on the edge, leaned back on the rope, saw the open air beneath me. When I leaned out into empty space to about a thirty-degree angle, I pulled on the rope and stood back up straight. I think I was trembling. This was not going to work.

Once you let go, they said, you will be fine. The very phrase "let go" filled me with terror.

On the third or fourth try, I finally stepped over the edge. The rope held me. I crept down the face, playing out line as I went. Once or twice, I lost my footing and ended up hugging the face. Laboriously, I stood out from the face again, making a triangle whose sides were the cliff, my body, and the rope. The rope was the lengthening hypotenuse. It took me about fifteen minutes to get down the eighty feet to the bottom of the pitch. My hands hurt, my shoulder hurt, my back hurt, and I was so tense that had you touched me, you would probably have plucked a note.

Less than a week later, I was hooking up, taking a flying jump, and caroming down the same face, seeing how far from the cliff I could spring. Because the pitch was broad, we sometimes rappelled in pairs, each of us trying to outdo the other in jumping and in speed. This was likely a very bad idea, but we survived it. For all the years that I climbed after this time, rappelling was my favorite part. I think the exquisite adaptation of living beings to the place they must live has as much of this adventure in it as it does of sheer need. The beginning of variation is trying something new.

Breath turns a place into a habitat. If you can breathe there, you can live there. The living have succeeded in occupying the entire air, from bottom to top—an area four times as great as all the water in the oceans—and over the full range of possible climates. An isopod lives happily an inch beneath Sahara sands, while a Rüppell's griffon, a vulture, flies at an altitude of thirty-six thousand feet (one was sucked into a jet engine above the Ivory Coast). There are tide pool mollusks that breathe water when the wave rolls in, and breathe air when the wave rolls out. Fish, worms, mollusks, and aquatic insects in Ugandan swamps have been air breathers since the Devonian. A turtle can hold its breath for months. Some salamanders have lungs, others have gills, many breathe through their skin, and some can do all three.

Darwin used the pigeon breeder as a proxy for natural selection, but when it comes to breath, human breeding can be worse than inefficient. Turkey breeders want more and more meat per turkey, which is obviously a good thing for the consumer, so they select generation after generation of turkeys for a greater proportion of meat to organs. All is well until the super turkey suffers a fright, runs around in terror, and suddenly dies when its aorta explodes. The volume of flesh outran the bloodstream's ability to supply it with oxygen.

Natural variation has about it an element of adventure, not planning. It goes where none has gone before. Consider the tarpon. When I was a boy, I had a fetish for tarpon because my parents took me to a restaurant in Port Aransas, Texas, called the Tarpon Inn. The walls of that restaurant were papered with tarpon scales, each inscribed with the name of the person who caught the fish, the date, and the weight of the fish. Each of these scales was as big as my five-year-old palm. I thought tarpon must be immense and powerful. I longed to catch one. I imagined them to be fierce and solitary. In fact, they are social and gregarious. And they have an unusual talent. Like most fish, they have an air bladder that can be filled or emptied in order to adjust their buoyancy. This way, a fish swimming at depth can adjust the bladder to maintain itself at that depth without other effort.

The tarpon takes in air through the mouth, a primitive feature in fish. It must rise to the surface to refill, whereas the more evolved fish can refill the bladder with air from their bloodstreams at depth. But the primitive tarpon has developed a rare ability. Its air bladder also has four rows of honeycombed spongy vascular tissue. Air passing through this tissue transfers its oxygen to the tarpon's blood cells. The blood carries the oxygen through the fish's body. In short, the tarpon has a basic lung.

Gills are easy to use because they don't dry out. All oxygen—whether delivered by lungs or gills in animals—must be delivered moist, so a dry gas-exchange organ won't work. If a lung were on the surface of our bodies as gills are on the surface of a fish, we would lose about 133 gallons of body water per day. A lung has to defend its wetness. On the other hand, lungs are terrifically more efficient than are gills, because there is forty times more oxygen in a quart of air than there is in a quart of water.

Tarpon did not convert exclusively to lung breathing, but they have learned to do both. An adult tarpon has a mouth as big as a five-gallon bucket, but the fry start life slender and transparent, with tiny heads, rather like little pennants or streamers. They are spawned offshore, but for some reason they drift inshore, sometimes into swamps or even into water that becomes seasonally landlocked, where oxygen levels can drop below the minimum needed to sustain fishy life. These low-oxygen environments are the nurseries for young tarpon, where they live the first year of their lives. (Tarpon have a life span of thirty to fifty years.)

From the beginning, they supplement gill breathing with air breathing. A young fish rises to the surface every five minutes or so to gulp air into its bladder-like lung or lung-like bladder. If it doesn't do this, it will die. Adult tarpon, which usually live in better-oxygenated waters, still breathe air. The fish is nicknamed silver king, for the flash a watcher sees when the tarpon rises and rolls on the surface, or jumps into the air.

This air-breathing behavior may give tarpon a reproductive advantage, since their young grow up along banks and in swamps where predatory fish are less common and more easily evaded. On the other hand, the shallow water makes tarpon a tempting target for fishing birds, and alligators eat large numbers of them. Perhaps tarpon breath is also the consequence of adventure, of one or ten or a hundred episodes of swimming along and ending up willy-nilly in this interesting but awful low-oxygen water. Ninety-nine times the fry died of it. One or more times they did not.

Given their vulnerability to birds, young tarpon do something inexplicable from the point of view of pure adaptation. They get together in groups to exercise their bladder lungs, as though they were teenagers responding to the suggestion, "Hey, let's go down to the mangrove roots and breathe air!" Three times out of four, when one young tarpon rises to the surface to breathe air, at least one other fish will follow within one second. Sometimes, a dozen will rise, one after another. Even though no single fish needs to rise more than once every five minutes to get the oxygen it requires, they can keep up the rising game for hours.

Researchers Arthur Schlaifer and C. M. Breder studied this behavior in the 1940s. They used not only live fish but also red rubber tubing and even a glass rod. If the tubing or the rod swam to the surface in the right way—its "head" angling up and "tail" angling down as it rose—then young tarpon would follow it. They just love to rise.

Fenchel's Dance

The first living things on earth breathed all right, but they did not breathe oxygen. When oxygen first appeared, it was to them a toxic pollutant. Biologist Lynn Margulis refers to the "oxygen holocaust." The rise of free oxygen in the air poisoned the astonishing diversity of living organisms that existed *prior* to this event. Dramatic as it sounds, however, this holocaust did not eliminate the ultimate ancestors of the living. It sent them to live in refuges that the pollutant cannot reach. There, they still thrive today. And there they show a world of life where sharing and exchange are as important as devouring. It is a world of flexibility and cooperation.

Wherever the music of variation may lead—from the simplest archaean organism exchanging electrons with a ferric iron, to the barheaded goose breathing the thinnest air at thirty thousand feet above the Himalayas, to the honeybee generating from its spiracled breath the greatest strength gram for gram in the whole animal kingdom, to the child who sleeps against its mother's breast—the indispensable mediator is respiration. Breath requires an exchange. It requires an inside and outside, and it requires give-and-take. A breath of air comes across a membrane, interacts with an inside, exchanges its elements with others from both inside and outside, and returns to the outside, bearing the products of its exchange. The process transforms food into energy for the breather, and the breather can thus live and grow. What the breather breathes out, as often as not, some other creature breathes in. Reproduction is consequent, not precedent, to this activity. Both the chicken and the egg come second.

We are accustomed to associate respiration with the bellows of our mammalian lungs, with the intake of oxygen and the output of carbon dioxide. But when life began on earth, oxygen was comparatively rare, and living in the open air bombarded by ultraviolet radiation was impossible. The first creatures lived protected by an envelope of water. They took their air from it. Most of the early air came from volcanoes, some of them belching under the sea, some erupting into the air. They provide carbon dioxide, hydrogen, ferric iron, sulfur, sulfate, hydrogen sulfide. The first to breathe breathed these. These creatures were not rare or struggling. They were diverse, common, thriving. They depended on one another. Indeed, they sometimes became one another. And all you have to do is dig a little in the mud to find them at work today.

The Danish ecologist Tom Fenchel has been doing this for more than a quarter century. He once examined a sliver of muddy sand about the size of a little finger, taken from a shallow bay near Copenhagen. In it he found about forty billion archaeans and bacteria, about a hundred million photosynthesizers (including cyanobacteria, diatoms, and others), around ten thousand amoebae and flagellates (tiny protists that move by waving their tails), another two to four thousand ciliates (protists that move by rhythmically waving little hairs called cilia), and the occasional passing giant of a clam, a springtail, or a bristle worm. And all of them were engaged in a dance, making and changing partners.

The bay bottom is a shallow, churning landscape, where opportunity and disaster are near neighbors. A big storm stirs the bottom sands, mixing oxygen deeper and killing millions who cannot bear it and cannot escape deeper still. A polychaete worm burrows down four inches. Oxygen seeps in along its channel, and the whole community beside the hole must flee or change. When bright daylight comes, the cyanobacteria residing in a blue-green mat on the surface photosynthesize like crazy, and the zone of oxygenated sand creeps deeper, causing havoc among those to whom oxygen means death. At night, the pressure relaxes, and the oxygen-free zone climbs almost to the top of the sediment.

The surface of the bay is six feet above where Fenchel found his sliver. Patches of green eelgrass, attached to the sandy bottom, wave in the moving water. Dead eelgrass decays on the bottom. Here and there, the sand is covered with a blanket of bright red or pink, a mat made of billions of photosynthetic sulfur bacteria; a fuzzy blue-green mat of cyanobacteria; or a yellow-brown sand full of diatoms. A little brant goose dives, ripping up and swallowing the green spaghetti of the eelgrass.

There is a whole world in that finger's worth of sand. The creatures there are tiny compared to us, but they encompass a size range about the same as that of the vertebrates. The smallest of the bacteria are about half a micron in diameter. (There are 25,400 microns in an inch, a little more than six hundred in the period at the end of this sentence.) The very largest of the ciliates are about a millimeter long. Thus, the biggest creatures in this little world are a thousand times bigger than the smallest, about the same as the difference in size between a shrew and whale.

And the world they inhabit is about the same size to them as ours is to us. Given nature's propensity to make endless self-similar shapes at every different scale, it is not impossible to think of the bacteria, ciliates, and flagellates inhabiting a world full of pathways through the sand, through the stations where their food is found, all presided over by the green sky of eelgrass. Their world has a similar shape and similar possibilities to ours, though the most adventurous ciliate of the bunch travels about sixteen inches (forty centimeters) from its place of birth. But there is as much variety of life here as there is in the open air above the surface of the bay. Creatures that long ago fled from the rising tide of oxygen in the atmosphere still live in vast numbers on the bottom of the bay. They live chiefly by cooperation, mutualism, symbiosis, and exchange.

Oldest and deepest are the methanogens, one-celled archaeans that make a living from two of the most common components of the earth's early atmosphere, carbon dioxide and hydrogen. When the methanogens were earth's leading creatures, very little land had formed, but water had condensed to form the oceans, and the best places to live were in the wide shallow seas. The methanogens breathe hydrogen the way we do oxygen, reducing the carbon dioxide to methane and water. The water and methane pass back across the creatures' membrane, leaving a small increment of fixed and available energy, by means of which the methanogens can live. Very little energy is generated by this

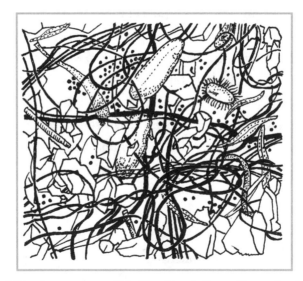

A part of the microscopic world in Tom Fenchel's small sample of sand.
The filaments and spheres are two species of sulfur bacteria. There are also
cyanobacteria, a nematode, ciliates, diatoms and flagellates.
(Illustration by Nora H. Logan)

reaction, only about 6 percent of what is made by breathing oxygen, but it is enough for a life.

The sulfate reducers breathe better, or at least, more efficiently. These are found in a layer of the sand above the methanogens. The sulfate reducers eat the remains of other creatures or swallow the methane of the methanogens. The waste and the dead of one are the food of another. These bacteria respire sulfate, transform carbon compounds into sugars, and thus create the energy to live. They breathe out sulfide, which rises upward through the mud.

Purple sulfur bacteria breathe the sulfide in. They are purple because their light-harvesting organ is the same compound— anthocyanin—found in trees' leaves as they turn in autumn. These creatures use the light energy, the sulfides, and the carbon dioxide to create sugars and breathe out water. The sulfate breathers and the sulfide eaters are a matched pair. Neither thrives without the other.

The biggest group of bacteria that shun oxygen are the ones that respire by means of the organic carbon left in their world by the dead. They ferment sugar to make energy. They exhale hydrogen. The trouble with hydrogen is that it stops fermentation. These bacteria can only live, then, if something gets rid of the hydrogen. The sulfate breathers use the hydrogen. So do the methanogens. So do purple sulfur and nonsulfur bacteria.

Oxygen sometimes intrudes higher in the sand. It is likely that oxygen played a role even in the early earth, but all that was produced was quickly reabsorbed. Along with the purple sulfur bacteria, which cannot tolerate oxygen, are other purple nonsulfur bacteria, which can. But they do not need to. When no oxygen is present, they use the energy of light to transform hydrogen and carbon dioxide into sugar and water. When oxygen appears, they do the opposite, breathing in oxygen to harvest energy from the sugar they made.

These are the sort of flexible bacteria that one day were eaten by another bacterium, but instead of being digested, they became partners, or endosymbionts. The formerly free-living purple nonsul-furs became the specialist in energy production for a larger, high-powered kind of cell, the kind that could use the jet fuel of oxygen. The mitochondria—organelles that today convert sugar into chemi-cal energy inside every cell of every animal and every plant—are the descendants of these purple nonsulfurs, which, upon entering into their partners, became a part of them.

Even the bigger creatures have partners. Kentrophoros is a single-celled ciliate, an organism that moves by means of short waving hairs at its edges. This beast swims about with a garden of sulfide-eating bacteria on its back. These bacteria can only exist right in the bor-derland of little (but not no) oxygen. Too much oxygen and their sulfide food will turn to sulfate, starving them. Kentrophoros oblig-ingly moves in the corridors of the sand, up and down, right and left, to maintain its garden of bacteria where they can live and thrive. In exchange, every once in a while, the ciliate engulfs a few of its passengers.

Above them is the land of oxygen. The cyanobacteria live there, often making a blue-green mat. Indeed, their photosynthesis is the source of the oxygen. They excrete it as they make sugar from carbon dioxide and water, and they use the oxygen up again, as they respire, making energy. At night, as no oxygen is produced and what is there becomes depleted, most cyanobacteria turn straightway into fermen-ters or sulfate breathers, returning to photosynthesis in the morning.

On the surface waves a strand or two of long slender eelgrass, blue-green like the cyanobacteria. In fact, they *are* in a sense the cyano-bacteria, since just as the purple nonsulfurs became mitochondria inside complex cells, so the cyanobacteria became chloroplasts inside the photosynthetic cells of plants. That worm with its hardened jaw burrowing in the mud, the crab sidestepping among the holdfasts, the perch swimming overhead—all of them are full of what were once purple nonsulfur bacteria living in a world of little oxygen.

This visible life and the lives of all of us rest on the base of these organisms deeper in the sand that grew little but developed a flexible network of relationships to sustain them. Their life is a weaving, not a tree. It is not a question of bifurcating paths, which part never to meet again, but of wanderings, partings, reconnections, and re-partings.

Even the lonely methanogens deepest in the sand and poorest at making energy are not left alone to fend for themselves. Ciliates that ferment their food keep methanogens inside them to metabolize the hydrogen that would otherwise kill them. Cows too keep methanogens safely in their guts, and so do we. They are the universal last-step organism that permits the final transformation of digested organic matter into its original inorganic parts. Yet they come from the deepest stratum of life times, about four billion years ago.

The Quantity of Breath

How much breath is in the air around us? I can try to make a rough count for a given space. Let's take a walk and count the breaths on a two-thousand-acre nature sanctuary in the hills north of the Catskills in upstate New York. There are two ponds, three streams, and a series of waterfalls set in a forest that alternates maple and beech hardwoods with a few surviving stands of hemlock. A lot of the older houses in the area have enormous floor planks, up to three or four feet wide, from the original hemlocks forests. The boards were cut at the local sawmill, which ran on power from the cataracts. Most of the hemlocks were cut for tanbark. The wood was the by-product that got used in town. The stripped hills were farmed and grazed until the 1930s, when this place was a mini-Appalachia and was cleared by the federal government to save the starving and provide cheap labor for the cities. Everybody from the Civilian Conservation Corps to local schoolchildren jumped in to save the soil on the abandoned farmlands by installing plantations of white spruce and red and scotch pine. These plantations were never harvested, and now begin to fail, making a cat's cradle of parallel and diagonal lines in the woods, where some trees stand, some fall, and some lean on others.

I have to admit that I am going to cheat slightly by adding to the counting area the eight-tenths of an acre of my orchard of young apple trees. It abuts the preserve, right enough, but I want to put it in because I know for a fact that it is full of mice, voles, and shrews. I know this because my small slender black-and-white blotched cat Wicked Beast—"Wickie" for short—brings them to me. There is a flat gray slab of bluestone more or less in the center of our south-facing slope, where the ground is wetter than elsewhere. Often, when I am out doing an orchard task—watering, pruning, weeding, mow-ing the orchard floor—Wickie occupies herself by catching vermin and presenting them on the rock to the god of cats. It is a kind of orchard altar, with a holocaust of rodents. For my purposes, Wickie is an excellent field biologist because within an area clearly delimited by our eight-foot deer fence she collects a good sampling of the small mammals that live there unseen by me.

The hill-bottom gate swings out fast. You have to hold it. I was not really happy to have to add this fence, but had I not, my three-foot apple whips would have been one-inch rootstock stubs within a week or two of planting. There is no shortage of deer around here. The preserve may have a couple hundred in all, each breathing on average 21 times per minute. I wonder if they would breathe slower or faster when masticating a nice young green apple stem?

At the start, I seeded the whole orchard to rye grass, which went fine for one year, but the garlic mustard was back the next. The best result was that controlling the perennial weeds gave a real boost to the native Myosotis plants, the blue forget-me-nots. The next year, I raked over the soil and frost-seeded with timothy and clover in the early spring. It was a wet year. The grass took, and wonderfully, the forget-me-nots remained. Now, by mid-April each spring, half the orchard is carpeted in crowds of small blue flowers.

I hope these flowers are attracting bees. Honeybees are meant to pollinate about one trillion apple blossoms each year in the state of New York. They surely have time to add my thirty-six trees to the list. As we saw, bees do not breathe in the way that we do, but their spiracles take in the air at a rate of about ten milliliters, or a third of an ounce, per hour, and there are perhaps six hundred thousand bees around the preserve at this moment.

Wickie's work has kept me apprised of the unseen rodents, against whom I must ring my young trees with hardware cloth down to four inches below ground level. (Come winter, the mice and voles dote on fresh apple stem, harvested by tunneling in beneath the snow.) On the cat's altar have appeared white-footed mice, masked shrews, and short-tailed shrews, along with meadow voles and others whom I cannot readily identify. I have not found out how often a vole breathes, but the white-footed mouse breathes about 135 times per minute, and the shrews, 800 and 152 times per minute, respectively. (The smaller an animal is, the more frequently it breathes, so you can see that the masked shrew is tiny.) There are perhaps 1,800 white-footed mice, 2,000 masked shrews, and 650 short-tailed shrews on the preserve.

And at least two *Homo sapiens*, each breathing an average of 19 times per minute, though as we are walking up the steep slope of the orchard, that rate might be somewhat higher. Let's also assume that on this lovely May afternoon, there are perhaps another two-dozen humans hiking or working the preserve.

As we approach the orchard's top gate, we hear a bird sing, "BEE BEE pidDAW PEE piSHAW PEE PEE PEE PRRRRRRR." There it is, sitting on a honeysuckle branch just outside the fence. Small, flat, with black stripes lengthwise down its breast, it is a song sparrow, and it breathes about 63 times each minute. This spring, there might be about sixty more song sparrows on the approximately two thousand acres.

It's a struggle to open the padlock on the top gate. It isn't supposed to rust, but it does. I have to jiggle the key to get it to engage. When we are out, we stoop through a tangle of grape and honeysuckle, coming out at the edge of a pair of buried tanks and a small cinderblock room, which is attached to one of the tanks. This is the town's water supply, drawn from the lake in the preserve. (We use the runoff from its settling tank to water the orchard by gravity feed.)

A road leads to the tanks, then bends right uphill to a pair of private houses that border the preserve. One of the houses has a fenced vegetable garden. Downhill along the edge of the road a fat groundhog trundles toward us. Perhaps it has just come from the garden. When he sees us, he slides off noisily into the preserve. We will count him: he breathes about 30 times per minute. There might be about fifty of his brethren in the sanctuary.

High overhead a pair of turkey vultures patrol, gliding down, finding thermals, circling up, and gliding down again. In a minute, each breathes 9 times. Birds breathe at a lower rate than mammals of the same size, in part because they breathe so much more efficiently. Their lungs do not expand or contract, so they need none of the supporting tissues that allow human lungs to expand, contract, and extract oxygen. Birds have a much denser, finer, and more sensitive network of cell surfaces to extract oxygen as it passes over the lungs. The air sacs that push the air over these tissues are located all over the bird. (Some even have them in their wing bones.) They push the air once through the lungs on its way in and once through the lungs on its way out. This afternoon, there might be about eighteen vultures working the preserve.

Where we turn to enter the forest road that marks the edge of the preserve, there is a scattering of feathers, the remains of a chicken from one of the nearby houses. It was taken probably by a coyote. The latter breathes 15 times each minute; the former breathed 13 times per minute. There may be about twenty coyotes on the land. (Perhaps we should subtract the chicken's breath?)

The edge of the forest road is framed in Oriental bittersweet, the orange-berried invasive vine that I have seen take over whole landscapes. Here, it has cloaked and killed a group of sumac on both sides of the wood edge, but inside the wood the shade defeats it.

Young maple and beech are growing in dense stands of slender trees on steep slopes that run down to the waterfall and the creek. Usually, the loudest sound here is the wind or the creaking of stems as they shift or rub.

It seems as if only the trees live here, but really the main business of the forest is taking place all around us. A young beech may have thirty-five thousand leaves; a young white pine, about two hundred thousand needles. Herbivores living in the forest will eat about 20 percent of the leaves and fruits and flowers available to them. Of this amount, about one-fourth will be digested and become parts of the animals. The rest will be shit and peed back to the forest floor. Eighty percent of each tree's annual production will simply fall to the forest floor, uneaten. So better than 90 percent of what the trees have made is lying beneath them in one form or another as the year goes on.

We would be several miles deep in the stuff were it not for the invisible armies that digest this litter. There are two and a half million invertebrates and six million nematodes per square yard breaking down the litter. If we take a handful of litter and pick through it with a 10× loupe, we will see some of them: pill bugs, springtails, tiny spiders, worms. They do about one-tenth of the work. The rest is done by the microbes. There are easily ten billion bacterial cells in a gram of forest soil. Two tons of fungi and bacteria live in the top eight inches of each acre of deciduous forest soil. Though we cannot see and hardly sense them—except from the faintly sweet odor of decay or the occasional sighting of a mushroom or bracket or cup fungus—the forest is alive with breathing microorganisms.

Coming out of the trees, we stand in a sudden sunny clearing at the top of a waterfall. There are pioneer birch and poplar here. A couple of red oak seedlings have taken hold in a sunny spot. There is honeysuckle blooming against a hump of piled spoil beside where a small dam has been placed. A ruby-throated hummingbird is sampling the flowers, taking in air at a rate of 250 breaths per minute. There are maybe a dozen of these hummingbirds now in the preserve.

From a dense thicket of viburnum comes the mewing call of the catbird. The large gray bird breathes 57 times per minute, and there are maybe two-dozen individuals on the property.

Turning north, we walk along the east side of the creek climbing toward the lake through a combination of red pine plantation and regenerating deciduous forest. There is the definite odor of pole cat, a striped skunk, rising out of the hollow beside the creek. It breathes 36 times a minute, and there might be about a hundred of them in all in the preserve.

The trail emerges from the mixed forest at the edge of the lake. A broad-winged hawk circles overhead. It breathes only about 20 times per minute on its perch, but up to 130 times per minute after takeoff. Cruising in the air above our heads it might be breathing about 75 times per minute. There are likely about four pairs of broad-winged hawks on the two thousand acres.

Halfway around the lake is a parking area, and a lawn that slopes down to the water. There are small structures, a cabin and outhouses, nearby. This is the town swimming hole. Every morning in the summer the lifeguards have to sweep up the poop that the Canada geese have left the night before. The staff has tried everything from installing trip wires along the shore to placing faithful imitation coyote statuary to scare the geese away, but they keep coming. The Canada goose breathes an average of 12 times per minute. Maybe only two pairs nest here, but two hundred or more are constantly stopping in.

Gently upslope is a trail that connects the lake to the smaller, shallower pond above it. There is a small marsh between them, and there we see a yellow-bellied flycatcher seize an insect in midair. This is the very southernmost part of this bird's summer range. It may be a transient. Perhaps it is the only one on the preserve. It breathes 74 times per minute.

317

The upper pond is home to a biological field station, with labs and living quarters. A house wren, brown with its stout curved beak, has nested in a box at the forest's edge. It calls loudly as it zips through the underbrush, drawing us away from the nest. It breathes 83 times per minute, and there are about four of them in the preserve.

We cross a road and start on the trail around the pond. We see the feet, some fur, and the tail of what appears to have been a Norway rat, which must have lived in or under one of the houses. It was out at the wrong time last night and met a screech owl or a great horned owl. The unfortunate rat had breathed about 90 times per minute. A screech owl breathes 29 times per minute, while the great horned breathes 45. There are maybe two-dozen rats on the preserve, a couple of screech owls, and four great horned owls.

At the far end of the pond, where it peters out into a bog, float two groups of ducks. The mallards take 14 breaths a minute; the black ducks, 27. In spring there are perhaps three dozen each of mallards and black ducks on the pond or the lake.

Along the trail that leads through the bog are the distinctive footprints of several raccoons. The forepaws leave an impression that looks like tiny human hands; the back paws, like tiny human feet. The raccoons, which breathe about 42 times per minute, seem to have been hunting crayfish. There might be about forty coons in the preserve.

Rounding the bog, we come back along the pond's wildest side. Turning over stones, we find one red-backed salamander after another. There are said to be about one of these voracious little amphibians per square yard through much of the Northeast. There might be as many as three million of them in the preserve. It is hard to count their breath, though, since they breathe continuously through their skin. Under one rock, we discover—surprise!—a large yellow-spotted salamander.

Circling back by the cabins, we turn off right down the far side of the lake, bound back toward our starting point. This area is even wilder than the far side of the pond. It is the heart of the preserve. And as if to prove the point, we surprise a black bear rooting in a rotten log. She makes off west. She breathes 22 times per minute, just a little faster than we do, though at the time we are certainly almost hyperventilating. There are perhaps three more bears on the preserve.

Heading downslope around the top of the falls and descending their opposite side, we walk into a patch of old-growth hemlock. It is on a slope too steep for logging, and while spruce and pine have fallen away around them, the hemlocks keep standing through fire and storm. At the edge, a blue jay greets us, vociferating at the top of his lungs. It breathes 49 times per minute as it squawks, and there are maybe about seventy-five or eighty jays on the preserve.

Among the hemlocks, there should be a lot more mice, but we do not see them. We do see a red squirrel ascending a stem. A few minutes later, a chipmunk scurries across the thick layer of hemlock duff and disappears into the crotch between two roots. There may be fifteen hundred red squirrels on the land, and in the same area as many as twenty thousand chipmunks. I do not know how often the red squirrel breathes, but the chipmunk breathes 65 times per minute.

At the foot of the hemlock stand runs a creek, flowing away from the base of the upper falls toward the lower falls, which drop where the road crosses a bridge. Although near the edge of the preserve, this habitat is rich and fast changing. Water has been flowing in great quantity down the slope on its opposite side. I tried to trace the water back to its source but ran into private property. At any rate, the trees on that slope—pine, ash, red maple, sugar maple, basswood—are dying. They are pierced by boring beetles and decayed by fungi. There are said to be more species of wood-boring beetles in the world than there are of mammals, birds, reptiles, and amphibians combined. Most of these types of beetles live in symbiosis with wood-decay fungi.

On the creek bottom itself is an equally various life. There the larvae of mayflies, stone flies, black flies, caddisflies, dragonflies, damselflies, and other insects that spend years in the stream, and a day or a month in the air, thrive in huge numbers. On the stones, there are maybe 50 larvae per square foot; on the moss and algae, maybe 750; on the rafts and sunken packets of decaying leaves, 900 larvae.

Over the red bridge and down the last trail to the parking lot by the state road, we start to see invasive plants again. The barberry is doing its best to spread upstream but hasn't gotten more than about fifty feet. Grapes are draped over the honeysuckles, the two invasives fighting it out. Burdock sends up its woolly leaves, like dozens of green outthrust tongues along the edge of the parking lot. A robin, breathing 48 times per minute, lights on the serviceberry that was planted last year. The population of robins on the land this year is perhaps one hundred. A house mouse runs along the sill of the preserve office, breathing 120 times per minute. There are many house mice in town, but perhaps only six or seven hundred on the preserve.

The sun has just set as we walk back onto the public street where it bends, crosses the bridge, and goes steep uphill. Over the old red mill a big brown bat celebrates its staccato flight, plucking bug after bug out of the evening air. In winter torpor, this bat can breathe as little as 4 times per minute and may go five minutes or more without breathing at all. In rapid flight, as now, she breathes 600 times per minute or even more. Until recently, there may have been about three hundred big brown bats on the preserve, though their numbers are increasingly threatened by a devastating fungal infection.

So what has our afternoon walk revealed? If we take each creature that we saw as a representative of its species, multiply it by the rough number of that species living on the preserve at that moment, and then by its rate of respiration, and add all the numbers up, we get around 19 million breaths per minute, 1.1 billion breaths per hour, 27 billion breaths per day. And that is only the breathing of the very small number of creatures whom we saw that afternoon and early evening. It says nothing of those we did not see, or of those who are too small for us ever to see without help.

Of course, some of our breathers do not take in much air in a single gulp. One breath of a shrew, for example, is about the size of a single couscous grain. What then is the total volume of air that is breathed in this place in a day? The amount breathed by the visible creatures is astonishing. On the preserve alone, the mammals breathe 650,000 gallons of air per day; the birds, about 30,000 gallons; and the reptile and amphibians, about 450 gallons. (Many reptiles breathe hardly at all when not in motion.) But this is nothing compared to the breath of the invisible. Insects, spiders, and worms breathe about one million gallons per day. The champions are the microbes and the plants. Together, these breathe better than eight and a half million gallons of air per day. (This is not to mention the slightly greater volume of air that plants take in for photosynthesis.)

In all, the living on the preserve breathe better than ten million gallons of air in a single day. If you ran a hose nonstop, it would take about ten thousand hours for that volume of water to come out. It is then perhaps neither a poetic way of speaking nor an exaggeration to say that the atmosphere is regulated by the living. From air and water, all the living are derived through the medium of breath. Perhaps it is fair to say that breath *is* being, and that creatures are the expressions of its existence.

Fogging the Mirror

The mirror used to be a tool of the coroner and the doctor. They would hold a small one before a dying person's nose and mouth. If the mirror did not fog, the person was declared dead. Moist warm air from the lungs—all air that is breathed must dissolve in a thin film of water—touches the cold mirror. The vapor cools and condenses. Or there is none.

Breath is the measure of life. In Genesis 2:7, human life begins when God breathes life into clay. Among practitioners of yoga, that life is counted not by the number of years but by the number of breaths. The yogins assert that every breath contains an unconscious prayer. Note that whenever you breathe in and out through the nose, the inhale makes a sound like "SSSSS," the exhale a sound like "AHHHH." According to them, the inhale pronounces "So-ham," which literally means "He am I." The exhale says, "Hamsah," or "I am He." By "He" is meant the immortal spirit.

Breath is the difference between life and death, not only in us but all the way back to the single-celled archaeans. There are only three places on earth that a creature can live: in the atmosphere, in the water, or in the dirt. Air penetrates all three, and in all three the air is regulated by breath.

The air is the kingdom of breath. The average person takes about thirty thousand breaths per day, or about eleven million breaths per year. The human population of the earth takes more than eight trillion breaths per hour. If the air were visible, we would see a constant torrent passing in and out of all of us. And that is not to mention the trillions upon trillions of breaths taken by animals, microbes, and plants. Each breath of this invisible air sustains some part of the visible world.

Breath does not belong to anyone. Scientists love to calculate the number of molecules of Caesar's last breath that pass through each and every human lung in a day—the estimates vary from four to eighteen—but they are talking through their hats. The breath was no more Caesar's than yours or mine in this instant is now ours.

A breath contains oxygen, nitrogen, carbon dioxide, a wide variety of other compounds, dust motes, pollen grains, bacteria, dead skin, plant hairs, and spores. (A person is liable to consume about two tablespoons of solid and liquid particles, along with the gases, each day.) Quickly the air recycles them again.

In crowds, you can envision breath emerging from the mouth, swirling, only to be taken right up again, in arabesques like the decorations on Mozarabic tiles. So if Brutus and his friends were with Caesar at his death, you can be sure that each breath you take of Caesar's has a good chance of having been in Brutus and Cassius too. Even if they fled immediately, did the eddies they left in the air draw Caesar's last breath with them?

On the other hand, where does a lonely breath taken above tree line at fourteen thousand feet go? I think of John Muir studying glaciers, alone with his rucksack and his pound of coffee, pound of flour, pound of sugar, and hunks of acorn bread. He has just taken a mouthful of the bread, and a swallow of cold water caught in a cup from the glacier melt. His exhalation includes a little tannin from the acorn bread and a little glucose in its aerosols. His breath is a lot less full of the usual gases, because at fourteen thousand feet the air is 30 percent less dense.

At the top of Middle Palisade in the Sierra Nevada there is a stiff west wind, as there almost always is. It skips over the summit, picks up Muir's breath, and immediately plunges it into the vortex on the other side. The water rises from the mix and condenses at the edge of a lenticular cloud that hangs over the mountain's lee, never moving. The gases and the aerosols are entrained in the westerlies. Soon, a grove of ponderosa pine makes use of some. The algal partners of orange crustose lichens take up some of the oxygen, while the fungal partner makes use of the carbon. The tannins are carried back up over the lip of the summit, where they form condensation nuclei—the indispensible centers on which raindrops form—for the afternoon's thunderstorm.

Though breath may not belong to us, there is a matchless pleasure to breathing. Babies do it in the womb before there is a need, breathing in and out amniotic fluid, while their oxygen is still supplied directly by their mothers. Doctors say they are doing this to get ready for the first breath, which is a good thing since the first breath is not easy.

Remember trying to blow up a balloon? The smaller the balloon, the harder it was to get it started. This is because the elastic of the balloon is resistant to expansion, and the smaller its radius the more resistant it is. You could go red in the face and develop a rasping pain in the lymph glands before anything at all happened to the balloon. Sometimes I just gave up. So would babies, they say, were it not for their lung practice and for the fact that just before birth a kind of wash runs through the tissues of the lungs' little balloons (the alveoli), softening them and making them stretchier.

But there is delight in breath as well as a compulsion. It is the body's constant ceremony as long as we live. When I hold my breath, I feel the discomfort as an increasing weight in my chest and as a pressure between my eyes. When at last I release the breath, I feel the pleasure on the exhale, not on the inhale. Were it only the oxygen

I craved, I think I would not feel good until I got it inside. Instead, it is the reestablishment of the rhythm that delights. Certainly, this promises oxygen, but before that it brings back my connection to everything around, my communion with the rest of the existing.

Breath is the one activity of the body that is both voluntarily and involuntarily controlled. I might starve to death intentionally, but I will never asphyxiate intentionally without some mechanical aid (like a noose with a difficult double knot in it). If I try to hold my breath, I will pass out, and in unconsciousness my other self will take up the breathing again. It is good proof that there really are two parts to the self. One is instinctual, and its job is to preserve the self, against all others (and even against the self) if necessary. The other is personal, volitional, able both to love and to despair. Aquinas called these two the individual and the person. The person may decide to do without breathing, but the individual will beg to disagree.

The Buddhists put great store in breath meditation. Anapanasati, one of the two forms of Theravada Buddhist meditation, has the meditator sit relaxed, focusing on the breath, whether by counting the number of inhalations or exhalations, or by focusing on the place between nostrils and lips where the breath enters and emerges from the body. This practice was taught by the Buddha himself. The point is to separate the meditator from all thoughts of past and future and so to allow the meditator to put aside greed and distress. It is the work preparatory to the second form of meditation, insight meditation. In the first, through focus on the breath, one is enabled to stop the clamor of life, and through the second, one can then discern the cause of that clamor and escape it.

Breathing is both personal and impersonal. It occurs usually without our noticing. When we stop to pay attention to it, we become aware of our connection to the whole of the universe that is not us. It gently shakes our sense of isolated existence.

Attention to breathing is the foundation of yoga practice. The mind, according to yogic teaching, is a chariot pulled by two horses. One is breath, the other desire. When desire is stronger, the mind is dragged after it. Trouble follows. When the breath is in control—regulated and even—it controls desire and guides the mind to contemplation and joy. One whole branch of yoga—pranayama—is devoted to the regulation and cultivation of the breath.

Something similar is behind the breath training for music and for sports. As a child I learned to play the clarinet—very badly but I valued it nevertheless. Here, for the first time, I had to learn something difficult that was neither exactly mental nor physical. Of course, I did have to learn to hold my mouth in a tight purse called the embrochure. That was certainly physical and painful, but the point was to make it possible to efficiently transmit the breath to the reed.

The little I learned, however, did create a separate place in me. Breathing in through the nose and out through the poor pursed mouth created a focused rhythm onto which the tones, the rhythms, and the qualities of sound could be laid, like paint on canvas. Though it was all I could do to get out the melody of "I Dream of Jeannie with the Light Brown Hair," I could sense the power of it. Here was access—for others perhaps, not for me—to a world less creaturely and more personal, a world of fundamental and beautiful relationships that were also possibly eternal. I began to love the word "woodwind"—though my clarinet was made of plastic—and to hear in it the arousing of music through the regulation of the breath.

I could experience this better when hiking. I learned songs to develop walking rhythms, and I sometimes resorted to German marching rhythm—*ein, zwei, drei, vier*—but in the practice of the rest step I made a different effort. I took deep breaths through the diaphragm at high altitudes. I stepped and breathed in through the nose, rested and breathed out through the mouth. It was always hard to start this rhythm in the morning, and I used it only on the hardest trails, but once I got it I let it carry me thirty-five miles a day while I was carrying a fifty-pound pack. This was not possible through physical exertion, but through the rhythm of breath. Past and future both dropped away.

Breath as an action also has a result. It creates an atmosphere. In the largest sense, the troposphere—that part of the atmosphere where the air constantly changes and where the living live—is the product of all of our respiration and photosynthesis. All those daily breaths. The air is not a thing or a place. It is the continual product of communion.

Perhaps breath becomes only truly personal when it stops, for in that moment the individual is no more. What of the person? On our father's last night, my brother and I sang and played to him. We read to him his favorite work, *Cyrano de Bergerac*. Now, I am a little afraid it might have annoyed him or that he did not understand a word, but I am not all that afraid. It is just the habit of worrying about the future or the past. As my friend Mark says, "Anything done with reverence is well done." Our hero in *Cyrano* dies, foully murdered with a falling log, but as he declares in the end, he keeps *mon panache*, the flamboyant white feather waving in his hat. The honor, the good humor, the faithfulness of the person.

That night, we watched our father's breath get shallower and shallower. On doctor's orders, we had been giving him morphine to lessen the pain, which probably eased his end. His old dear friend and fellow doctor Ed Rubenstein had told us that his lungs would likely slowly fill with fluid and that he would drift away. "That's the best way, it really is," said Ed, shaking his head. "Cancer," he muttered. "We all die of cancer in the end."

After all that rhythm—more than 500,000,000,000,000,000 breaths in a life of seventy-five years—a last one comes. It goes out, and the white T-shirt settles against the chest one more time. You think you see it stir again. No, it does not.

Shall These Bones Live?

This is the question God asks Ezekiel. He has set him at the edge of a desert full of the dry bones of soldiers long dead. God tells Ezekiel to prophesy to the bones and so to cause them to knit together again. The prophet does as he is told, and the bones compose themselves into bodies once more. But they are still stone dead. Prophesy to the wind, God tells Ezekiel. And say to the wind, enter into these bodies that they may live. Ezekiel does so. The wind does as it is told. And up stand the once-dry bones as men, "a very great army." A wonderful poetic way of speaking! It is also exact.

Breath is the measure of life. Three minutes after we stop breathing we will be brain dead, and in six minutes stone dead. But this is not what I mean by "exact." I mean that the wind—the enveloping, ever-moving atmosphere—is exactly where our breath comes from, and that by its entering into our bodies and exiting them again, we join a community that has been producing and sustaining Earth's air for around four billion years.

But to start with, where did this atmosphere come from? And why did it stay? After all, the solar wind—a constant stream of ionized hydrogen and helium atoms—blows ceaselessly through the solar system. Why did the air not just blow away? So far as we can tell, there is no other heavenly body within twenty parsecs that has the like of Earth's air.

In our solar system, three of the so-called terrestrial planets started out in life more or less the same. A garden-variety supernova exploded in the vicinity, ejecting not only light elements such as hydrogen and helium, but also heavier elements, including carbon, iron, silicon, and oxygen, and even very heavy radioactive elements. Some of these formed a rotating nebula that began to collapse under the force of gravity.

The nebula separated into concentric rings. The rings sorted themselves out as they did so. Light elements at the center started fusing, creating the incandescent sun. Comparatively near the young sun, heavier elements like the metals and the earths began to form a set of smaller bodies, while farther away large amounts of gas and volatiles, such as water, ammonia, and methane, froze, creating immense planets with no solid surface at all. If, for example, you tried to land on Jupiter or Saturn, you never would. You would go through layer after layer of atmosphere until the immense pressure crushed you. Bodies coming from outside the solar system often meet just this fate. Attracted to the huge, fast-spinning outer planets, they disappear into them. In this way, the outer planets shield the inner terrestrial planets.

Mars, Venus, and Earth are the three terrestrial neighbors, all made out of approximately the same stuff. The dust and gases in their rings began to stick together, making larger bodies in each ring. The larger bodies in each ring collided, first asteroid-sized objects and finally whole proto-planets slamming into one another. The three resultant planets probably had the beginnings of a solid surface, with an ocean of volcanic magma roiling on the surface and island arcs of dry land. The force of the impacts, the energy of gravitational collapse, and the decay of radioactive elements kept the magma liquid.

Each planet began to arrange itself. Lighter and more easily melted elements like silicon—the backbone of rocks and soils—rose to the surface and solidified. The air cooled and evaporated. For millennia water fell as rain, creating oceans. Heavier metals like nickel and iron sank quickly toward the center, making a core. The sinking itself heated the elements, as the iron super-compressed. Deep in the interior it was as hot as 9,000 degrees Fahrenheit, but so dense as to be solid. Atop this solid core, however, where the pressure was less, the iron remained molten.

Volcanoes punched through the new solid surface, ejecting above it the world's first air. It was likely mainly carbon dioxide and hydrogen, with water and methane.

Heated by the hot solid core, by the continuing decay of radioactive elements, and by the energy transmitted by fresh collisions between the early planets and wandering planet-lets, the liquid iron of the outer core circulated like water in a boiling pot. Turning in this hot liquid matrix, the solid inner core acts like an induction motor, inducing an electric current and a magnetic field. Without the shield of a magnetic field, a planet won't hold water. In fact, its whole atmosphere will slowly sputter away in the constant solar wind. If a planet has no charged envelope to protect it, the solar wind will gust over the top of the atmosphere, energizing and scavenging molecules so that they flow away into deep space.

Since the formation of Mars, that planet has lost about as much atmosphere as Earth today possesses. At the beginning, Mars had its own hot core, molten mantle, and magnetic field. There was plenty of water on the planet. But Mars is 50 percent farther from the sun than is Earth. The light intensity that reaches it is only half what reaches us. And Mars is much smaller than Earth, only a little larger than our moon.

As Mars cooled, it lost its core convection and its magnetic field. Low gravity let the water and everything else in the early Martian atmosphere rise to the top of the air. There, the solar wind began to erode away carbon dioxide and free water. The air on Mars today is thin, about 1 percent of the atmosphere of Earth, and cold. There is little greenhouse effect to moderate temperatures because the two gases that most enhance the greenhouse effect—carbon dioxide and water—are scarce. Highs are about 68 degrees Fahrenheit, lows about –125 degrees. Some water remains on the planet, but it is locked up as ice.

Venus lives at the opposite extreme from Mars. It is closer to the sun than both Earth and Mars. The air on Venus is dry, thick, and hot. The air there is a hundred times thicker than is ours. Because of their extremes, Mars and Venus have suffered almost the same fate. Venus is about the same size as Earth, but it rotates much more slowly (243 days for one turn). When it was newly coalesced, Venus likely had a strong magnetic field, and it still has volcanoes. Although it is impossible to see through the thick atmosphere, infrared photographs have revealed a surface landscape of high plateaus surrounded by large basins. The light color of some of the rocks in these plateaus suggests that they are granite, metamorphic rock recycled by volcanic action. If this is so, then Venus, like Mars, may once have had oceans of free water to fill the basins.

But Venus is too close to the sun (30 percent closer than Earth is) and therefore too damn hot. Early in the planet's history, it is likely that the heating drove more and more carbon up from the surface and into the air. As we are now experiencing, carbon dioxide is an effective greenhouse gas. It holds in the energy that would otherwise radiate back to space from the surface of the planet. As it does so, it heats the air still more. The more carbon dioxide in the air, the more it heated, and the more it heated, the more carbon dioxide was released.

Any water on the surface of Venus would soon have turned to vapor. Imagine a situation in which all Earth's oceans evaporate. It must have been something like that. Rising fast through hot air, the vapor reached the edge of the atmosphere, where much was simply blown off into space. The charged particles from the sun separated the remaining water into hydrogen and oxygen, and blew each of them away.

No water, no photosynthesis. No photosynthesis, no free oxygen. No free oxygen, no aerobic breath. On Mars or on Venus, Ezekiel's dry bones will be dry forever. Even on Earth, oxygen might have remained a minor component of the air. There could have been the abundant microscopic photosynthetic cyanobacteria—the first creatures to put oxygen into the air—but no more complicated organisms, and Ezekiel's bones would have stayed dry had not one additional, strange, and improbable catastrophe occurred.

Maybe half a billion years before the first signs of life appeared on Earth, when Earth already had a convecting core and a magnetic field, a body about the size of Mars slammed into the young planet. Big deal! A little late, but it was not so unusual for the young solar system. What was strange was that it broke off a large chunk of Earth's mantle, and this chunk went into orbit around the planet, creating the moon. No other planet has a single moon so relatively large as ours. Its regular rotation tugs at the ocean basins, creating tides. The tides exchange fresh salts with upwelling water, with the ocean-side land, with the mid-oceans. It was in these rich tidal basins on the edge of the seas that breath began.

The moon also acted as a counterweight, stabilizing the tilt of Earth's orbit. Thus the sun's path is never more than twenty-three degrees south or north of the equator. The regular alternation gives rise to a dependable (if not predictable) pattern of shifting temperatures and rainfall. The moon makes it possible for us to have a climate, and for the world's creatures to sort themselves according to their use of it. With this stability, the creatures of Earth could learn to breathe and so begin to regulate and maintain the planet's air.

Consider the alternative. Mars has two small moons that do not regulate the planet's tilt. Mars shifts back and forth from a tilt of zero degrees to a tilt of sixty degrees, on a cycle of about ten million years.

As a result, there are times when it is extremely cold at the equator and warm at the poles, and vice versa. Life on Mars would have been in constant flight to keep up with the careening weather.

With its more stable climate, Earth let the breathers live. The living took carbon dioxide out of the air and buried it deep in the earth—as carbonate rocks and hydrocarbons. (Venus has no more carbon dioxide than we do, but all of Venus's carbon dioxide is in its air.) And the living contributed oxygen, which, rising to the stratosphere, capped the air. The magnetic field kept water in—well, in reality it does not work perfectly, so we lose about three feet of water every billion years—while the ozone shield kept ultraviolet radiation out and cradled the mass of the atmosphere beneath its warmth.

Ezekiel's bones are not dry on this Earth and the breath can come into them only because of two highly improbable facts: First, the planet is just the right distance from the sun. Second, it suffered a catastrophe late in its development, and so acquired its moon. You may call this chaos if you like, but if you do, then what does that word mean?

Shining

Why the Daytime Sky Is Light

Whole books have been written about why the daytime sky is blue. This is not one of them. My wife, Nora, who is a landscape painter, does not believe the sky is blue. Or when it is blue, in her opinion, it is so with infinite qualification. It is robin's egg blue, or cerulean blue, or over there it may be more navy blue. Sometimes it is a clean crisp middle blue, but then there's often green in the sky and rose and yellow too. At the zenith it may be more or less blue, but at the horizon it has usually gone a lovely rich cream color. The blue of the sky doesn't come out of any one paint tube. You have to mix ultramarine and Prussian blues—at least!

And what about all the clouds? she will ask, as though you had somehow intended to defraud her of them. For these, you must start with unbleached titanium, that is a white with pink and beige in it. Often, she says, the sky is much warmer than you think. The clouds have a cast of light on them, and that fills their color with warm yellow and pink. At sunset, she adds, the clouds may go a deep rich gray, and the light around them is mauve and rose with little streaks of red and yellow. She thinks a moment. And also some light yellowish green.

She puzzles over why the sunrise colors are so pale and the sunset colors so rich. At sunrise, she says, you see the sun as this pure red ball, but the colors all around it are very pale and fleeting. They are dissipating, she thinks, flying upward toward the full light of day. At sunset, by contrast, the light is withdrawing from the sky. As it sinks down, it gets richer and richer, until it is gone.

The more interesting issue, to my mind, is not why the daytime sky is blue, but why it is light, since there are no days and nights in outer space. The sky is light because of the air. When the astronauts look out the window of their craft in orbit, they see the sun and they see the stars and the moon and the blue-green earth—all of these are very bright, but everything else is basic black. The thin film of gases surrounding the earth, the dusts, the spores, the vapor, the droplets, the height, the kind and the thickness of the clouds, the angle at which the sun is shining—all of these go to make a sky that has such a range of color in it. Sun and the weather make the sky. Color belongs to this world.

There Is Only One Sun

On a summer Friday evening in 1973, I rode on a bus toward the setting sun, to an inn in western Japan. I had traveled all day from Tokyo, first in the Shinkansen, or Bullet Train, then in a regional train, then in a local train with wooden walls that stopped when people waved it down, and finally in this bus. The driver pointed me across the street to a two-story modern building that had a sliding shoji front door. All around in the darkening valley were ranks of pear trees, each laden with fruit, and each fruit covered in a white sleeve that gave the pears the look of a thousand lamps.

I had come this far on a whim, to see the place where a movie I loved—called *Woman in the Dunes*—had been filmed. In the film, the dunes seemed impossibly extensive and impossibly deep.

I was tired and apprehensive. I had studied Japanese for two years in college, enough to get by but scarcely enough to read more than the most ordinary communications and hardly enough, I thought, to understand a word spoken in the dialect of this, the smallest and most rural prefecture in Japan. I crossed the street. There was a sweet damp smell in the air. I didn't see any sign indicating that this was an inn, so I was glad that the driver had pointed to it. On the other hand, there was not a single other building in sight. Perhaps we had not understood one another? Perhaps he had let me off at somebody's house?

I took a breath and slid back the door. Inside, it seemed, in a wide deep room, were gathered every man, woman, and child in the valley. And they were all talking at once. When they looked up and saw me at the door, every single one fell instantly silent and stared. A woman of about thirty-five or forty came toward me, and I said shyly, in my best Tokyo Japanese, that I believed I had a reservation to stay with her. *Irashaimase!* She crowed. Welcome! And so did everyone else in the room. For the next two hours at least, I became the focal point of a dance.

There are three sizes of beer bottles in Japan: *kobin, chubin,* and *oobin*—little, medium, and big. If you are drinking alone, you buy a *kobin*, but hardly anybody drinks alone. Rather, you buy an *oobin*, and you share it with your friends. In return, they do the same for you. You pour for your friends. They pour for you. If it is just one friend, you might split *chubins*. I was passed from table to table, splitting *oobins* with all and sundry.

Wave after wave of goodwill washed over me. Between that and the effects of the beer, I was soon carelessly speaking the best Japanese I could muster. It was becoming fluid enough that I thought it even sounded a bit like the dialect that was coming at me. Tottori Japanese was indeed different from Tokyo Japanese. I understood parts of many sentences, but while my hosts talked on, I would spend most of our time together trying to piece out the puzzle of the first few things they had said, adding in later phrases as clues. It was entertaining, and my new friends did not seem to mind that I was responding to questions they had not asked.

Somewhere in the latter part of the evening, I sat down with two older men at their table. The one who had a stubble beard fixed me with a gaze and smiled warmly. It occurred to me that he was old enough to have fought in the Second World War. Perhaps the last American he had seen up close had been an enemy. Gravely and with ceremony, he said, *"Taiyoo wa hitotsu."* This was evidently not a pleasantry, and since I was on the wavelength of casual conversation, I understood not a word. "*Sore de, minna tomodachi,*" he continued. He put emphasis into the *minna* part, so it sounded like "meeeeennn-naa." He ended, "*Kereri was rippa na hito deshita.*"

I must have looked quite blank, so he repeated himself. Then he repeated the same phrases again. And again. At last, I started to get the meaning.

Taiyoo wa hitotsu. There is only one sun.

Sore de meeennnaa tomodachi. Therefore we are all friends.

Kereri was rippa na hito deshita. This one puzzled me. Somebody named Kelly or Kerry, he was saying, had been a fine man.

Kereri . . . Kereri . . . Kennedy! He was complimenting President Kennedy.

"Now Kennedy, there was a fine man." I agreed with his sentiment. We repeated the phrases in unison. And finished our *oobin*, laughing.

He was perfectly correct, at least about the sun. The sun drives the sky here in western Japan, where the trains have wooden walls and the pears are protected one by one on their branches; in Tokyo, where the lights never go out and you can find a crowd at two in the morning; in Boron, California, where it is 104 degrees in the shade; and in New York City, where you can also find a crowd at two in the morning but a completely different one.

From the smallest breeze that turns a candy wrapper on the sidewalk to the great convection that carries warm air north from the equator aloft and returns cold air from the poles south, the sun is the single motive power. But here in this place and moment I saw the truth of the simultaneity of irreducible unity and irreducible multiplicity. It is the source of both beauty and friendship, as well as a source of our fascination with the air and the weather. It is the clear perception that there is one source of all the changes in the air, and at the same time infinite different effects in each and every place. At the same time, the goodwill of these people was one and the difference in our ways of life irreducible. That man had likely been out bagging pears earlier in the day, while I had been reading a work by William Faulkner. One day, he may read Faulkner and I may bag pears, but we will still and always come to each other from far away. Our lives would always remain irreducibly different, and in their midst, we might be (even for a moment) friends sharing the one sun.

Several days later, when I was preparing to leave, the-five-year-old daughter of the innkeeper came up to me shyly toting a heavy encyclopedia volume. She set it in my lap. It was open to the entry *Nyuu Yokku*, written in katakana, New York. Across the top of the page ran a photograph of the skyline of midtown Manhattan. "Where," she asked me in her slowest and most careful schoolgirl Japanese, "in all of that do YOU live?" I had to inform her that I did not live in the picture at all, but way off to the left of it, uptown. "*Upputown*," she repeated. And went away, intoning, "*Upputown*."

The Sap Rising

Wherever there are plants in all the world, the sun powers the ascent of the sap and so sets in motion the processes by which all creatures live. Trees are the largest, the most massive, and the longest-lived creatures on earth. If you count all plants, green growing things outweigh all other life on the planet by a factor of ten to one. There are ten pounds of plants for each pound of the rest of us. One-half of the organic carbon in the world is cellulose. Another fourth is lignin. The two polymers weave the nets of cells that keep trees bending and standing in the air. Trees make 250 billion metric tons of sugar every year.

Trees are heavy, solid, stable, and persistent, and they never move until they fall. The air is quick, transparent, ephemeral, ever moving, ever changing, never still. But, joined together by the sun, trees and air are the planet's greatest symbionts. They form a community of mutual need. They depend on each other. They feed each other. They egg each other on. One of them cannot exist in its actual form without the help of the other. The sun brings them together.

What does a tree give to the air? First of all, water. The tree transports liquid water from the ground, pumps it through a labyrinth of tiny pipes, and emits it as a gas—water vapor—through the stomata, tiny holes on the back side of each leaf. The scale of this process is hard to fathom, but as a rough beginning, consider that an oak leaf has about nine thousand stomata per square inch, and a good mature red oak has maybe ninety million leaves. That makes about 1.6 trillion tiny outlets through which the liquid water in the ground becomes the gas of water vapor in the air. And that is just one tree. In the air, the water vapor is the source of clouds and of future rain and snow. When it condenses into clouds, it releases heat energy that propels the circulation of the atmosphere. The power, the pattern, and the range of storms are all in large measure the gifts of the trees and plants to the air.

The second gift is oxygen. Trees and plants produce all of the free oxygen in the air by means of photosynthesis. Oxygen makes ozone, which protects the living from ultraviolet rays and puts a lid on the sky.

What does the air give a tree? First of all, carbon dioxide. Trees pull the gas in through the same trillions of stomata beneath the leaves. Carbon dioxide is the component in photosynthesis that gives form and shape to all the molecules of life. It is the foundation of all life's fuel, all its structure, and all its behavior. All the solid flesh of the living has its origin in the carbon dioxide absorbed from the air.

The second gift is water, because it is the power of the air that draws the water through the tree. Most of that water goes as vapor into the atmosphere, but a small amount remains in the leaves. That water is the key to the first step in photosynthesis. The energy built in the chloroplasts through the absorption of the sun's rays is used to split the water molecules, releasing oxygen and building the stores of chemical energy that will be used to make flesh out of carbon dioxide gas.

The air may pull as much as a hundred gallons of water through a single tree in a day. Each year it pulls twenty inches of rain from the ground through the trees of an oak-hickory forest in the southern Appalachians. Less than a tenth of the water that comes in through the roots is used inside the tree. The rest just passes through, trillions upon trillions of streams rising every day of the growing season and coiling upward into the sky like smoke.

Wherever there is enough water on earth, there will be trees and forests. Savannahs, grasslands, and deserts occur only where there is too little water in the ground to support the streams of water that rise through trees. Hopeful settlers west of the one-hundredth meridian in the United States laboriously planted trees to shade their prairie houses. The trees grew well for a few years, especially if they were wet years, but eventually they simply drew down the water table beneath them and the young trees sucked air. The trillion of internal rivulets lost their streams of water, and the trees collapsed.

There is nonetheless enough water around the world for forests to be the largest ecosystem in it. Almost nine-tenths of all the live carbon-based organisms on our planet are forests and their creatures. The rate of global warming is even slowed by the ability of the growing forests to turn more and more carbon into flesh. The Amazon rain forests alone take up five billion metric tons of carbon each year.

All the symbiotic exchanges between the trees and the air take place because of this hidden transport from the roots, through the trunks and branches and twigs, and out the stomata of the leaves. It is easy to understand how roots suck up water from the soil, and not so hard to see that leaves give off vapor, but how does the water get from one to the other? As the sun rises, the leaf warms. Some of the heat is radiated right back, some makes the felt heat in the air, a tiny amount is absorbed by the chloroplasts to begin the day's photosynthesis, and the rest is used to start the transformative flow of the hidden streams.

The stream from ground to crown and out into the air is driven by simple differences in pressure. Each stream stretches from a root to a leaf stoma. The water at the very end of the stoma forms the crescent moon of a meniscus where it meets the air. The intermolecular forces of surface tension hold this crescent in place against the sides of the stoma. On the surface of the crescent, the rising temperature supplies the heat to start evaporation. The first molecules of water break their bonds with the fluid and float off into the sky. As they do so, they make space in the stream, reducing the pressure and increasing the tension. Water moves up to replace what has evaporated, pulling the stream upward through the tree. Down in the roots, a few molecules of water are pulled in from the soil by the same pressure drop. The day's work has begun.

As the streams flow upward into the sky, driven by solar heat, there are moments of greater and lesser tension. During the latter, carbon dioxide seeps into the leaf from the air. At the same time, a small amount of water is diverted to the food-making centers in the leaf. The water and the carbon dioxide are used to make the sugars that will be the basis for both the structure and the fuel that lets the tree live and grow. As the water is decomposed, its oxygen is released from the stomata into the air.

The path from root to stoma is labyrinthine. The channels of the streams are lines of cells, called tracheids in conifers and vessels in broadleaf trees. Each of these cells must die so that the tree can live. The cells extend and link to one another by pits and valves and elliptical connectors that resemble air-conditioning ducts. Combining into linked pipes, they climb the tree in lines, in zigzags, in spirals, and even in circles. A vessel might be from a fraction of an inch to ninety feet long. It might function for a day or for a hundred years. It might be wide enough to see with the naked eye, or so narrow it can't be seen unless stained and placed under the microscope. Every vessel forms connections to as many vessels as it crosses in its winding climb, so there is not one but a huge number of pathways through the labyrinth of pipes.

When the channels are formed, all the cells die. Only then, when the insides of the cells have dried and decomposed, do the streams of water begin to flow between the surviving cell walls and through the twisted, ever-ramifying, anastomosing network.

Although the labyrinth is astonishingly complex in structure, it nonetheless transmits strong pressure from the stomata ends. An ingenious botanist decided to see how strong a pull it was. First, he measured the pull of leaves on the columns of water. Then he took away the leaves and hooked up a vacuum pump. The leaves outpulled the pump. One reason for this is the way water behaves in the wilderness of tubes. Molecules cling to the walls of the vessels and remain there, unmoving. The molecules not clinging to the walls cling to each other. Together, they create a smooth passage that under normal conditions during the growing season is impervious to bubbles and to blockage. The inner volume of molecules passes hand over hand along the chain, shielded on its edges by the sheath of molecules clinging to the walls. In this way, the water acts both as though it were a liquid and as though it were a solid.

Another test of how well the pull works is what happens when you break it. If you make a cut into the stem of a large-vessel tree like an oak, you can hear the hiss as air rushes into the broken pipes. Oaks, and other trees like them, bet on large pipes to quickly carry all the water the tree needs. They renew these pipes each year. Other broadleaf trees and all conifers prefer a larger number of smaller-diameter tubes. Though these cannot carry the volume that the oak vessels can, they are less prone to damage and may keep working for several years.

Every channel is vulnerable. There is always air dissolved in the water that comes in through the roots. The tight seal of the vessels, and the way water works along their walls and in their stream, make it hard for bubbles to form—but not impossible. And a large bubble that fills a vessel from wall to wall is likely to put it permanently out of commission. Water might be stored in that vessel, but it will never again circulate.

There are two times when bubbles form. The first is during drought, when the vapor pressure in the stem sinks so low that the air comes out of solution. This is how most drought damage happens. Trees prevent it by closing the stomata and trapping the water in the vessels before the pressure gets too low.

The second problem cannot be avoided. In most temperate climates there are freezes during the winter. Air is a thousand times less soluble in ice than in water, so when the water in the vessels freezes, bubbles inevitably form. If the vessels are small with small diameters, they often can reabsorb the bubbles when the spring thaw comes. If not, they localize the damage inside a small vessel segment. When a bubble occurs in a vessel, it causes the membranes that connect to other vessels to seal shut, limiting their spread.

The circulation that generates the power of storms, the oxygen for breath, the stratospheric shield, and the making of all flesh depends on this strange internal labyrinth of dead, connected cells. The secret of their success is not to be ironclad and invulnerable. Rather, it is to be flexible, replaceable, and to create as many mutual connections as they possibly can. That way, if one pathway fails, another is available. The secret is resilience.

The Air Is a Slow Cold Flame

Early in my study of air, I heard an atmospheric scientist say that one of her teachers had told her this: "The air is a slow cold flame." I was instantly attentive. What did your teacher mean? I asked. But she was out of time, and she would not say more. I have thought about the sentence ever since. What does it mean?

Partly, it simply notices that the very highly reactive element oxygen—or more precisely the molecule O_2, dioxygen—has its primary reservoir in the air. Oxygen reacts with just about everything else, and the reactions always produce heat and sometimes produce light. Most of the aerosols that rise into the air react with the oxygen there, so in that sense the air is slowly burning.

Real visible flames—say, of a candle—are indeed the product of a reaction of fuel with oxygen. When you light a match to a candle, the wax vaporizes, and the resulting rapid reaction of the fuel with oxygen gas produces heat and visible flame. The heat of the reaction vaporizes more wax, creating a chain reaction that persists as long as the fuel, the oxygen, and the heat are present.

You can do this trick with other oxygen reactions as well. Rusting is a slow burn. You can prove this by letting some steel wool rust. Put the rusted wool in a closed jar with a thermometer and read the temperature. Then, take it out and clean off the rust with a vinegar bath.

Now, put the wool back in the jar with the thermometer. As the wool begins to rust anew, the temperature will exceed that of the already rusted wool, but only slightly. A small amount of heat is released, but there is no visible flame. The entire surface rusts, but the metal beneath the rust remains unchanged and unreacting.

If, on the other hand, you start a fire by means of flint and steel, you are essentially rusting a flame into being. The flint flakes off a very small thin strip of iron. This strip is all surface area and almost no depth. As it rusts all at once, the chip begins to glow. That is the glow that lights the tinder and starts the fire.

The greatest of all the oxygen reactions is the one that in the present world sustains most of the planet's living beings. Respiration is the means by which creatures combine oxygen with a carbon fuel to produce the energy to grow, hunt, feed, digest, defend themselves, heal themselves, and reproduce. The common name for the process is the equation of burning. But where is the flame?

Recently, I awoke around three o'clock in the morning, as I often do, the witching hour. I imagined a candle flame in my drowsy brain— its shifting shape and colors—when I suddenly opened my eyes. The room around me was not black. It was dark but not black, and if I looked right and left attentively, I saw a symphony of gray, some with more brown, others with more yellow, still others with cool blue in them. I knew that if I did not manage to get back to sleep, God help me, I would watch the light gradually rise. Soon there would be yellows and reds and greens. Soon I would see dawn, and if I looked out the window, the white of clouds, the blue of the clear sky, the red then yellow of the sun, the yellow green of the trident leaves, the red gray of the maple bark.

It suddenly occurred to me that the entire envelope of air in which we live and move and have our being is *actually* a slow cold flame. Not some piece of it, or process in it, but the whole unending, restless concert of it. We are accustomed to look down on the moth for being attracted fatally to flame, just as we look askance at the lemming for supposedly running over cliffs, but if the air were a slow cold flame, however it might be with the lemmings, the moth joke was on us. For we, as much as moths and lemmings, are living inside the flame.

Think of it this way. The content of the air is regulated by the earth and by the living. The oxygen that comprises 20 percent of the air is put there by the photosynthesis of plants. The nitrogen that comprises more than 70 percent of the air is regulated and replaced by bacterial fixation, by the decomposition of the dead, and by the deposition of urine and feces. When the high energy of sunlight glances off the atoms of nitrogen and oxygen, a part of it scatters, so in the regions of the sky farther from the sun, we see the most easily scattered color, blue. When we look closer to the solar disk, we see yellow, or when the sun is setting or rising and so must travel through the greatest thickness of air, we see the least easily scattered yellows, the longer-wavelength yellow, and the longest red.

But the air is by no means composed only of these gases. Water is vaporized by the solar heat and rises into the atmosphere. Sulfur compounds rise from the surface sea or are spewed high into the stratosphere by volcanoes. Nitrates rise into the air from the sea, from fields, from the dead. All kinds of carbon—both organic and inorganic—are swept up into the air. All of these chemicals burn slowly with oxygen in the air, and combine with one another, forming the nuclei on which water can condense to form cloud droplets, and so eventually to make it rain or snow. Bacteria and fungal spores also travel in the air, some of them too contributing to the formation of clouds.

The sun, when it strikes cloud particles, is rather focused than scattered. The light goes through them as through a lens, making the whole range of tinted whites. As the distance it must travel through the clouds increases, the white darkens to a palette of grays.

Isn't this precisely a slow cold flame? A flame occurs when a gas is excited and emits light of a particular set of wavelengths. In the air, the gases are excited, liquids are vaporized, and aerosols are sent aloft, either directly by solar energy or by the solar energy that has been translated into work by the living. In the atmosphere, these gases and the aerosols meet incoming solar energy, bending and scattering it electromagnetically to produce the whole range of hue, chroma, shadow, intensity, and pallor in which we exist.

We, and everything around us, live in the midst of a slow cold flame.

Notes

xv "And in this bright confusion": From Edwin Denby. 1973. "Group and Series," in *Collected Poems* (New York: Full Court Press), 49.

Introduction

8 "The clouds pass": From Wilhelm and Bayne (1950), 4. It is interesting that so ancient a book has so "modern" an understanding of the role of water in creating and sustaining life.

12 In 1947 Dave Fultz: Scientist Edward Lorenz had an early and abiding interest in the dishpan experiment. He was fascinated by the fact that three completely different regimes were possible and that one of them was completely unpredictable. See Lorenz (1965, 1979, 1993). For Fultz's own account, see Fultz (1960).

15 "Only subjects exist": See "The Human Subjectivity" in Maritain (1966), 60. Devoted to the work of Thomas Aquinas, Maritain viewed abstraction and quantification as wrong turns for wisdom. He and his friend Gabriel Marcel viewed the truth of human life in immanence and relationship, rather than in mind or in any Platonic ideal realm.

15 Federico García Lorca: In García Lorca's *Poet in New York*, from García

Lorca (2002), 682–683. The line here is my translation. Among the many people writing about New York at the beginning of the Great Depression, García Lorca had the clearest vision of the spiritual dangers of a commercial culture. See particularly "Sleepless City," "New York," "Cry to Rome," and "Ode to Walt Whtiman."

16 "the world of nature and adventure": See Maritain (1957), 24–28, and Maritain (1966), 354. Maritain insists that meaning is not extractable from events, but rather is revealed through them.

Floating

25 huge dust storms had arisen: An excellent resource on this time is Worster (1979). The Dust Bowl was a classic example of faux science and promotion working together to create a disaster. When the promoters' saying "Rain follows the plow" proved false, a whole pseudoscientific system called dry farming was created to keep the fantasy alive. As the twentieth century dawned, Americans pushed out into the plains, west of the one-hundredth meridian, into western Kansas, eastern Montana, the Dakotas, Oklahoma, Texas, Colorado, and Wyoming. "Rain follows the plow," they were told, so although these lands had formerly been known as the American desert, they had confidence that soon the lands will flower, and the rains will fall. It was not a completely implausible idea. At the beginning, the soils were fertile, never having been tilled and having been covered with prairie grasses, some of whose root systems reached down twenty feet. If crops are planted, the reasoning went, they will soak up moisture and transpire vapor into the atmosphere. Then, more rain will be able to fall. Why then, someone should have asked, do the roots of the native plants grow three to twenty feet deep in the ground? The roots of our wheat go only about a foot and a half to three feet. Rain in this part of the world may total ten to twenty inches a year, while it is thirty-five to fifty inches in Ohio. How do we get the scarce water to the roots of our plants, and why should it rise up in the soil to meet us? It didn't. Droughts were too frequent, reducing yields to less than half what Ohio got. Fortunately, science was ready to save the day. State Agricultural Experiment Stations, university professors, and some elements of the U.S. Department of

Agriculture conceived of dry farming. It was a rational system that made just enough sense. If there were too little rain to support even the most drought-tolerant wheat on a regular basis, then the solution was twofold: (1) leave *half* the farmland unplanted and fallow each year, storing that year's rain for next year's crop, so when the crop is planted in that half in the second year, the wheat will get twice the water that one year's rain could bring, and (2) treat the soil by repeated plowing and subsoil compaction to lessen evaporation and keep the water in the soil until the roots can take it up. However, neither rain nor soil was saved. The weather thought little of dry farming. A drought year following a drought year left even the fallowed fields with too little water to bear a healthy crop. The farmers went deep into debt buying the machinery needed to do the repeated plowing, disking, and subsoil packing, while the price of wheat fell. Worst of all, the fine topsoil layer above a firmed subsoil had no structure and no roots to hold it. The prairie winds lifted the fine-tilled topsoil into the air and blew it away. By 1935, one-fifth of the farmland in the southern plains had been left idle, and one-fourth of farms had been abandoned. In every county, at least 30 percent of the farmers were on the dole, and in some counties more than 90 percent were.

25   Charles Darwin began to realize: See Darwin (1989), 6.

26   He later reported: Darwin (1846) represents Darwin's study of dusts encountered at sea. The reference is on page 267.

26   Darwin had not forgotten the dust: For his account of the dust, see Darwin (1846). For an account of what C. H. Ehrenberg found, see Gregory (1961), p 13. "I may remark": Darwin's conclusion to the article Darwin (1846), 274.

30   "We believe the dependence": See Swap et al. (1992), 133.

31   "It is input from the atmosphere": See Chadwick et al. (1999), 496.

32   Darwin was moved to write: Darwin (1989), 89.

33   The fungi were once classed with the lower plants: For a wonderful Internet resource about the world of fungi, see *The Fifth Kingdom* (n.d.).

35   John brought out books: The books are Gregory (1961) and Dennis (1968). There has perhaps never been a book: The citation is from Dennis's precise observations of the ascomycetes. This description is located in Dennis (1968), 24.

48 this small selection: All the locations are from the pages of Dennis (1968).

51 The fungi travel for their work: The best resource about how they get there is Ingold (1965).

58 The wonderful amateur mycologist Mary Banning: It was New York State mycologist John Haines who discovered the lost Banning watercolors. He organized a traveling show of them. Selected images can be found online at the website of the New York State Museum (www.nysm.nysed.gov/treasures/department.cfm?dept=Biology). Haines also created a moving dialogue play that replays the long correspondence between Banning and pioneer American mycologist Charles Horton Peck. The cited Banning quote is from that unpublished play. It is extracted from the text of her unpublished manuscript.

59 The fungi, when they are not: For a well-written compendium of the fungi as agents of disease, see Large (1940). It is worth remembering that the potato blight that led to Irish famine and emigration, as well as the phylloxera that almost destroyed the French wine industry, and many more epidemic diseases of food plants, are all fungal in origin.

59 *Claviceps purpurea*: See Dennis (1968), 227.

63 Consider your bedroom: The count of skin cells in the bedroom air is from Gregory (1961).

64 it is only through the work of certain bacteria: For an account of both natural and industrial nitrogen fixation, see Leigh (2004). What the bacteria do at room temperature or below, the industrial Haber process to fix nitrogen must do at very high heat and pressure, with concomitant high energy costs.

65 Viable bacteria have been found: For descriptions of bacteria as aerosols, see Andreae and Rosenfeld (2008), Burrows et al. (2009), Conen (2011), and Perfumo and Marchant (2010).

66 Pollens are the giants: For a general account of pollen function and a good anthology of the forms and shapes, see Ogden et al. (1974). For a brief but thorough account, see Echlan (1968).

68 Palynology is built: For a very thorough account of palynology, from the oldest strata to the present, see Traverse (2007).

69 "It is premature": See Traverse (2007), 463.

71 Pierre Miquel was not so interested: A good account of Miquel's work

is found in Gregory (1961). Miquel's own account is contained in his *L'organismes vivants de l'atmosphere* (1850).

75 The lung tissues change: Material about tissue remodeling is derived from an interview with Dr. Jesse Roman, pulmonologist and chief of medicine at the University of Louisville Medical School. Dr. Roman emphasized how lungs are impaired by this remodeling, whether it is the building of useless masses of fiber to fill the lungs or the kind of hollowing out of tissues that occurs with emphysema.

77 China has created a system: See Chen et al. (2007) for chilling data on Chinese air pollution. There has been a long-running dispute between Chinese authorities and the American embassy in Beijing. The embassy publishes daily an accounting of the fine particulate pollution in Beijing. The official Chinese figures only account for coarse (PM10) air pollution, while the embassy figures single out the more dangerous fine (PM2.5) pollutants. So the Chinese authorities say the air is fine, while the embassy says it is terrible. Pressure was put on the embassy by the Chinese to stop releasing its figures, but the embassy refused to comply.

78 It used to be thought: For data on formaldehyde, see Azuma et al. (2006), Bernstein et al. (2008), Pope et al. (2009), Slaughter (2009), World Health Organization (2008), and Xiang et al. (2010). For pollutants like formaldehyde, a wide range of sensitivities exist in different individuals, so what may stimulate a severe allergic reaction in one person will have no discernible effect on another.

79 In Atlanta, a pulmonologist: The doctor was Dr. Jesse Roman, now chief of medicine at University of Louisville.

80 Perhaps they should have proudly proclaimed: In *The Chronicles of H. Bustos Domeca*, Jorge Luis Borges and Adolfo Bioy-Casares created witty faux reviews of art and architecture, which they published under the pen name H. Bustos Domecq.

80 A World Bank study: See World Bank (2011). It is interesting to note the high levels of emphysema seen among rural people using biomass stoves with poor ventilation. Although they do not smoke, they suffer the same hollowing transformation of lung tissues as do heavy smokers.

80 Dr. Roberto Accinelli Tanaka instituted: For Dr. Tanaka's study and

results, see Tanaka (2004). The improvements in health resulting simply from a change in stoves and ventilation is dramatic everywhere.

82 Within an hour and a half, both buildings: For data on the materials put into the air after the planes struck, see Landrigan et al. (2004) and Wu et al. (2010).

82 "the air is safe": Rudolph Giuliani's comments are reported in Fred Mogul's WNYC audio report "Rudy Giuliani and Air Quality after 9/11" broadcast on January 24, 2008.

82 "glad to reassure the people": Christine Whitman's comment on the safety of the air at the World Trade Center is reported in a press release from the Environmental Protection Agency dated September 18, 2001, titled "Environmental News: Tuesday, September 18, 2001. Whitman details ongoing agency efforts to monitor disaster site, contribute to cleanup efforts."

84 the EPA had been in there way ahead of us: See McKee et al. (2003).

87 Ten years later, the number of people: See Ahearn (2010).

87 Seven of the worst-affected patients: The study is reported in Wu et al. (2010).

88 When Christine Whitman was severely criticized: Whitman testified before the Committee on the Judiciary of the House of Representatives on June 25, 2007. The transcript can be found online at http://judiciiary.house.gov/hearings/printers/110th/36342.PDF.

Spinning

91 By no means is the air empty: Data on the number of aerosols in the atmosphere come from many sources. Among the ones I used are Andreae and Rosenfeld (2008), DeMott et al. (2010), and Schwartz (2004).

92 Consider the sky above: See Poschl et al. (2010).

94 there were perhaps twice as many aerosols: See Rosenfeld et al. (2008), 1309.

95 In places like Beijing, China: See Menon et al. (2002).

100 the plankton sink out of sight: The effect of hurricanes on fishing and global warming were described to me by atmospheric scientist Kerry Emanuel.

100 Max Margules, who in 1903: See Margules (1910).

102 "Look for the worst weather": See Buck (1998), 28.

102 The strongest winds naturally occurring: A thorough, somewhat technical, but understandable and well-illustrated introduction to tornado genesis and structure is found in Davies-Jones et al. (2001). Howard Bluestein of the University of Oklahoma is the best resource overall for the study of tornadoes, their genesis, and power. See Bluestein and Weiss (2004) and Bluestein et al. (2003).

104 The Fujita Scale: The Fujita Scale is widely used to assess the strength of tornadoes. One place to see the full scale is on the web at http://www.tor nadoproject.com/fscale/fscale.htm. The quotation is from this web page. Accessed 2/12/2012.

105 Most Atlantic hurricanes begin: The best accounts of hurricane origin and dynamics are by Kerry Emanuel, especially Emanuel (1988). See also Black et al. (2007).

110 a weather chart called a SkewT diagram: A very good introduction to this diagram is the U.S. Air Force publication from Air Weather Service (1979). SkewT diagrams show graphically the steepness of temperature decline with altitude and the spread between temperature and dew point. They are thus a fast and reliable way to assess how much water is in the atmosphere, how fast the air is rising, and when precipitation is likely to fall.

115 El Greco's Clouds: For links to the paintings discussed in this section, please go to www.williambryantlogan.com.

115 "The sky": John Constable's remark about the sky as the chief organ of sentiment is perhaps his best-remembered phrase. Here it is in the Victoria and Albert Museum's study of Constable's best-known painting: http://www.vam.ac.uk/content/articles/s/constables-studies-for-the-hay-wain/ (accessed 1/10/2012). The phrase is a touchstone for Thornes's *John Constable's Skies* (1999), a very interesting study of Constable's paintings that considers both their art and science. The book is beautifully illustrated not only with Constable's paintings but also with comparisons from other great landscape painters, including Bellini.

116 How different is the atmosphere of: The Bellini painting *Madonna of the Meadow* has an iconography that is difficult to grasp. I was helped in the

effort by Cast (1969), with thanks to Maud Humphrey and Sally Cornelison for tracking the article down.

122 The young Lorenz: A good introduction to Lorenz's biography is his own reflection, in Lorenz (1991). Another is Kerry Emanuel's brief biography (Emanuel 2011). Lorenz was a brilliant scientist and a very shy man, and like most great atmospheric scientists, he was what Howard Bluestein calls "a weather nut." Bluestein recalled a time when his office was right next to the bulletin board at MIT where all the fresh weather data were posted. In the time before smart phones and the Internet, this is where all the weather nuts came to satisfy their curiosity. He remembers one day when he looked up from his desk to find Lorenz standing in the doorway, using every means short of actually speaking out loud to indicate that he had a very interesting weather observation to discuss. They pored over the observation together.

124 Lorenz used twelve equations: The experiment is reported in Lorenz (1963b).

126 "The controversy had not yet been settled": Ibid., 432.

126 "There is no way of knowing": Lorenz made the remark in his Kyoto Prize acceptance spreech, Lorenz (1991).

128 William Cobbett spent: Cobbett (1985), 226.

129 More ingenuity and more computing power: For an account of the ENIAC work, see Platzman (1979). For Charney's report on the work, see Charney et al. (1950).

129 The first man to publish: Edward Lorenz had a deep interest in Fitzroy's pioneering work. See Lorenz (1966). Fitzroy, given to bouts of depression, was in many ways a difficult and disappointed man. He committed suicide by cutting his throat in 1865. Nevertheless, his efforts to make weather observations and forecasts on a regular basis were among the most enlightened public projects of his day.

131 The first to actually use: For a brief, engaging biography of Richardson—including his work on the causes of war and on what would later be called fractals—see Hunt (1998). Like many atmospheric scientists—Margules, Lorenz, and Fitzroy among them—Richardson was a somewhat solitary man. He was also a Quaker and pacifist. He gave up on his efforts to make

numerical weather forecasts when he believed that they might be used to give an advantage in warfare.

136 This ensemble forecasting: Thanks to Kerry Emanuel for his descriptions of ensemble forecasting, including the MIT competition between Model Output Statistics (MOS) and Ensemble.

139 They jostled, yelled, scribbled: For a full account, see Fleming (2004).

141 The two British teams: For a valuable firsthand recollection of the events by one of the participants, Lawrence Hogben of the Admiralty Office, see Hogben (1994).

143 The Germans believed that the weather: See Lettau (2002), though the part of the interview that focused on the D-day events was lost.

143 later a revered professor: For a university memorial resolution about Professor Emeritus Heinz Lettau, see University of Wisconsin, Madison (2008).

145 After the war, German Admiral Friedrich Ruge: See D'Este (2002), 529.

146 Gavin Schmidt is an Englishman: I am indebted to Gavin Schmidt and his colleague Kostas Tsigaridis, for their elucidation of aerosol and other processes in the atmosphere, and on the workings of climate models.

151 As composter Clark Gregory: Gregory was a master of large-scale composting. I met him and traveled with him to composting sites in Florida during the late 1980s. He was a wonderful source of knowledge and wisdom. I once asked him if there weren't some things that just had to go to the waste dump. He replied, "It isn't waste until it's wasted."

152 "Who can sound the depths": Artist Charles Burchfield was a great observer (and painter) of weather. This citation is from Davenport (2004), plate 2. Burchfield painted wind and weather with a combination of expressionist imagination and accurate observation that make his paintings exhilarating to see, even when the subjects are cold and windy.

152 in 1781, the French physicist: For a description of Marcellin Ducarla-Bonifas's thought experiment and for much else on the history of ideas about rain and snow, see Strangeways (2007). The quoted phrases are from the section on Ducarla-Bonifas in Strangeways (2007).

160 Pilot Jack Knight reported: See Knight (2008).

161 As a child living in the Bay Area: Both the Sandburg and the Lowell citations can be found in Untermeyer (1919).

162 "War is the struggle": See Weil (1938).

163 they could create a firestorm: For a complete account of the Dresden firestorm, see Addison and Crang (2006). It seems incredible that people could regard the horrors of wartime as an element of everyday life, but they did. Daily air raids were a part of life in many major German cities. Among the most moving accounts of life in wartime and its attendant worries are the letters between the pastor Dietrich Bonhoeffer and his family and friends, written while the pastor was in prison. See Bonhoeffer (1953). There are frequent references to the nightly bombings, often stated simply as a series of inconveniences. Bonhoeffer's mother reported, for example, that it had become necessary to take all the pastor's books from his room and store them in a safer place, but she was unable to find a book when he needed it. One can imagine that such letters and exchanges occurred frequently among Dresdeners in the months before the firestorm killed so very many of them.

163 around the town of Peshtigo: A historical account of the Peshtigo fire is found in Brown (2004). A moving firsthand account is that of the local parish priest, Reverend Peter Pernin (1971). Wherever a firestorm occurs, it is the updrafts caused by the heat of the fire that draw more oxygen into the system and so exponentially increase the power and spread of the fire.

166 "Night after night": Quotes in Wohl (2005), 309. Antoine de Saint-Exupéry, most often known as the author of *The Little Prince*, was in fact an aviator who worked for the first trans-ocean mail carrier, Aéropostale. His books for adults were best-sellers and were deeply admired by the likes of novelist André Gide. Saint-Exupéry uniquely evokes the heroism and loneliness of flight in his early works, but as aviation became a means to military supremacy, he became disgusted with the destruction that flying made possible.

Flying

168 The one published report: I read about efforts to follow ballooning spiders in Suter (1999).

169 One arachnologist kept count: See the wonderful study of ballooning by

Suter (1999). Of course, this ballooning flight is the same as occurs in E. B. White's *Charlotte's Web*.

170 Some scientists had suggested: The account of their observations is found in Schneider et al. (2001).

175 The downstroke is the power stroke in the bird: For good accounts of the physics of flapping flight and of soaring, see Alexander (2002) and Rayner (1982).

177 Colin Pennycuick once studied: For an engaging account of the crane's flight and the human pilot's effort to follow them, see Pennycuick et al. (1979).

178 "Initially thermals were good": Ibid., 244.

181 My teacher—thirty years my junior: Thanks to Brian Monga, then of Air Fleet Training in Caldwell, New Jersey, for his patient instruction.

184 It does not matter so much: The best resource for the study of aeronautics is Anderson (2011). A less technical account of the work of wings is to be found in Alexander (2002). A good and well-illustrated account of the bound vortex is found in Denker (2008). The idea that a wing flies because of the way it is enveloped by spinning air is fascinating. The much more supple ability of birds and insects to fly is in part owed to their greater mastery of the vortices created by wings.

185 In every takeoff, however, the Kutta condition: For more on the Kutta condition, see Anderson (2011), 330.

190 Beryl Markham, who was a bush pilot: See Markham (1983). The quotation is on page 11. Hers is among the most interesting and accessible accounts of the camaraderie and the difficulties of early fliers. Much of her time was spent searching for friends who may have had mechanical problems and had to set down somewhere in the middle of nowhere.

191 Wilbur and Orville Wright went to: An account of the Wrights' experiments, their triumph, and their subsequent flights can be found in Wohl (1994), 5–30. There exists a photograph of all the wing shapes that they tried in their miniature wind tunnel. There are at least three hundred of them. The picture is found in Anderson (2011), 8, and the quotation from Wright is on page 7.

193 Alone among the mammals, bats: John Maina's (1998) book about breath contains valuable material on the way bats get the energy to fly. A good

article on bat flight energetics and means is Kalko et al. (2008). A comparison between bat and bird flight is Hedenstrom et al. (2009).

194 One in five mammals is a bat: For all their solitary flight, bats are among the most social of mammals. A large bat roost is as populous as the city of Chicago, although bats may shift roosts very frequently . . . like everyone in Chicago moving to Moline, overnight. There is little competition for roost space since in most places there are more choices of roost than there are bats to occupy them. And since many species delight in large numbers, there is no need to kick out an extra ten thousand or so. Birds migrate, but bats hibernate. The fat that birds store to fuel their flight, bats store to help their long sleep. There is an obvious advantage to a large colony in a cold winter, the many bats keeping each other warmer than they would otherwise be. But the sociability of bats goes well beyond central heating. Mother bats, in particular, very often share the same roosts with the same group of mothers through a life that spans from five to thirty years. The roosts may shift but the colony contains the same individuals, with the periodical addition of recruits from the younger generation. Males sometimes join these colonies or sometimes go their own way. In the colonies, bats groom each other, warm each other, babysit each other's young, and sometimes even feed each other. There is no evidence of a pecking order in these colonies, and helpful behaviors are not limited to relatives but are spread through the whole group. Vampire bats—not those you would think generous—will feed hungry members of their roost, whether they are related to them or not. (Bats relinquished large digestive tracts in order to make flight possible, and can starve to death in a few days.) Unrelated females often form pair-bonds with another female, to ensure that both get enough to eat. Bats have occupied a place in nature that gives them first pick of insects and fruits, so they are frequently living with plenty. Under those circumstances, they seem to cooperate at least as much as they compete.

195 The honeybee has no lungs at all: Honeybee flight energetics are discussed in Altshuler et al. (2005), Harrison et al. (1996), Heinrich (1974), (1993), Roberts and Elekonich (2005), Suarez (2000), and Woods et al. (2005). Again, the context for the breathing feats of the honeybee is wonderfully provided in Maina (1998). For information on the beeline, I am indebted

to beekeeper Richard Ronconi. The system of spiracles in all insects makes it important for anyone who applies pesticides to exercise great care. The system is vulnerable to poisons, and many of the pesticides aimed at an attacking organism might also kill nontarget insects, like bees. One way to avoid this is to be sure that no bees are present when you spray. Another is the development of new classes of insecticide that target only the pests, not the beneficials. Some insect growth regulators (IGRs) fulfill this criterion.

196 It must then have seemed like sour grapes: For the French study, see Magnan (1934). Here is another example, if we needed one, of how we humans go wrong when we assume that we are the crown of Creation and that everything we do is done in the best-possible way. Magnan's mistake was to think that an insect could not fly better than a human. A similar study by the U.S. Navy once proved that dolphins could not really swim in the way that they actually did.

197 At the top of its arc: Again, Maina (1998) is a good resource to set the goose's achievement among that of other birds. For more specific accounts, see Black and Tenney (1980), Javed et al. (2000), and Koppen et al. (2010). Several studies emphasize that the birds don't choose passes or valleys when these are present. They regularly travel over the crests.

199 In all living things, the constituents: For the fundamental ideas of the neutral theory of molecular evolution, see Kimura (1979). For application of this idea to the goose's hemoglobin, see Liu et al. (2001). Kimura's ideas are, I think, consonant with Jacques Maritain's notion of a world of nature and adventure. Variations occur, each an offer of adventure. One may lead nowhere or lead only to maladaptation and death. Another may lead to a different way of life.

200 Adventure leads all creatures on: The hotel is located in Nipton, California. This monument—set at the desert edge of a native cactus garden, with only the tracks of the Union Pacific between it and the playas and mountains of the high Mojave—is both lonely and magnificent. It makes me wish that I had known Ken Trongo and perhaps traveled with him up into that desert. I know from my own early childhood there that it was full of surprises: rivers flowing upside down, abandoned towns, mine shafts, sudden bursts of flowers.

203 One of the most notable areas: An account of the Sierra Wave Project is

found in Grubišić and Lewis (2004). It is worth surfing the Internet to look at images of the rotors as they descend after crossing the Sierra into Owens Valley. Also beautiful are images of the lenticular clouds found there.

223 One evening in Vietnam: Dave Oguss is an instructor for Flight Safety International. In the 1960s, he wondered whether to join the Peace Corps or to fly. He loved to fly, so he joined the Marine Corps. He noted that when you are flying a fighter and it malfunctions, you can bail out and go get a new one. A passenger jet is a whole other ballgame.

Telling

226 The world is awash in perfumes: A broad and thorough introduction to the world as sensed through pheromones is Wyatt (2003). See also E. O. Wilson's early and cogent account (1963), Holldobler and Wilson's account of ant pheromone behavior (1990), and Eisner (2003).

226 As Vincent Dethier pointed out: See Dethier (1987).

227 Writer François Rabelais: See Rabelais (1990), 202.

229 The Japanese honeybee: Careful observation of the bees' response to a hornet attack is reported in Ono et al. (1995). It is interesting to note that beekeepers often have their bees sent through the mail, and that in this way some European honeybees have reached Japan. The European bees, however, do not know how to defend against the hornet and are consequently devoured.

231 Not only is there communication: See the studies of Dicke and Dijkman (1992) and Turlings et al. (1995).

233 Yet very few babies have any trouble at all: For a study of the chemicals produced by the mother, see Vaglio et al. (2009).

234 "are an Ariadne's thread": Ibid., 131.

234 Within an hour of birth: See Porter and Winberg (1998).

234 The mother learns a similar trick: See Porter et al. (1983) and Weller (1998).

235 Robert Frost got it exactly: The poem is to be found online at http://www .etymonline.com/poems/tramps.htm. Accessed 2/16/2012.

237 "But when from a long-distant past": From Proust (2008), 43.

241 Though many odors allure me: Two book-length and absorbing accounts of the human response to scents—both natural and perfumes—are Classen et al. (1994) and Stoddart (1990).

243 Immanuel Kant put smell in its place: See Kant (2006), 50.

244 In 1886, a Frenchman: See Galopin (1886). This is a very French and very lovely book in celebration of what the sense of smell contributes to our love lives.

244 "Odor is the precursor of love": Ibid., 88. My translation.

246 "Love Perfumes All Parts": Herrick (1876), 102.

247 a scent has three notes: Stoddart (1990), 158.

251 There are over six thousand species of bark beetles: Two classic studies of bark beetle behavior are Raffa and Berryman (1983) and Raffa and Dahlsten (1995). A moving and very intelligent account of the destructive spread of bark beetles in recent decades, as well as good accounts of their ecology and habits, are found in Nikiforuk (2011).

252 Predators also get the message: The data on numbers of beetles and their predators are from Raffa and Berryman (1983).

255 When attacked by a predator, an aphid: For three valuable studies of the interactions of aphids with their protectors and other symbionts, see Nault et al. (1976), Pasteels (2007), and Stokl et al. (2010).

258 In *New Seeds of Contemplation*: See Merton (1961), 290.

258 The bolas spider is a fine example: A good account of the methods of the spider, including the work of *Mastophora dizzydeani*, is provided in Haynes and Yeargan (1999).

Calling

262 Orientation—a sense: See Maturana and Varela (1998).

265 "a single furious gesture of advance": Federico García Lorca, from "Cielo vivo." My translation.

267 Indeed the great student of the Central American yellow-naped Amazon parrot: For Wright and Dahlen's studies of the yellow-naped Amazon parrot's vocalization, see Dahlen and Wright (2009) and Wright and Dahlen (2007).

269 linguists like Jerrold Katz and Jerry Fodor: See Katz and Fodor (1963).

Notes

269 "Colorless green ideas sleep furiously": See Chomsky (1957), 15.

272 Bats ask and the universe answers: For recent studies of bat echolocation, see Au and Simmons (2007), Jones (2007), and Schnitzler and Kalko
(2001).

273 It wasn't until 1938: The key study, with excellent illustrations of the
experiment, is Griffin and Galambos (1941).

274 Nectar-feeding bats: See the study by Simon et al. (2006).

275 A few blind people: Human echolocation studies have shown that the
sight-impaired can learn to echolocate well enough to play basketball. See
Schenkman and Nilsson (2010) and Thaler et al. (2010, 2011).

278 The builders of the twelfth century: An excellent local publication on
the architecture of the abbey of Sénanque and other Cistercian abbeys
is available from the monastery gift shop. It is L'art des bâtisseurs romans
(1987).

279 Every day, eight times a day: For an outline of Cistercian liturgical prac-
tices, see Kerr (n.d.).

279 "Through the beauty of": This sentence of Bernard's is cited in Guillier
(2002), 26.

279 There was only proportion and stone: For a good introduction to the abbey
of Sénanque, with excellent pictures, see Guillier (2002).

280 All the proportions of the building: For studies of the resonant acoustics
in the abbey of Sénanque and other Cistercian abbeys, see A. Magrini and
U. Magrini (2005) and U. Magrini and A. Magrini (2005).

280 "the terrible snorting of a bellows": Aelred's no-nonsense response to what
he thought of as inflated or pompous church music is included in Kerr
(n.d.).

284 The Orphic Hymns: An interesting eighteenth-century English translation of the hymns is in Taylor (1792).

284 Ficino was polite compared to his contemporary: Bruno's career and
thought are well assessed in Yates (1964, 1966).

284 In his Incantations of Circe: An English translation of the books is available
in Bruno (2009). The Latin original of Bruno's Incantations of Circe is represented online at http://www.esotericarchives.com/bruno/circaeus.htm.
Accessed 02/16/2012. The citations are found in Circe's fourth speech in
the First Dialogue.

286 The folklorist Alexander Carmichael: There are hundreds of incantations, many of them very beautiful in Carmichael's English versions (1992), with Gaelic on facing-pages. There are prayers for everything from going to bed, to milking the cow, to herding, to fishing, to weaving.

287 "The sacred Three": Carmichael (1992), 234–235.

287 "An angel white": Ibid., 236–237.

289 "If all musical sounds": Davenport (2004), 72.

292 All over the world the same pentatonic scale: Leonard Bernstein in his 1973 Norton Lectures at Harvard University provided a captivating introduction to musical form and tonal possibilities. The work is available as both book and video. See Bernstein (1976).

293 Early writers about the sonata form: For a translation and commentary of Francesco Galeazzi's late-eighteenth-century prescriptions for sonata form, see Churgin (1968).

293 Likewise, the sonata depends: For scholarly descriptions of sonata form, see Caplin (1998) and Hepokoski (2006).

295 Lord Rayleigh—the same person: See Raleigh's account (1915) of Aeolian tones.

295 Emerson, who was so delighted: For Emerson's response to the Aeolian harp and for his poems about it, see Matteson (1963). For a broader view of the Romantic fascination with the wind harp, see Abrams (1957). The poem is quoted in Matteson (1963), 7.

297 "Waldo asks if the strings": Emerson's recording of his son's question is cited in Matteson (1963), 6.

Breathing

301 Breath turns a place into a habitat: For a marvelous account of breathing in all living creatures, see Maina (1998).

301 Darwin used the pigeon breeder: Darwin developed *The Origin of Species* out of a chapter entitled "Variation under Domestication." Beginning in my edition (1968), 81, Darwin considers both his knowledge and his experience of pigeon breeding.

302 Consider the tarpon: As did Schlaifer and Breder in their inventive and very interesting work (1940, 1941).

305 Biologist Lynn Margulis: Margulis developed the idea of the oxygen

holocaust in her important book (1981). An earlier version of the book was roundly criticized when it appeared in 1970, but by 1981 her idea of the symbiotic origin of eukaryotic cells had become a cornerstone of biology.

306 The Danish ecologist Tom Fenchel: Fenchel's wonderful Tansley Lecture of 1992 is a description of this bay-bottom ecosystem and its microscopic life.

314 I have not found out how often a vole breathes: To find rates of oxygen consumption and rates of breathing, I consulted many articles on allometric breath calculations, and many articles on the measured respiration of and in forest ecosystems. Among the key references are Cook (2004), Frappell et al. (2001), Harrison and Roberts (2000), Holmes and Sturgis (1975), Houston et al. (1998), Nagy (2005), Niven and Scharlemann (2005), Reich et al. (1995), Sullivan et al. (1996), and Tang et al. (2008). Allometry is itself a way of estimating breath, so the totals are estimates only. I mean to get an order of magnitude calculation for the volume of daily breath in this limited area. It is astonishing and makes more believable the notion that our air is indeed produced by the living.

322 Among practitioners of yoga: A classic, fine account of yoga practice, with an entire chapter on breath, is Iyengar (1965).

325 Aquinas called these two: See Aquinas (1989), 68.

328 This is the question: Ezekiel 37:3.

329 Mars, Venus, and Earth: For accounts of the early atmospheres, I am indebted to Butcher et al. (1992) and to David Brownlee.

Shining

342 the sun powers the ascent of the sap: Perhaps no one has ever understood better than Mel Tyree how water travels through a plant. His account in Tyree and Zimmermann (1983) is well worth wading through the seas of mathematics.

Bibliography

Abrams, M. H. 1957. "The correspondent breeze: a romantic metaphor." *Kenyon Review* 19 (1): 113–130.

Addison, Paul, and Jeremy A. Crang. 2006. *Firestorm*. London: Pimlico.

Aguado, Edward, and James E. Burt. 2007. *Understanding Weather and Climate*. Upper Saddle River, NJ: Pearson Prentice Hall.

Ahearn, A. 2010. "nine years later: health effects in World Trade Center responders, with Philip Landrigan." *Environmental Health Perspective*. Available at http://ehp03.niehs.nih.gov/article/fetchArticle.action?articleURI=info%3Ad oi%2F10.1289%2Fehp.trp090110. Accessed 2/12/2012.

Airborne Microbes. 1967. Seventeenth Symposium of the Society for General Microbiology. Cambridge, UK: Cambridge University Press.

Air Weather Service. 1979. *The Use of the SkewT Log P Diagram in Analysis and Forecasting*. Illinois: Scott Air Force Base.

Aldrich, Thomas K., et al. 2010. "Lung function in the rescue workers at the World Trade Center after 7 years." *New England Journal of Medicine* 362 (14): 1263–1272.

Alexander, David E. 2002. *Nature's Flyers: Birds, Insects and the Biomechanics of Flight*. Baltimore: Johns Hopkins University Press.

Altshuler, Douglas L., et al. 2005. "Short-amplitude high-frequency wing strokes determine the aerodynamics of honeybee flight." *Proceedings of the National Academy of Sciences of the United States of America* 102: 18213–18218.

Anderson, John D. 2011. *Fundamentals of Aerodynamics.* New York: McGraw-Hill.

Andreae, M. O., and D. Rosenfeld. 2008. "Aerosol-cloud-precipitation interactions. Part 1. The nature and sources of cloud-active aerosols." *Earth Science Reviews* 89: 13–41.

Aquinas, St. Thomas. 1989. *Summa Theologiae: A Concise Translation.* Allen, TX: Christian Classics.

L'art des bâtisseurs romans. 1987. Crots, France: Association des amis de Boscodon.

Au, Whitlow W. L., and James A. Simmons. 2007. "Echolocation in dolphins and bats." *Physics Today* 60: 40–45.

Azuma, K., et al. 2006. "The risk management for indoor air pollution caused by formaldehyde in housing." *Facilities* 24 (11): 420–429.

Bazzaz, F. A. 1979. "The physiological ecology of plant succession." *Annual Review of Ecology and Systematics* 10: 351–371.

Bernstein, Jonathan A., et al. 2004. "The health effects of air pollution." *Journal of Allergy and Clinical Immunology* 114: 1116–1123.

———. 2008. "The health effects of nonindustrial indoor air pollution." *Journal of Allergy and Clinical Immunology* 121: 585–591.

Bernstein, Leonard. 1976. *The Unanswered Question: Six Lectures at Harvard.* Cambridge, MA: Harvard University Press.

Black, Craig Patrick, and S. M. Tenney. 1980. "Oxygen transport during progressive hypoxia in high-altitude and sea-level waterfowl." *Respiration Physiology* 39: 217–239.

Black, Peter G., et al. 2007. "Air-sea exchange in hurricanes." *Bulletin of the American Meteorological Society* 88: 357–374.

Bluestein, Howard B., and Christopher C. Weiss. 2004. "The vertical structure of a tornado near Happy, TX on 5 May 2002." *Monthly Weather Review* 132: 2325–2337.

Bluestein, Howard B., et al. 2003. "Mobile Doppler radar observations of a tornado in a supercell near Bassett, Nebraska, on 5 June 1999: part II: tornado-vortex structure." *Monthly Weather Review* 131: 2968–2984.

Bonhoeffer, Dietrich. 1953. *Letters and Papers from Prison.* New York: Touchstone.

Brown, Hutch. 2004. "'The air was fire': fire behavior at Peshtigo in 1871." *Fire Management Today* 64: 20–30.

Bibliography

Browne, Janet. 1995. *Charles Darwin: Voyaging*. Princeton, NJ: Princeton University Press.

———. 2002. *Charles Darwin: The Power of Place*. Princeton, NJ: Princeton University Press.

Bruno, Giordano. 1995. *The Ash Wednesday Supper*. Translated by Stanley L. Jaki. The Hague: Mouton.

———. 2009. *Cantus Circaeus: The Incantations of Circe*. Ouroboros Press.

Buck, Robert N. 1998. *Weather Flying*. New York: McGraw-Hill.

Burrows, S. M., et al. 2009. "Bacteria in the global atmosphere—part 2: modeling of emissions and transport between different ecosystems." *Atmospheric Chemistry and Physics Discussions* 9: 9281–9297.

Butcher, Samuel S, et al., eds. 1992. *Global Biogeochemical Systems*. London: Academic Press.

Camp, J. Parks, and T. Montgomery. 2001. "Hurricane maximum intensity: past and present." *Monthly Weather Review* 129: 1704–1717.

Caplin, William Earl. 1998. *Classical Form: A Theory of Formal Functions for the Instrumental Music of Haydn, Mozart and Beethoven*. New York: Oxford University Press.

Carmichael, Alexander. 1992. *Carmina Gadelica*. Aurora, CO: Lindisfarne Press.

Cast, David. 1969. "The stork and the serpent, a new interpretation of the *Madonna of the Meadow* by Bellini." *Art Quarterly* 32: 247–257.

Chadwick, Oliver, et al. 1999. "Changing sources of nutrients during four million years of ecosystem development." *Nature* 397: 491–497.

Charney, Jule, et al. 1950. "Numerical integration of the barotropic vorticity equation." *Tellus* 2: 237–254.

Chaston, Peter R. 1997. *Weather Maps*. Kearney, MO: Chaston Scientific.

Chen, Tse-ming, et al. 2007. "Outdoor air pollution: overview and historical perspective." *American Journal of the Medical Sciences* 333 (4) 230–234.

Chomsky, Noam. 1957. *Syntactic Structures*. The Hague: Mouton.

Churgin, Bathia. 1968. "Francesco Galeazzi's description (1796) of sonata form." *Journal of the American Musicological Society* 21: 181–199.

Clark, Kenneth. 1949. *Landscape into Art*. London: John Murray.

Classen, Constance, et al. 1994. *Aroma: The Cultural History of Smell*. London: Routledge.

Cobbett, William. 1985. *Rural Rides*. London: Penguin Books.

Conen, F., et al. 2011. "Biological residues define the ice nucleation properties of soil dust." *Atmospheric Chemistry and Physics Discussions* 11: 16585–16598.

Cook, Bruce D., et al. 2004. "Carbon exchange and venting anomalies in an upland deciduous forest in northern Wisconsin, USA." *Agricultural and Forest Meteorology* 126: 271–295.

Curtis, Luke, et al. 2006. "Adverse health effects of outdoor air pollutants." *Environment International* 32: 815–830.

Dahlen, Christine R., and Timothy F. Wright. 2009. "Duets in yellow-naped Amazons: variation in syntax, note composition and phonology at different levels of social organization." *Ethology* 115: 857–871.

Darwin, Charles. 1846. "An account of the fine dust which often falls on vessels in the Atlantic Ocean." *Geological Society Journal* 2: 267–274.

———. 1896. *On the Power of Movement in Plants.* New York: D. Appleton.

———. 1968. *The Origin of Species.* London: Penguin Books.

———. 1989. *The Voyage of the Beagle.* New York: Penguin Putnam.

Davenport, Guy. 2004. *Charles Burchfield's Seasons.* San Francisco: Pomegranate.

Davies-Jones, Robert, et al. 2001. "Tornadoes and tornadic storms." *Meteorological Monographs* 28 (50): 166–221.

Day, John A. 2006. *The Book of Clouds.* New York: Sterling.

DeMott, P. J., et al. 2010. "Predicting global atmospheric ice nuclei distributions and their impacts on climate." *Proceedings of the National Academy of Sciences of the United States of America, Early Edition.* Available at www.pnas.org/cgi/doi/10.1073/pnas.0910818107.

Denker, John H. 2008. *See How It Flies.* Available at www.av8n.com/how.

Dennis, R.W.G. 1968. *British Ascomycetes.* Lehre: Verlag von J. Cramer.

D'Este, Carlo. 2002. *Eisenhower: A Soldier's Life.* New York: Henry Holt.

Dethier, Vincent G. 1987. "Sniff, flick and pulse: an appreciation of interruption." *Proceedings of the American Philosophical Society* 131: 159–176.

Dicke, Marcel, and Herman Dijkman. 1992. "Induced defense in detached uninfested plant leaves: effects on behavior of herbivores and their predators." *Oecologia* 91: 554–560.

Dudley, Robert. 2000. *The Biomechanics of Insect Flight.* Princeton, NJ: Princeton University Press.

Dyson, Freeman. 2006. "A failure of intelligence." *Technology Review* 109 (5): 62–72.

Echlan, Patrick. 1968. "Pollen." *Scientific American* 218: 80–93.

Eisner, Thomas. 2003. *For Love of Insects*. Cambridge, MA: Belknap Press of Harvard University Press.

Ellis, Martin B., and J. Pamela Ellis. 1985. *Macrofungi on Land Plants*. New York: Macmillan.

Emanuel, K. A. 1988. "Towards a general theory of hurricanes." *American Scientist* 76: 370–379.

———. 1997. "Some aspects of hurricane inner-core dynamics and energetics." *Journal of Atmospheric Science* 54: 1014–1026.

———. 2006. "Hurricanes: tempests in a greenhouse." *Physics Today* 59: 74–75.

———. 2011. *Edward Norton Lorenz 1917–2008: A Biographical Memoir*. Washington, DC: National Academy of Sciences.

Emanuel, K., et al. 2008. "Hurricanes and global warming." *Bulletin of the American Meteorological Society* 89: 347–367.

European Centre for Medium-Range Weather Forecasting (ECMWF). n. d. "Analyzing and forecasting the weather for early June 1944." ECMWF Reanalysis and Forecasts of D-day Weather. Available at www.ecmwf.int/research/era/dday. Accessed 12/14/2011.

Faegri, Knut, and Johs Iversen. 1964. *Textbook of Pollen Analysis*. New York: Harper.

Federal Aviation Regulations/Aeronautical Information Manual 2011. 2010. Newcastle, WA: Aviation Supplies and Academics.

Fenchel, Tom. 1992. "What can ecologists learn from microbes: life beneath a square centimetre of sediment surface." *Functional Ecology* 6 (5): 499–507.

The Fifth Kingdom. n. d. Available at www.mycolog.com/fifthtoc.html. Accessed 1/20/2012.

Finlay, Bland, and Tom Fenchel. 1989. "Everlasting picnic for protozoa: many protozoa form consortia with other microbes or with chloroplasts stolen from microscopic plants. Some of these partners are 'milked', some are digested, while others mop up metabolic waste." *New Scientist* 1671: 1–4.

Fleming, James R. 2004. "Sverre Petterssen, the Bergen School, and the forecasts for D-day." *Proceedings of the International Commission on History of Meteorology* 1 (1): 75–83.

Frappell, P. B., et al. 2001. "Scaling of respiratory variables and the breathing pattern in birds: an allometric and phylogenetic approach." *Physiological and Biochemical Zoology* 74 (1): 75–89.

Fultz, Dave. 1960. "Experimental models of rotating fluids and possible avenues for future research." *In Dynamics of Climate*, edited by R. L. Pfeffer. New York: Pergamon Press.

Galopin, Augustin. 1886. *Le parfum de la femme, et la sens olfactif dans l'amour.* Paris: E. Dentu.

García Lorca, Federico. 2002. *Collected Poems.* New York: Farrar, Straus and Giroux.

Garrison, V. H., et al. 2006. "Saharan dust—a carrier of persistent organic pollutants, metals and microbes to the Caribbean?" *Revista de Biologia Tropical* 54: 9–21.

Gould, Stephen Jay. 2002. *The Structure of Evolutionary Theory.* Cambridge, MA: Belknap Press of Harvard University Press.

Gregory, P. H. 1961. *The Microbiology of the Atmosphere.* New York: Interscience.

Griffin, D. R., and R. Galambos. 1941. "The sensory basis of obstacle avoidance by flying bats." *Journal of Experimental Zoology* 86: 481–506.

Griffin, Dale W., and Christina A. Kellogg. 2004. "Dust storms and their impact on ocean and human health: dust in Earth's atmosphere." *EcoHealth* 1: 284–295.

Griffin, Dale W., et al. 2001. "Dust in the wind: long-range transport of dust in the atmosphere and its implications for global public and ecosystem health." *Global Climate and Human Health* 2 (1): 20–33.

———. 2002. "The global transport of dust." *American Scientist* 90: 230–237.

Grubišić, Vanda, and John M. Lewis. 2004. "Sierra Wave Project revisited: 50 years later." *Bulletin of the American Meteorological Society* 85: 1127–1142.

Gu, Lianhong, et al. 2003. "Response of a deciduous forest to the Mount Pinatubo eruption: enhanced photosynthesis." *Science* 299: 2035–2038.

Guillier, Gerard. 2002. *L'abbaye de Sénanque.* Paris: L'imager.

Haines, John, et al. 1999. *Mycology of the Air.* Tucson, AZ: Pan American Aerobiology Association.

Harrison, John F., et al. 1996. "Achievement of thermal stability by varying metabolic heat production in flying honeybees." *Science* 274: 88–89.

Harrison, Jon F., and Stephen P. Roberts. 2000. "Flight respiration and energetics." *Annual Review of Physiology* 62: 179–205.

Bibliography

Haynes, Kenneth F., and Kenneth V. Yeargan. 1999. "Exploitation of intraspecific communication systems: illicit signalers and receivers." *Annals of the Entomological Society of America* 92: 960–970.

Hedenstrom, Anders, et al. 2009. "Bird or bat: comparing airframe design and flight performance." *Bioinspiration and Biomimetics* 4: 1–12.

Heinrich, Bernd. 1974. "Thermoregulation in endothermic insects." *Science* 85 (4): 747–756.

———. 1993. *The Hot-Blooded Insects.* Cambridge, MA: Harvard University Press.

Hepokoski, James A. 2006. *Elements of Sonata Theory.* New York: Oxford University Press.

Herrick, Robert. 1876. "Love perfumes all parts." In *The Complete Poems.* London: Chatto and Winus.

Hogben, Lawrence. 1994. Letter to the editors. *London Review of Books* 16 (May 26): 21.

Holldobler, Bert, and E. O. Wilson. 1990. *The Ants.* Cambridge, MA: Belknap Press.

Holmes, R. T., and F. W. Sturges. 1975. "Bird community dynamics and energetics in a northern hardwoods ecosystem." *Journal of Animal Ecology* 44 (1): 175–200.

Houston, A. P. C., et al. 1998. "Microbial processes and fungal community structure in soils from clear-cut and unharvested areas of two mixedwood forests." *Canadian Journal of Botany* 76: 630–640.

Hunt, J. C. R. 1998. "Lewis Fry Richardson and his contributions to mathematics, meteorology, and models of conflict." *Annual Review of Fluid Mechanics* 30: xiii–xxxvi.

Ingold, C. T. 1965. *Spore Liberation.* Oxford, UK: Clarendon Press.

Iyengar, B. K. S. 1965. *Light on Yoga.* London: George Allen and Unwin.

Javed, Salim, et al. 2000. "Tracking the spring migration of a bar-headed goose (*Anser indicus*) across the Himalaya with satellite telemetry." *Global Environmental Research* 4: 195–205.

Johnson, Kirk. 2003. "Uncertainty lingers over air pollution in days after 9/11." *New York Times* (September 7): 39.

Jones, Gareth. 2006. "Echolocation." *Current Biology* 15: R484–R488.

Kalko, Elizabeth K. V., et al. 2008. "Flying high—assessing the use of the aerosphere by bats." *Integrative and Comparative Biology* 48: 60–73.

Kant, Immanuel. 2006. *Anthropology from a Pragmatic Point of View*. Cambridge, UK: Cambridge University Press.

Katz, J. J., and J. A. Fodor. 1963. "The structure of a semantic theory." *Language* 39: 170–210.

Kellogg, Christina A., and Dale W. Griffin. 2006. "Aerobiology and the global transport of desert dust." *Trends in Ecology and Evolution* 21: 638–644.

Kerlinger, Paul. 1995. *How Birds Migrate*. Mechanicsburg, PA: Stackpole Books.

Kerr, Julie. n. d. "An Essay on Cistercian Liturgy." Cistercians in Yorkshire, University of Sheffield, Sheffield, UK. Available at http://cistercians.shef.ac.uk. Accessed 2/1/2012.

Kimura, Motoo. 1979. "The neutral theory of molecular evolution." *Scientific American* 241: 1179–1198.

Knight, Jack A. 2008. "Crossing the Alleghenies in 1919." *Air & Space*. Available at http://www.airspacemag.com/history-of-flight/Crossing_the_Alleghenies_in_1919.html. Accessed 9/1/2011.

Koppen, Ulrich, et al. 2010. "Seasonal migrations of four individual bar-headed geese *Anser indicus* from Kyrgyzstan followed by satellite telemetry." *Journal of Ornithology* 151: 703–712.

Lamb, Hubert. 1991. *Historic Storms of the North Sea, British Isles and Northwest Europe*. Cambridge, UK: Cambridge University Press.

Landrigan, Philip J., et al. 2004. "Health and environmental consequences of the World Trade Center disaster." *Environmental Health Perspectives* 112: 731–739.

Large, E. C. 1940. *The Advance of the Fungi*. New York: Henry Holt.

Leigh, G. J. 2004. *The World's Greatest Fix: A History of Nitrogen and Agriculture*. Oxford, UK: Oxford University Press.

Lester, Peter F. 2001. *Aviation Weather*. Englewood, CO: Jeppersen Sanderson.

Lettau, Heinz (2002). Oral history interview with Heinz Lettau. Interview by Sharon Nicholson, March 10. Boston, MA: American Meteorological Society, University Corporation for Atmospheric Research.

Liu, Xiao-Zhou, et al. 2001. "Avian hemoglobins and structural basis of high

affinity for oxygen: structure of bar-headed goose aquomet haemoglobin."
Acta Crystallographica Section D 57: 775–783.

Lorenz, Edward N. 1955. "Available potential energy and the maintenance of
the general circulation." *Tellus* 7: 271–281.

———. 1963a. "Deterministic nonperiodic flow." *Journal of Atmospheric Science*
20: 130–141.

———. 1963b. "The predictability of hydrodynamic flow." *Transactions of the New
York Academy of Sciences Ser. II* 25: 409–432.

———. 1965. "Energetics of atmospheric circulation." *International Dictionary of
Geophysics*, 1–9. Oxford, UK: Pergamon Press.

———. 1966. "Large-scale motions of the atmosphere: circulation." In *Advances
in Earth Science*, 95–109. Cambridge, MA: MIT Press.

———. 1969a. "How much better can weather prediction become?" *Technology
Review* 75 (July/August): 39–49.

———. 1969b. *Studies of Atmospheric Predictability. Final Report.* Bedford, MA:
Air Force Research Laboratories, Office of Aerospace Research, U.S. Air
Force.

———. 1973. "On the existence of extended-range predictability." *Journal of
Applied Meteorology* 12: 543–546.

———. 1979. Dynamical and Empirical Methods of Weather Forecasting.

———. 1991. *A Scientist by Choice. Kyoto Prize Acceptance Speech.* Available at
http://emuseum.kyotoprize.org/future/_/img/laureates/EdwardNorton-
Lorenz_doc_lct_e.pdf. Accessed 2/15/2012.

———. 1993. *The Essence of Chaos.* Seattle: University of Washington Press.

Magnan, August. 1934, *La locomotion chez les animaux.* Vol. 1 Paris: Hermann.

Magrini, Anna, and Ugo Magrini. 2005. "Measurements of acoustical properties in Cistercian abbeys." *Forum Acusticum* (Budapest). Conference Report.

Magrini, Ugo, and Anna Magrini. 2005. "Measurements of acoustical properties in Cistercian abbeys." *Building Acoustics* 12: 255–264.

Maina, J. N. 1998. *The Gas Exchangers.* Berlin: Springer.

———. 2005. *The Lung-Air Sac System of Birds.* Berlin: Springer.

Marcel, Gabriel 1964. *Creative Fidelity.* New York: Fordham University Press.

———. 1965. *Being and Having.* New York: Harper Torchbooks.

Margules, Max. 1910. *On the Energy of Storms.* Translated by Cleveland Abbe.
Washington, DC: Smithsonian Miscellaneous Collection.

Margulis, Lynn. 1981. *Symbiosis in Cell Evolution.* New York: W. H. Freeman.

Maritain, Jacques. 1957. *On the Philosophy of History.* New York: Scribners.

———. 1966. *Challenges and Renewals.* Cleveland: Meridian Books.

Markham, Beryl. 1983. *West with the Night.* New York: North Point Press.

Maturana, Humberto R., and Francisco J. Varela. 1998. *The Tree of Knowledge.* Boston: Shambala.

Matteson, Robert S. 1963. "Emerson and the Aeolian harp." *South Central Bulletin* 23: 4–9.

McKee, John K., et al. 2003. "Chemical analysis of World Trade Center fine particulate matter for use in toxicologic assessment." *Environmental Health Perspectives* 111: 972–980.

Menon, Surabi, et al. 2002. "Climate effects of black carbon aerosols in China and India." *Science* 297: 2250–2253.

Merton, Thomas. 1961. *New Seeds of Contemplation.* New York: New Directions.

Miquel, Pierre. 1850. *L'organismes vivants de l'atmosphere.* Paris: Gauthiers-Villars.

Nagy, Kenneth N. 2005. "Field metabolic rate and body size." *Journal of Experimental Biology* 208: 1621–1625.

Nault, L. R., et al. 1976. "Ant-aphid association: role of aphid alarm pheromone." *Science* 192: 1349–1351.

Nikiforuk, Andrew A. 2011. *Empire of the Beetle.* Vancouver, BC: Greystone Books.

Niven, J. E., and J. P. W. Scharlemann. 2005. "Does metabolic rate at rest and during flight scale with body mass in insects?" *Biology Letters* 1 (3): 346–349.

O'Connor, Patrick M., and Leon P. A. M. Claessens. 2005. "Basic avian pulmonary design and flow-through ventilation in non-avian theropod dinosaurs." *Nature* 436: 253–256.

Ogden, Eugene C., et al. 1974. *Manual for Sampling Airborne Pollen.* New York: Hafner Press.

Ono, Masato, et al. 1995. "Unusual thermal defence by a honeybee against mass attack by hornets." *Nature* 377: 334–336.

Pasteels, Jacques M. 2007. "Chemical defence, offence and alliance in ants-aphids-ladybirds relationships." *Population Ecology* 49: 5–14.

Pennycuick, Colin J., et al. 1979. "Soaring migration of the common crane *Grus grus* observed by radar and from an aircraft." *Ornis Scandinavica* 10: 241–251.

Perfumo, Amedea, and Robert Marchant. 2010. "Global transport of thermophilic bacteria in atmospheric dust." *Environmental Microbiology Reports* 2: 333–339.

Pernin, Reverend Peter. 1971. *The Great Peshtigo Fire: An Eyewitness Account.* Madison, WI: State Historical Society of Wisconsin. Reprinted from the *Wisconsin Magazine of History* 54 (Summer 1971): 246–272.

Platzman, George W. 1979. "The ENIAC computations of 1950: gateway to numerical weather prediction." *Bulletin of the American Meteorological Society* 60 (4): 302–312.

Pope, C. Arden, III, et al. 2009. "Fine-particulate air pollution and life expectancy in the United States." *New England Journal of Medicine* 360: 376–386.

Porter, Richard H., and Ian Winberg. 1999. "Unique salience of maternal breast odors for newborn infants." *Neuroscience and Biobehavioral Reviews* 23: 439–449.

Porter, Richard H., et al. 1983. "Maternal recognition of neonates through olfactory clues." *Physiology and Behavior* 30: 151–154.

Poschl, U., et al. 2010. "Rainforest aerosols as biogenic nuclei of clouds and precipitation in the Amazon." *Science* 329: 1513–1516.

Proust, Marcel. 2008. *Swann's Way.* Translated by C. K. Scott Moncrieff. Available at Forgottenbooks.org.

Purcell, E. M. 1977. "Life at low Reynolds number." *American Journal of Physics* 45: 3–11.

Rabelais, François. 1990. *Gargantua and Pantagruel.* Translated by Burton Raffel. New York: W. W. Norton.

Raffa, K. F., and A. A. Berryman. 1983. "The role of most plant resistance in the colonization behavior and ecology of bark beetles." *Ecological Monographs* 53: 27–49.

Raffa, K. F., and D. L. Dahlsten. 1995. "Differential responses among natural enemies and prey to bark beetle pheromones." *Oecologia* 102: 17–23.

Rayleigh, Lord. 1915. "Aeolian tones." *Weather Review* October: 511.

Rayner, J. M. V. 1982. "Avian flight energetics." *Annual Review of Physiology* 44: 109–119.

Reich, P. B., et al. 1995. "Different photosynthesis-nitrogen relations in deciduous hardwood and coniferous evergreen species." *Oecologia* 104: 24–30.

Richardson, Lewis Frye. 2007. *Weather Prediction by Numerical Process*, 2nd ed. Cambridge, UK: Cambridge University Press.

Roberts, S. P., and M. M. Elekonich. 2005. "Muscle biochemistry and the ontogeny of flight capacity during behavioral development in the honey bee, *Apis mellifera.*" *Journal of Experimental Biology* 208: 193–198.

Rosenfeld, Daniel, et al. 2008. "Flood or drought: how do aerosols affect precipitation?" *Science* 321: 1309–1313.

Samet, Jonathan M., et al. 2000. "Fine particulate air pollution and mortality in 20 U.S. cities, 1987–1994." *New England Journal of Medicine* 343 (24): 1742–1749.

Schaefer, Vincent J., and John A. Day. 1981. *A Field Guide to the Atmosphere.* Boston: Houghton Mifflin.

Schenkman, B. N., and M. E. Nilsson. 2010. "Human echolocation: blind and sighted persons' ability to detect sounds recorded in the presence of a reflecting object." *Perception* 39: 483–501.

Schlaifer, Arthur, and Breder, C. M. 1940. "Social and respiratory behavior of young tarpon." *Zoologica* 25: 493–511.

———. 1941. "Aspects of respiratory behavior in small tarpon." *Zoologica* 26: 55–60.

Schneider, Jutta M., et al. 2001. "Dispersal of *Stegodyphus dumicola* (Araneae, Eresidae): they do balloon after all!" *Journal of Arachnology* 29: 114–116.

Schnitzler, Hans-Ulrich, and Elisabeth K. V. Kalko. 2001. "Echolocation by insect-eating bats." *Bioscience* 51: 557–569.

Schwartz, Stephen E. 2004. "Aerosols and climate change: a tutorial." Brookhaven National Laboratory, Upton, NY. Available at *http://www.ecd.bnl.gov/steve/schwartz.html.*

Shaw, George H. 2008. "Early atmosphere—Hadean to Early Proterozoic." *Chemie der Erde* 68: 235–264.

Simon, Ralph, et al. 2006. "Size discrimination of hollow hemispheres by echolocation in a nectar feeding bat." *Journal of Experimental Biology* 209: 3599–3609.

Slaughter, Powell. 2009. "The formaldehyde factor." *Home Furnishings Business* 4 (5): 32–36.

Smith, E. Grant. 1986. *Sampling and Identifying Allergenic Pollens and Molds.* Vol. 2. San Antonio: Blewstone Press.

Stockl, Johannes, et al. 2010. "Smells like aphids: orchid flowers mimic aphid alarm pheromones to attract hoverflies for pollination." *Proceedings of the Royal Society B: Biological Sciences* 278: 1216–1222.

Stoddart, D. Michael. 1990. *The Scented Ape*. Cambridge, UK: Cambridge University Press.

Strangeways, Ian. 2007. *Precipitation: Theory, Measurement and Distribution*. Cambridge, UK: Cambridge University Press.

Suarez, Raul K. 2000. "Energy metabolism during insect flight: biochemical design and physiological performance." *Physiological and Biochemical Zoology* 73: 765–771.

Sullivan, M. H., et al. 1996. "Estimates of net photosynthetic parameters for twelve tree species in mature forests of the southern Appalachians." *Tree Physiology* 16: 397–406.

Suter, Robert B. 1999. "An aerial lottery: the physics of ballooning in a chaotic atmosphere." *Journal of Arachnology* 27: 281–293.

Swap, Robert, et al. 1992. "Saharan dust in the Amazon basin." *Tellus* 44B: 133–149.

Tanaka, R. A. 2004. "Efecto de los combustibles de biomasa en el aparato respiratorio: impacto del cambio a cocinas de diseno mejorado." Instituto de Investigaciones de la Altura, Universidad Peruana Cayetano Heredia, Lima, Perú.

Tang, Jianwu, et al. 2008. "Ecosystem respiration and its components in an old-growth forest in the Great Lakes region of the United States." *Agricultural and Forest Meteorology* 148: 171–185.

Taylor, Thomas, trans. 1792. *The Hymns of Orpheus*. London: Printed by the author.

Thaler, Lore, et al. 2010. "Human echolocation I." *Journal of Vision* 10: 1050.

———. 2011. "Neural correlates of natural human echolocation in early and late blind echolocation experts." *Plos One* 6: 1–16.

Thomas, Steven P., and Roderick A. Suthers. 1972. "The physiology and energetics of bat flight." *Journal of Experimental Biology* 57: 317–335.

Thorne, John E. 1999. *John Constable's Skies*. Birmingham, UK: University of Birmingham Press.

Tobalske, Bret W. 2007. "Biomechanics of bird flight." *Journal of Experimental Biology* 210: 3135–3146.

Traherne, Thomas. 1960. *Centuries*. Wilton, CT: Morehouse.

Traverse, Alfred. 2007. *Paleopalynology*. Berlin: Springer.

Turlings, Ted C. J., et al. 1995. "How caterpillar-damaged plants protect themselves by attracting parasitic wasps." *Proceedings of the National Academy of Sciences of the United States of America* 92: 4169–4174.

Tyree, Melvin T., and Zimmermann, M. H. 1983. *Xylem Structure and the Ascent of the Sap*, rev. ed. Berlin: Springer.

University of Wisconsin, Madison. 2008. *Memorial Resolution of the Faculty of the University of Wisconsin-Madison on the Death of Professor Emeritus Heinz H. Lettau*. Faculty document 2038. April 8.

Untermeyer, Louis, ed. 1919. *Modern American Poetry*. New York: Harcourt, Brace, and Howe.

Vaglio, Stefano, et al. 2009. "Volatile signals duing pregnancy: a possible chemical basis for mother-infant recognition." *Journal of Chemical Ecology* 35: 131–139.

Weil, Simone. 1938. "The Coming World War." *International Review* 1 (1): 10–15.

Weller, Aron. 1998. "Communication through body odour." *Nature* 392: 126–127.

White, C. R., et al. "The scaling and temperature dependence of vertebrate metabolism." *Biology Letters* 2 (1): 125–127.

Wilhelm, Richard, and Charles F. Bayne. trans. 1950. *The I-Ching or Book of Changes*. Princeton, NJ: Bollingen Foundation, Princeton University Press.

Williams, Charles. 1943. *The Figure of Beatrice*. Cambridge, UK: D. S. Brewer.

Wilson, E. O. 1963. "Pheromones." *Scientific American* 2081: 109–114.

Wohl, Robert. 1994. *A Passion for Wings*. New Haven, CT: Yale University Press.

———. 2005. *The Spectacle of Flight*. New Haven, CT: Yale University Press.

Woods, William A., et al. 2005. "Honeybee flight metabolic rate: does it depend upon air temperature?" *Journal of Experimental Biology* 208: 1161–1173.

World Bank. 2011. *Household Cookstoves, Environment, Health, and Climate Change*. Washington, DC: World Bank.

World Health Organization. 2008. *Indoor Air Pollution: Children's Health and the Environment*. Available at www.who.int/ceh/capacity/Indoor_Air_Pollution.pdf. Accessed 10/5/2011.

Worster, Donald. 1979. *Dust Bowl: The Southern Plains in the 1930s*. New York: Oxford University Press.

Wright, Timothy F., and Christine R. Dahlen. 2007. "Pair duets in the yellow-naped Amazon (*Amazona auropalliata*): Phonology and syntax." *Behaviour* 144: 207–228.

Wu, Maoxin, et al. 2010. "Case report: lung disease in World Trade Center responders exposed to dust and smoke: carbon nanotubes found in the lungs of World Trade Center patients and dust samples." *Environmental Health Perspectives* 118: 499–504.

Wyatt, Tristram D. 2003. *Pheromones and Animal Behavior.* Cambridge, UK: Cambridge University Press.

Xiang, Zhao, et al. 2010. "Indoor air pollution effects on human beings and healthy building design measures." Bioinformatics and Biomedical Engineering (ICBBE), 2010 Fourth International Conference, 1–5.

Yates, Frances A. 1964. *Giordano Bruno and the Hermetic Tradition.* Chicago: University of Chicago Press.

———. 1966. *The Art of Memory.* Chicago: University of Chicago Press.

Zannoni, Davide, ed. 2004. *Respiration in Archaea and Bacteria: Diversity of Prokaryotic Respiratory Systems.* Berlin: Springer.

Zimmermann, Martin H., and Claud L. Brown. 1977. *Trees: Structure and Function.* Berlin: Springer.

Index

Page numbers in *italics* refer to illustrations.
Page numbers beginning with 352 refer to end notes.

Index